INSPIRATION
for all
SEASONS

INSPIRATION for all SEASONS

CELTIC WISDOM FOR TODAY

JOHN SCALLY

BLACK & WHITE PUBLISHING

First published in 2020
By Black & White Publishing Ltd
Nautical House, 104 Commercial Street
Edinburgh EH6 6NF

1 3 5 7 9 10 8 6 4 2   20 21 22 23

ISBN: 978 1 78530 316 6

Interior illustrations © Shutterstock.com

The publisher has made every reasonable effort to contact copyright holders
of material used in this book. Any errors are inadvertent and anyone who for
any reason has not been contacted is invited to write to the publisher so that a
full acknowledgement can be made in subsequent editions of this work.

A CIP catalogue record for this book is available from the British Library.

Typeset by Iolaire, Newtonmore
Printed and bound by CPI Group (UK) Ltd, Croydon, CR0 4YY

Benedictus

To the memory of the late, great John O'Donohue.
May he continue to be a real presence.

Beannachtaí

CONTENTS

FOREWORD

I T'S SO EASY TO FIND YOURSELF TRAPPED inside a never-ending cycle of negativity these days. Stress and anxiety seem to have become the familiar trademarks on a journey that so many people feel they have no control over.

It is very worrying; more so because it's almost impossible to find a way to step back from it and reclaim a sense of who you used to be before it all became such an uphill struggle.

Life has lost its sense of mystery and wonder. We have lost our sense of self, of who we are, of what we mean to ourselves.

It is as though we no longer recognise ourselves because we feel surgically attached to an endless routine that we can't break out of. It's difficult to sleep because the problems we just can't seem to solve are never far from our thoughts. We worry about children, jobs, relationships, and money to pay a never-ending list of important bills. Unfortunately, the single most important aspect of our lives that becomes overlooked and neglected is our health.

I was diagnosed with a neurological disorder called Multiple System Atrophy in 2018. It is a progressive and incurable neurological illness. Since then I have undergone huge changes in my life. Of course I wish I didn't have to go through them, but ironically it is not affecting my outlook.

Or maybe I should say that I am *not allowing it* to affect my outlook. My sense of humour hasn't changed. I still laugh as much as I can, and continue to live my life to its fullest. Everything is changing, except my mind, which has stayed sharp. But I work hard on keeping everything within the day.

No darkness lasts forever. Life is precious and shorter than we realise. Life is so unique and amazing. It lives on in our love for others, if they can open themselves to it, and can be remembered always and recalled in a way that only open hearts will know.

Real living has nothing to do with technology. We surround ourselves with the latest gadgetry we can afford in order to feel connected to a world that ironically leaves us feeling more alone and on our own than we have ever felt before.

Technology carries a high price if we begin to believe it can serve all our needs. It can't come anywhere close. Despite its many benefits and its ability to keep us connected, modern technology has isolated us from real living.

It is easier to text than to talk. Valuable words and emotions are reduced these days to a simple screen emoji, when often such words spoken at the right moment give rise to valued reflection. Inner reflection waters the seeds of inner growth and belonging. Everyone needs to know they truly belong. That feeling is more important than anything else.

Enjoy every minute of what life offers. Never forget that time and space is all we have. It's easy to surround ourselves and fill that important space we call life with distractions; but that space is all we have, and none of us knows how much time we have left before that space is taken away forever.

There are times when the journey of life takes us down a difficult, hard road that we could never have imagined before. It is usually then that we realise we have to look deep inside ourselves in order to find the strength we need to lift us to a level of hope that will sustain us through the dark times.

Sometimes it can become so difficult that we want to give up. But giving up can never be an option, only because the road constantly changes; often when we least expect it. Each of us is on a journey, but it doesn't have to be a journey travelled alone.

Be YOU while you have the opportunity. Paint your own picture. Don't waste time colouring in someone else's. Show your love and share it every chance you get. There is a huge shortage of love out there, and the demand for it has never been so high.

Inspiration for all Seasons is a wonderful book to keep close to you, to dip in and out of, when you are searching for strength and trying to make sense of the journey you are on. It is filled with inspirational thoughts and reflections. I hope you find something here that might speak to you especially if your spirit might need a lift.

Keep strong and positive, even when you don't believe you can, and keep doing anything and everything that makes you feel better. Never doubt the courage within if you listen to your true self.

Gareth O'Callaghan
September 2020

INTRODUCTION

AY YOU LIVE IN INTERESTING TIMES. So says the Chinese curse.

As this book was being written, the Coronavirus pandemic struck the world with the ferocity of a tsunami. Apart from the global trail of illness, economic devastation and death, it sparked a tidal wave of fear. It struck at something deep inside us and shattered many of our cherished certainties. We thought we were in control, but nature reminded us of our fragility, vulnerability and mortality not with a gentle whisper but with a primeval scream. The experience had echoes of a medieval plague, but our twenty-first century world struggled to find an adequate response to it. So where can we find a pathway through this existential crisis?

As someone who lectures in theology, one resource I find helpful in troubled times is to turn to my Celtic heritage. It offers shafts of light into the darkness that so many people grapple with on a daily basis and provides prisms of hope into the despair I regularly feel while watching the news.

As our lives under the shadow of COVID-19 illustrated so vividly, the world today can be both disconcerting and disconnecting. However, the Celtic tradition offers connections, community and common sense. It presents itself as a rich vein to be mined of insight, imagination and inspiration. When we have an aching heart, Celtic wisdom can be a sanctuary of rest, renewal and reassurance. Long before the terms 'mindfulness' and 'well-being' were coined, the Celtic tradition offered pathways to peace of mind and serenity.

THE WRITE STUFF

I once visited the monastery of Saint-Gaul in Switzerland, which had a great medieval school. One of its most famous teachers was Iso. While his mother was pregnant with him, she had a disturbing dream of a hedgehog being stripped of its quills by a bunch of young boys who then went to write on the walls with these quills. Her husband went to the local hermit, an Irishman called Eusebius, who shared her anxieties about the dream. Eusebius calmed her down by explaining that the dream did not imply a threat, but the very opposite. Her boy would grow up to be a teacher and devote his life and career to educating generations of children with writing quills. It was ultimately an affirmation of the power of wisdom. In the Celtic tradition wisdom was valued above all else. This book mines some of that rich tradition.

The Celts had a distinctive sensibility. To take a small example. Every year, thousands of people visit the beautiful Glenveagh National Park in Donegal. The name Glenveagh comes from the Gaelic *Gleann Bheatha* which means 'glen of the birches'. In the Celtic tradition, birches have special powers. If a child had a cradle made of birch they had the protection of the gods.

Caoimhe was the name of the Queen of Ulster in days gone by. Caoimhe had the ears of the horse, a feature which made her feel angry and ashamed. Since she was not prepared to be laughed at by allowing her ears to be seen, she wore her hair very long, and the hairdresser visited the palace only once a year at festival time. It was a different hairdresser every year, because the poor hairdresser was put into prison forever so that she could never tell anyone about the queen's big ears.

One day the queen, who had a good heart, decided to let the hairdresser go free as long as she promised never to tell anyone her secret. The poor hairdresser, Mairead, was so afraid of telling anyone Caoimhe's secret that she went and asked her grandmother, who was famous far and wide for her wisdom, how she would keep her secret. So her grandmother advised Mairead to go to a forest and tell a tree her secret. Mairead did as she was told and immediately she felt better.

The tree was a willow tree and a few weeks later it was cut down to make a new harp for the queen's orchestra. On the big feast day, the whole kingdom of Ulster gathered for the annual concert, but when the music started the audience heard the sounds coming from the new harp saying: 'The Queen has horse's ears.'

There was stunned silence.

Then the harp started to play again and this time the words that came from it were:

> 'But do not mind her ears
> Because she has a good heart
> And that is all that matters.'

And everyone got to their feet and clapped and cheered for the queen's good heart. From that day on, the queen never worried about her ears again and all her hairdressers were released from prison. Soon Ulster became known as the kingdom of kindness. Such an idea paved the way for the later Celtic idea of *Cinéaltas Chríost*, the kindliness of Christ.

INTO THE MYSTIC

However, just as the Celts were happy to borrow wisdom from everywhere, this volume is happy to do the same. I have sought out stories, wisdom, poetry and prayers which resonate with the Celtic sensibility. One of Ireland's greatest singers is Van Morrison. He is a Celtic mystic for our times. One of his more recent songs is called 'Dark Night of the Soul'. He borrows this title from St John of the Cross. Like a Celtic magpie, I borrow wisdom shamelessly from other traditions. My hope is that, in the words of Alice Taylor, when the world is too much with us and our way forward is obscured by confusion these inspirational thoughts 'will be a ray of light to beam peace into stressful lives and focus us forward with renewed hope and serenity in our hearts'.

This collection is full of simple thoughts, but I hope with a depth of meaning. It offers a series of short reflections, which take only a few minutes to read but a lifetime to assimilate. Long before the phrase was coined, the Celts knew intuitively that laughter is the best medicine. So I hope the collection will bring a few smiles as well as lifting the spirits.

The Celtic year was based around the seasons and I have structured this book around the seasons to reflect that. As wisdom, stories, poetry, prayers, humour and letters are at the heart of the Celtic tradition I have broken the central sections of the book into subsections to reflect these threads in the Celtic tapestry. Much of my appreciation of the Celtic tradition was formed by my friendship with the late great, John O'Donohue. I conclude the book with a small tribute to a giant of Irish intellectual and spiritual life and I dedicate this volume to John's memory.

This book is not a nostalgic portal to what I imagine was a golden age of traditional Irish lyricism with mighty mists lolling lazily about the Celtic landscape, but a search for wisdom that will resound with the sort of truthfulness that will steer deep recognitions in the reader.

As this is a book of shared blessings I am donating all royalties to the Peter McVerry Trust who help those who need not a handout but a hand up.

PART ONE
SPRING

S PRING IS COMING.

St Patrick's Day was my father's birthday. He was called Paddy in honour of our national saint. We marked it each year with a visit to the cemetery. No cake. No candles. No presents. Just fresh flowers to replace the ones from a previous visit. Each visitation was emotionally debilitating. Generally a gentle rain fell. It was indeed right and fitting.

He died when I was five. A well-meaning priest told me to be happy for him because he was gone to a better place. I hoped he had, but those words gave me no consolation because the wounds were too raw. Decades later they have never healed. The passage of time would never deaden such painful memories. This explains why I never really have bought into the idea of St Patrick's Day as a time of celebration.

Since my father died I always have had ambivalent feelings about the nation's day of celebration. As a boy I rejoiced in the respite we were given from the rigours of our Lenten fast. However, when other people speak of festivity to me, the seventeenth of March is tinged with sadness. With each passing year my sorrow has increased as I reflect ruefully on all the might-have-beens. This unhappy association of ideas has been a forbidding impediment to the cultivation of a healthy attitude to St Patrick on my part. In recent times, though, I am beginning to think I have done him an injustice.

The past is a different country. The Ireland of St Patrick

was radically different from the society we are so familiar with today. Explorers from Europe generally looked on the island of Ireland as a remote outback not worthy of their attention. For this reason it escaped invasion by the Roman legions and therefore never became part of the mighty Roman Empire. Ireland was sometimes referred to as 'the back of beyond' or to use the Latin term *Ultima Thule*, the final stage of the journey. The population was a mere quarter of a million. One indication of the importance of farming to the economy was that the Gaelic word for 'road' was *bothar*, a path for the cows.

From a political point of view, Ireland was then nothing more than a geographical expression. Instead of a single government there were approximately one hundred and fifty small independent kingdoms known as *tuatha*, each ruled by its own king. Each *tuath* was rigidly divided into rich and poor.

Ogham was the earliest form of writing in Celtic Ireland. It involved notches etched on the edges of stones to indicate the different letters. Ogham stones were used to mark boundaries or graves.

The Celts did not believe in building great temples to their gods, but used groves in the forest or the land beside a sacred pool for their religious ceremonies. Sometimes they carved statues to their gods out of stone or wood, but often they would simply use a misshapen tree trunk as an image. Sacrifices were key elements of their religious ceremonies. The Celts considered that magic forces infused their surroundings. They felt that the gods were very powerful. They had many gods and goddesses, each one responsible for some aspect of their lives and they believed that woods and wells were sacred places. The chief god was Dagda, the good god and the father of the people, but there were others such as Lug the fertility god celebrated in the August festival, Lughnasa.

IN THE FAMILY

Patrick was born into a relatively affluent Roman family. They lived in a villa which nestled comfortably into a farm. His father, Calpurnius, was an esteemed member of the community. His job was on a par with a senior civil servant today; i.e., to ensure that the laws were kept and the taxes were paid and his title was *decurio*, an official Latin title used in the Roman Empire. Not only was Calpurnius an important figure in the civil life, he also had an official position in the life of the Church. As a deacon he undertook duties during the Church's services of worship. Patrick's grandfather, Potitus, was a priest, indicating that there had been some form of organised Church life in that part of Britain for some years.

Patrick was born and reared in a place called Bannavem Taberniae somewhere in Britain. It is a reasonable assumption that it was close to either the English or Welsh coast because he was snatched away from his home by a ship's crew from Ireland. Irish pirates would frequently raid the British coast in search of plunder – either material possessions or slaves.

As a boy Patrick enjoyed a comfortable lifestyle and learned Latin. Then his life changed forever just before his sixteenth birthday. A ship came over from Ireland, in search of plunder and slaves. Slaves could be sold for gold and were used as labourers on the land with farmers as their masters. Patrick wrote that he was one of thousands captured on that day.

KIDNAPPED

The Celtic culture was deeply enshrined in Irish society by the time Patrick first landed in Ireland as a slave boy to an unknown master. We next hear of him in the west of Ireland near 'the woods of Focult by the western sea' in County

Mayo. Interestingly this is the only place in Ireland that Patrick mentions by name although he is popularly associated with a number of places such as Tara and Armagh.

Although Patrick would later become Ireland's great spiritual shepherd he started life as a more humble one. He was entrusted with the burden of protecting his master's sheep from savage attacks by wild animals. Regardless of inclement weather, if sheep wandered in the woods or up on the mountain he would have to retrieve them. In his little shepherd's hut, his breath came out like diamonds on frosty nights as he prayed seeking solace from God in his solitary existence. After his death, the prayers he used were woven into a song called *St Patrick's Breastplate* which is one of his enduring legacies to us today. It includes the lines:

> Christ be within me,
> Christ be beside me,
> Christ be behind me,
> Christ be before me.

Patrick began to feel that God was calling him for a special task. As he slept he had visions. In one such vision, he saw himself as an immobile stone, stuck in the mud. Then something dramatic happened. In Patrick's own words, 'He that is mighty took hold of me, lifted me out of the mud, and set me out of the mud, and set me up on top of the wall.'

Patrick was convinced that he was being prepared for a divine commission.

THE SECOND COMING

Although the conventional wisdom is that Patrick brought Christianity to Ireland, this is not strictly true. We know from

Prosper of Aquitaine's *Chronicle* that, 'Palladius was ordained and sent as first bishop to the Irish who believed in Christ by Pope Celestine,' in the year AD 431. Although his name emerges in one of the early Church calendars, very little is known about Palladius. According to popular tradition there were other Christians, such as Declan from the Waterford region, in Ireland before Patrick. Given Ireland's maritime status it is a reasonable assumption that Ireland's shipping and trading contacts with Britain and France would have led to Christian travellers visiting the island.

At heart Patrick was obviously a frustrated Seamus Heaney. He spoke about his ministry in images. He described his pastoral work as 'hunting and fishing'. He got the phrase from the Biblical prophets and found it had a particular resonance in Ireland, as he journeyed as a pilgrim. He hunted people in need of the Good News. He fished patiently for them, constantly seeking a good catch. His aim was to persuade them to take the road less travelled and embrace Christianity. His message was full of Good News – God's love for people, hope, life, wisdom, truth and healing. As he 'wandered about the country for Christ', to many troubled people Patrick's presence was a silence, a voice that spoke without words, a quiet that was loud with conviction, the calm at the centre of a storm.

Patrick's God was a Trinitarian one. He wrote:

'He has a Son, co-eternal with Him, the Son is not younger than the Father nor is the Father older than the Son, and the Holy Spirit breathes in them. The Father and the Son and the Holy Spirit are not separate.'

He constantly spoke of God as Father, Son and Holy Spirit. He explained the idea of God as three persons in one to explain to his followers that God's love was shown first when he created the world, second, when Jesus became the Word made flesh, and third, through the Holy Spirit whose love and power works among all the peoples of the world. The Trinitarian emphasis is very evident in Patrick's *Breastplate*.

> I bind unto myself today
> The strong name of the Trinity
> By invocation of the same
> The three-in-one and one-in-three.

Patrick was steeped in the scriptures and there were frequent quotations from the Bible in his writings. Despite his whirlwind pace of missionary activity, Patrick also had a contemplative side. He was a man of constant prayer.

St Patrick's recognition of the importance of prayer is prophetic and particularly relevant to the Ireland of today. 'That's *only* a contemplative order' is a phrase one sometimes hears today when people are talking about religious life. Apart from what it betrays about our understanding of religious life, it also says something about our attitude to prayer. It is as if prayer is on the periphery of the Christian life, instead of at the very centre.

SUPERSTITIOUS MINDS

Patrick's Ireland was a world where superstition cast a long shadow and generated a lot of fear. He is the confirmation of Camus' assertion that, 'The particular obsession of a man is to understand the times he lives in.' Patrick invested great time and attention to understanding the engines that drove Irish society. Patrick was content to retain the established social order except in two areas: to replace the existing heathen priesthood with a Christian one and to eliminate the influence of the druids.

The druids had huge power in Celtic life. As the educated elite in Celtic society, they were pagan priests who carried out sacrifices to the gods and organised festivals. They were believed to have magical powers and to be able to foretell the future. A druid called Cathbad was said to have predicted that Cúchulainn would grow up to be a great hero. Training to become a druid was long and difficult and could take up to twenty years. Aspiring scholars came to schools of druids in pursuit of knowledge and wisdom. Accordingly, druids often advised rulers and settled disputes between people. Strabo the Greek historian, wrote in the first century: 'They used to stab a human being to death in the back with a dagger and foretell the future from his convulsions.'

Patrick felt he had a divine mandate to challenge the paganism of the druids. According to legend, every time he raised his arm to God a druid dropped dead. There is a strong emphasis in the *Breastplate* on God's protective power in reaction to the druids' malign influence:

> Against the demon snares of sin,
> Against all Satan's spells and wiles,
> Against the wizard's evil craft,
> Against the death-wound and the burning,
> The choking wave, the poisoned shaft.

In the fifth century, Ireland was ruled by approximately one hundred and fifty chieftains, but shortly after Patrick's death most of these warrior-kings had become Christian. This is one indication of Patrick's success as a missionary. Yet it would be a mistake to think it was all plain sailing. In his *Confession*, Patrick writes about an aristocratic young woman, of royal birth and great beauty. After she heard about the Christian message she wanted to give her life to follow and serve Jesus. Patrick exhorted her to remain single so that she might dedicate herself exclusively to the service of God. Her family were mortified about this and did not conceal their hostility. They persecuted their daughter and physically attacked Patrick!

On another occasion he was arrested and nearly killed. He was robbed and chained up in irons for two weeks. He needed his friends to rescue him. Although Patrick was grossly abused during his imprisonment he never lost his seeds of faith or hope. On the contrary, those virtues blossomed in adversity. Out of that difficulty he felt something emerging, despite the human failings which prompted his torture. Touching rock bottom, he abandoned himself to reach out to the transcendent.

Having entered a new world of suffering and fear without any familiar landmarks or comforting shoulder to lean on and stripped of all physical dignity in his vulnerability and power-lessness, Patrick experienced total dependence on God. This was not an academic exercise but an authentic human Calvary. Yet Patrick saw that in the darkness, physical and emotional, of his prison cell that God was with him in a very special way, transforming the savage into the sacred, making his pain redemptive.

Through all his suffering, Patrick felt a deep sense of being held in the loving embrace of God, an experience that brought him great consolation. Surrendering wholeheartedly to God, Patrick contemplated Jesus on the cross, and came to a new understanding of the depth of the mystery of God's love for us. He rejoiced in the Lord despite of – indeed, because of – all the sufferings he was subjected to. The joy and gratitude which mark his writing about this period seem strangely alien in the light of the suffering and degradation he was enduring at the time.

These experiences prompted some of his prayers which survive in his *Breastplate*:

> I bind unto myself today
> The power of God to hold and lead
> His eye to watch, his might to stay
> His ear to hearken to my need.
> The wisdom of my God to teach
> His hand to guide, his shield to ward;
> The word of God to give me speed,
> His heavenly host to be my guard.

Ireland is peppered with towns, mountains, wells and churches that get their name from Patrick; for example, Downpatrick, Croagh Patrick and Patrickswell. As Patrick had great success converting people to Christianity, he constantly marvelled at everything that God had accomplished through him.

THE CELTIC GENESIS

The Celtic year was divided into four parts, and the passage from one part to another was marked by a great festival. These were:

> *Samain* – celebrated on the first of November;
> *Imbolc* – celebrated on the first of February;
> *Bealtaine* – celebrated on the first of May;
> *Lughnasa* – celebrated on the first of August.

This was the spiritual environment Patrick was going to be immersed in. It is also the tradition we have inherited.

Geography played a big part in distinguishing Celtic Christianity from its Roman counterpart. The long distance, the difficulties with travel and the often-troubled political conditions in Europe militated against significant contacts between Rome and Ireland. Patrick's theology was local and contextual, incorporating existing cultural norms and values thereby ensuring a deeper understanding of the Christian faith in a Celtic religious milieu. For that reason, religious practice in Ireland developed a momentum of its own and took on a pronounced Celtic hue.

Spring was always a special time in the Celtic tradition because of its association with new life and new beginnings.

WISDOM
FOR
SPRING

Spring Comes

Sit quietly, do nothing, spring comes and the grass grows by itself.

ZEN SAYING

For Now

There exists only the present instant . . . a Now which always and without end is itself new. There is no yesterday nor any tomorrow, but only Now, as it was a thousand years ago and as it will be a thousand years hence.

MEISTER ECKHART, 1260–1328

Think Big

Dear Ones
Beware of the tiny gods frightened men create
To bring an anaesthetic relief to their sad days.

HAFIZ

Spring Fruits

The fruit of letting go is birth.

MEISTER ECKHART

Explosive Power

God is not nice, God is not an uncle, God is an earthquake.

TALMUD SAYING

Why Worry?

That the birds of worry and care fly above your head, this you cannot change.

But that they make nests in your hair, this you can prevent.

CHINESE PROVERB

Time Out

Yesterday is but today's memory, and tomorrow is today's dream.

KAHLIL GIBRAIN

Love and Happiness

For each new morning with its light,
For rest and shelter in the night,
For health and food for love and friends,
For everything Thy goodness sends.

RALPH WALDO EMERSON

Healthy Options

Be very careful of your health. The devil employs a trick to deceive good souls. He incites them to do more than they are able, in order that they may no longer be able to do anything.

ST VINCENT DE PAUL, 1581–1660

Who Dares Wins

To dare is to lose one's footing momentarily.
Not to dare is to lose oneself.

SØREN KIERKEGAARD, 1813–1855

Seeing is Believing

It is only with the heart that one can see rightly; what is essential is invisible to the eye.

ANTOINE DE SAINT-EXUPÉRY, 1900–1944

All You Need is Love

Keep love in your heart. A life without it is like a sunless garden when the flowers are dead.

OSCAR WILDE, 1854–1900

Honeytrap

Life is a flower for which love is the honey.

VICTOR HUGO, 1802–1885

Prisoners

To forgive is to release a prisoner within us.

ANON

Beauty

See deep enough and you see musically; the heart of nature is everywhere music if you can only reach it.

THOMAS CARLYLE, 1795–1881

All Things Bright and Beautiful

When you reach the heart of life you shall find beauty in all things, even in the eyes that are blind to beauty.

KAHLIL GIBRAN

True Character

Character is doing the right thing when nobody is watching.

J.C. WATTS, B. 1957

Ageing Gracefully

Do not regret getting older. It is a privilege denied to many.

AUTHOR UNKNOWN

Persistence

I do dimly perceive that while everything around me is ever changing, ever dying there is underlying all that change a living power that is changeless, that holds all together; that creates, dissolves and recreates. For I can see that in the midst of death life persists; in the midst of untruth, truth persists in the midst of darkness light persists.

MAHATMA GANDHI, 1869–1948

The Pursuit of Perfection

Here below, to live is to change and to be perfect is to have changed often.

ST JOHN HENRY NEWMAN, 1801–1890

The Wishing Well

It seems to me we can never give up longing and wishing while we are alive.

There are certain things we feel to be beautiful and good, and we must hunger for them.

GEORGE ELIOT

The Extraordinary Ordinary

Notice the intimate connection between God and what is otherwise everyday and ordinary.

POPE FRANCIS

Right Timing

Ní hé lá na gaoithe lá na scoth.
A windy day is no day for thatching.

IRISH PROVERB

TEN MOST IMPORTANT THINGS ...

Love
The Special Feeling that Makes You Feel
all Warm and Wonderful.

Respect
Treating Others as Well as You Would Like to Be Treated.

Appreciation
To Be Grateful for all the Good Things Life Has to Offer.

Happiness
The Full Enjoyment of Each Moment. A Smiling Face.

Forgiveness
The Ability to Let Things Be Without Anger.

Sharing
The Joy of Giving Without Thought of Receiving.

Honesty
The Quality of Always Telling the Truth.

Integrity
The Purity of Doing What's Right, No Matter What.

Compassion
The Essence of Feeling Another's Pain,
While Easing Their Hurt.

Peace
The Reward for Living the Ten Most Important Things.

AUTHOR UNKNOWN

YOU ARE . . .

You are *strong* . . .
When you take your grief and teach it to smile.
When you overcome your fear and help others
To do the same.
When you see a flower and are thankful
For the blessing.
. . . You are *loving* . . .
When your own pain does not blind you
To the pain of others.
. . . You are *wise* . . .
When you know the limits of your wisdom.
. . . You are *true* . . .
When you admit there are times
You fool yourself.
. . . You are *alive* . . .
When tomorrow's hope means more to you
Than yesterday's mistake.
. . . You are *growing* . . .
When you know what you are
But not what you will become.
. . . You are *free* . . .
When you are in control of yourself and
Do not wish to control others.
. . . You are *honourable* . . .

When you find your honour is to honour others.

...... You are *generous* ......

When you can take as sweetly as you can give.

...... You are *humble* ......

When you do not know how humble you are.

...... You are *thoughtful* ......

When you see me just as I am and
Treat me just as you are.

...... You are *merciful* ......

When you forgive in others the faults
You condemn in yourself.

...... You are *beautiful* ......

When you don't need a mirror to tell you.

...... You are *rich* ......

When you never need more than what you have.

...... *You are you* ......

When you are at peace with who you are not.

AUTHOR UNKNOWN

TALES
FOR
SPRING

Spring Singing

The abbot had a way of presenting all his opinions as well-established facts, and his certainties did have a sinuous power.

But the abbot was distressed. A few days ago, his problem seemed resolved. The problem had been dragging on now for a number of years. All the monks were getting very old and although they were still able to do their chores, their voices were well past their best and the community singing had suffered terribly. The main problem was of course, Br. Caomhín, who sang, if such a word could be used, in a high-pitched squeaky voice, doing violence to the ears of those unlucky enough to be in his immediate vicinity.

Then, one day, as if by a miracle, a young man joined the community who had the voice of an angel. When he sang solo, everyone was enthralled by the sheer beauty of his voice; time just seemed to stand still, like the fulfilment of an ancient dream. His solo singing brought a dramatic improvement to community worship, but not even he could cover up for Br. Caomhín.

Now the abbot faced a new problem. The local bishop had

unexpectedly sent a message to say he would be starting a three-day visit to the community. How could the abbot possibly subject the bishop to Br. Caomhín's singing? There was only one course of action; the abbot decided to instruct Br. Caomhín not to sing while the bishop was visiting. He did so with mixed feelings because normally he lived his life with the belief that an opportunity to do kindness is too precious to neglect. The abbot didn't want to hurt Br. Caomhín's feelings, but pleasing the bishop was more important than the pride of a simple monk.

The next day, Br. Caomhín sat quietly in the back of the chapel like a balloon gently deflating. Like eager first-time parents, waiting for their child's first words, the bishop and abbot waited attentively.

The singing went beautifully. The bishop was loud in his praise of the quality of the singing. The abbot went to bed, a happy man that night. He smiled contentedly, thinking that the day couldn't have gone any better. But that night an angel came to visit the abbot: 'What happened to the singing tonight? We didn't enjoy it as much as normal. We particularly missed Br. Caomhín's singing. He sings the Lord's praises so beautifully.'

The abbot couldn't believe his ears. 'Br. Caomhín is a terrible singer. He has a voice like a growling dog. How could you possibly enjoy his singing?'

'Ah, you don't understand,' said the angel. 'You see, in heaven, we listen to the heart.'

SHARING A MARCH MIRACLE

Growing up on a small farm in Roscommon, my favourite season was spring when the trees hummed with contentment. Rabbits made love in fields that proudly displayed their blankets of green. Thoughts of liberation filled all minds. Miracles of rebirth.

My grandfather's favourite music was birds singing. He especially loved the cuckoo, which sent its voice of mystery from out the woodland depths and wide-open spaces calling nature to rejoice at the advent of spring.

The song of the cuckoo was an echo of the halcyon days in paradise, rendering nature what it truly is: beautiful, poetic life at its innocent best, the world as it ought to be, the ideal for a moment realised. As we took refuge in a canopy of trees during spring showers everything seemed made from memory. The sound of the cuckoo enshrouded us with a redemptive feeling, melting away depression, pain and bitter disappointment. Her dulcet tones hinted at a bygone age of innocence and values that no longer obtain. The music was sweet and sensual, evocative of a higher world.

From my grandfather's point of view, the most disappointing feature of the change of landscape was the virtual disappearance of the corncrake. These small birds with their bright chestnut wings were the victims of progress; when silage came in, their natural habitat was destroyed. It was my father who first introduced me to the sweet sound of the corncrake. Once we had gone out in the still night to check a newly born calf, we drank together from the bird's symphony of raucous notes pleading in the night. She seemed to bring out not just good tidings but elation. I always associated that sound with sun-drenched days in the age of my innocence before my father died.

Some of my friends at school spent their evenings stealing birds' eggs and vandalising nests. My grandfather made me solemnly swear that I would not partake of such activity. He saw it as a crime against nature and psychologically and spiritually unhealthy, claiming: 'Every time we kill something; something inside *us* dies too.'

I never failed to get a little thrill from bringing a lamb into the world, especially after a very difficult birth. I felt I was part in some small way of achieving the miracle of new life. It would be melodramatic to say it was a religious experience, but a warmth flowed through my body like a sliding, sun-dappled river. The birth was a language of hope, lyrical yet maddeningly inarticulate, alive to the resonances of everyday life. The first sound of the breathing of the new lamb was the breathing of hope.

One March morning I witnessed the dawn breaking as I went out to check a sickly lamb. I woke early, long before the first faint vestiges of light illuminated the specklings of frost on the hard ground. As I pulled back the curtains I was compelled to watch the world take shape despite my haste. Sunrise so rose my spirits that I could later easily understand why dawn worship had been a powerful article of belief for the pagan Celts.

A tumult of sound greeted me, every bird in the fields singing its heart out, although it was still dark. Gradually the sky lightened and the low, bruised clouds began to be caressed with red. The faint horizontal threads of clouds were growing a fiercer red against the still grey sky, the streaks intensified to scarlet and to orange and to gold, until the whole sky was a breath-taking symphony of colour. Then, for a few moments as the dawn broke, the birds fell silent. The carollers drew close and paused to seek out instruments, searching for the string, the bow, the drum, to make the appropriate melody. That was the instant the sun appeared over the horizon. The birds went silent because of the wonder and that was the only possible response. Praise was secondary. It seemed that all of nature was affected by a tremor of excitement, adoring the creator. Timelessness breathed through the daybreak like the pulsebeat of a new baby. When the birds began to sing again, it was not the pre-dawn chorus at all, but something more reverential like a heavenly choir.

Subtle tunes resonated with ancient harmonies. It was like the first music ever made. All life was simplified. All thoughts were complete. Music was the best for this. The words of every day are unworthy vehicles to describe the transcendent. This was theological reflection at its most eloquent.

PRECIOUS TIME

Ní fiá scéal gan údar.
There is no story worth telling without an author.

With a timid voice and idolising eyes, the little boy greeted his father as he returned from work, 'Daddy, how much do you make an hour?'

Greatly surprised, but giving his boy a glaring look, the father said, 'Look, son, not even your mother knows that. Don't bother me now, I'm tired.'

'But, Daddy, just tell me please! How much do you make an hour,' the boy insisted.

The father, finally giving up, replied: 'Twenty euro per hour.'

'Okay, Daddy? Could you loan me ten euro?' the boy asked.

Showing his restlessness and positively disturbed, the father yelled, 'So that was the reason you asked how much I earn, right? Go to sleep and don't bother me anymore!'

It was already dark and the father was meditating on what he said and was feeling guilty. Maybe, he thought, his son wanted to buy something. Finally, trying to ease his mind, the father went to his son's room.

'Are you asleep, son?' asked the father.

'No, Daddy. Why?' replied the boy, partially asleep.

'Here's the money you asked for earlier,' the father said.

'Thanks, Daddy!' rejoiced the son, while putting his hand under his pillow and removing some money. 'Now I have enough! Now I have twenty euro!' the boy said to his father, who was gazing at his son, confused at what his son had just said.

'Daddy, could you sell me one hour of your time?'

> Time is too precious to spend it all on work.
> Appreciate your loved ones and don't take them for granted.
> Time is precious – Decide how you want to spend it.
>
> AUTHOR UNKNOWN

HEAD AND HEART

Head said: 'I am full of bright ideas.'

Heart said: 'I am full of tenderness and passion.'

Head said: 'I am reason. I am order. I am the lynchpin which holds everything together.'

Heart said: 'I am feeling. I am mystery. I am the creative energy which sparks wonder and authentic life.'

Then Head and Heart began to squabble.

Head said: 'You are easily swayed and misled. You live in a world without order.'

Heart replied: 'You are dispassionate and detached. You don't live. You just exist.'

So Head and Heart went to God and asked if they could be split up.

God laughed at them and said: 'You two belong together. Apart you are worthless. Head, you are the container. Heart, you are the contents. The container without the contents is as useless as an empty vessel, all sham and no substance. The contents without the container will scatter to the ends of the earth and blow into the empty wind. It's not possible for you to live apart and have productive lives.'

Head and Heart were puzzled: 'But we are total opposites. How can we find harmony?'

God said: 'Draw close and embrace like lovers. Protect each other. Look out for each other. Help each other to be equal partners. Then you will join together as one and I promise you something fantastic and wonderful will happen.'

At this Head and Heart asked in unison: 'What?'

God simply smiled and said: 'Wait and see.'

SMALL IS BEAUTIFUL

Once there was a great king who was preparing to go to war and he sent his servant to the blacksmith to be certain his horse was ready. The blacksmith told the groom he had no iron to shoe the horse. The king would have to wait. The groom said this was not on and he would make do with what he had. The blacksmith tried his best but he had not enough iron to correctly fasten the fourth shoe.

The battle began in earnest. The king was leading his troops from the front when his horse's shoe fell off. The horse stumbled and rolled over. The king was thrown to the ground. His men deserted him when they saw his plight. The king was captured and the battle was lost. And all because of a missing nail!

WITH A LITTLE HELP FROM MY FRIENDS

One day a magnificent lion lay asleep in the sunshine. A little mouse ran across his paw and woke him up. The lion was furious and was going to eat him up when the little mouse cried,

'Oh please let me go, sir. Some day I may help you.'

The lion laughed at the idea that the little mouse could be of any use to him. But he was a good-natured lion, and he set the mouse free.

Not long after, the lion got caught in a net. He tugged and pulled with all his might, but the ropes were too strong. Then he roared loudly. The little mouse heard him and he ran to the spot. He said, 'Be still, dear lion, and I will set you free. I will break these ropes.'

With his sharp little teeth, the mouse cut the ropes, and the lion came out of the net.

'You laughed at me once,' said the mouse. 'You thought I was too little to do you a good turn. But see, you owe your life to a poor little mouse.'

STICK AT IT

A father had a family of sons who were perpetually quarrelling among themselves. When he failed to heal their disputes by his exhortations, he determined to give them a practical illustration of the evils of disunion; and for this purpose he one day told them to bring him a bundle of sticks. When they had done so, he placed the bundle into the hands of each of them in succession, and ordered them to break it in pieces. They tried with all their strength, and were not able to do it. He next opened the bundle, took the sticks separately, one by one, and again put them into his sons' hands, upon which they broke them easily.

He then addressed them in these words:

My sons, if you are of one mind, and unite to assist each other, you will be as this bundle, uninjured by all the attempts of your enemies; but if you are divided among yourselves, you will be broken as easily as these sticks. The breach of unity puts the world, and all that's in it, into a state of war, and turns every man's hand against his brother; but so long as the band holds, it is the strength of all the several parts of it gathered into one.

SAMUEL CROXALL C. 1690–1752

MEMORY

Sometimes Fionn found it hard to sleep. His problems were compounded one night when in his semi-conscious slumber he became aware of an insistent sound of scraping and scratching. Eventually he lit his bedside candle. There was a silence, but the irritating noise resumed, and penetrated the stillness of the night, when he blew out his candle. 'It must be a mouse' thought Fionn to himself. He got up again and retrieved his old mouse-trap from its home in an old shoebox and delicately secured a morsel of cheese on its spike. After leaving the trap where he thought the noise of the scratching was he climbed into bed. He lay very still, determined not to fall asleep, but slowly his eyes got heavier and drifted slowly towards sleep.

The sudden, unmistakable snap of the trap jerked him out of his dozing. He sat up not quite sure, for a second, or two, where he was. Then he heard a pained squealing from the corner of his room. He groped in the dark for the matches to light his candle and dragged himself out of his bed. The rheumatism which so often crippled him was playing up again in the cold weather. There in the corner was the mouse, its tail firmly caught in the trap. It was vigorously, vainly, tugging at its tormentor, but it wouldn't let go.

'Hah, hah, you little devil you. I have you now you cheeky little bugger,' shouted Fionn in triumph. The mouse looked up at him. Its tiny black beady eyes screamed one emotion – fear. Fionn stopped dead in his tracks. He knew that feeling. His mind flashed back over fifty years.

Craving excitement, he had enlisted in the British army in 1940 and found himself deployed in the desert in North Africa. Fionn's American Sherman tank was isolated and attacked by the Germans. As he attempted to escape Fionn was shot in the leg. A young German soldier was dispatched to finish him off.

The throb of military vehicles was deafening in the misery enveloping the county.

As the blood oozed from his leg, Fionn lunged in manic desperation for his rifle. A sudden, despairing sickness ran through him as he felt the barrel of a gun on the back of his head. He raised his hands slowly. He tried to pray but his mouth seemed in a vice-grip and he could not will speech. Expecting a bullet to end his life at any second he ever so slowly began to turn his head. The German could have been no more than seventeen. Fionn was not going to beg:

'Why don't you get it over with and finish me off, sonny? You're just wasting your time and mine. For God's sake, just finish it.'

His executor seemed almost more afraid than he was – paralysed by indecision. He pulled back his gun. Fionn braced himself and closed his eyes. To his astonishment when he opened his eyes a few moments later the German soldier was running away. Fionn lay emotionally exhausted in the searing heat unable to make the effort to get back to camp. A few hours later he was rescued by his colleagues . . .

Reality rudely reasserted itself and obliterated Fionn's reminiscences and he was dragged back to the present by the sound of the mouse tussling with the awesome trap. Watching the mouse dragging the implacable contraption with his tail, jolted

Fionn into action. He tenderly took the mousetrap in his hand and set the mouse free.

Memory is central to all our lives.

EVENTUALITIES

Is áit an mac an saol.
Life is very strange.

One day there was a young prince who was meandering around distant lands looking for adventure. That morning he had opened a window shutter and watched dawn steal across the fields. His face was pale in the flickering light. First, the sky turned from black to dark blue, then to violet. The landscape became full of grey shadows, which gradually resolved into trees, hedges, fences and buildings. There was no sign of the sun, hidden as it was behind a layer of cloud, but the prince felt better once the night was over at last.

He came to a town which was near a pass into a fertile valley as he was thinking about the mysteries that confronted him. He had arrived just as the service was finishing and most of the congregation were leaving in a rush, eager to begin their festivities and enjoy their meals.

Nonetheless the prince was taken aback by the poverty in the town and inquired why the people did not move into the valley. The locals told him that they couldn't because a dragon was guarding the pass and that they were all afraid of him. The prince sighed, and the townsfolk saw lines of weariness etched into his face.

As princes so often do in stories like this, the prince decided that he was going to solve the problem irrespective of his own personal safety. With a brave smile but with a knot in his stomach, the prince made his way to the pass. It was accessed by a wooden bridge so dangerously ruinous that crossing the moat was an adventure in itself. The prince frowned a little but took it in his stride. With his sword waving, he reached his destination. He rubbed a hand through his fine hair, feeling his stomach tie itself in knots. To his great surprise all he could see was a tiny little dragon, who only was the size of his boot.

'Where's your father?' asked the prince, his voice loud and full of self-importance.

The dragon stepped forward to make a low and very sincere obeisance and said, 'I live here on my own.'

'But how can a tiny little beast like you so terrify the local people?' the prince asked, trying to keep the reproach from his voice, but not succeeding.

'Because of my name.'

'What's your name?'

'What Might Happen?'

THE SILVER SPOON

Cheered by the sight of a clear sky after so many overcast days, Br. Seán wandered into the yard of his community house, and watched the bright orange globe sink behind the trees at the bottom of the garden. He headed towards the homeless hostel he ran on behalf of his congregation.

He first spoke that evening with Peadar, who was shaking his head in tolerant resignation. Unfortunately, his eccentric way of moving as he talked to himself meant that he was seldom taken seriously outside the hostel. Normally he was compliant and patient, but that evening he was agitated and moody, oscillating between angry defiance and frightened tearfulness. Anxiety was written clearly on his pallid face that had survived over eighty birthdays. Br. Seán was anxious to do what little he could to alleviate the uneasy atmosphere and asked Peadar what he would like for his birthday. 'A spoon,' was the surprising answer.

Momentarily thrown, Br. Seán said, 'You are very low maintenance, Peadar. You look frozen. Let's go and get you some of the nice hot stew that Br. Micheál has been slaving over all afternoon.'

Peadar savoured every mouthful of the delicious meal. He was first in the line on his birthday for the lunch, which again he relished. There was a nice surprise for him after the enticing desert of mince pies and cream when Br. Seán approached him and presented him with a gift wrapped in lovely paper and with an impressive red bow. After he gasped his thanks, Peadar opened the present, which was a silver spoon. Peadar smiled his thanks before tears toppled in steady streams down his cheeks.

Br. Seán's dark eyes took in the scene with undisguised curiosity and he said, 'Peadar, please excuse my vulgar curiosity but why did you want a spoon? I know you have to take a lot of tablets. Is it because a spoonful of sugar makes the medicine go down?'

Peadar laughed heartily at first before almost being choked by a fit of wheezing coughing. 'No,' he said. 'The reason I wanted the spoon is that every time we have meals here whenever I see a spoon I know that something nicer is to come after we finish our main meal. I am not long for this world. We both know it will be you who will have to arrange my funeral because I have nobody who will miss me apart from you. When I die I want you to put the spoon with me in my coffin.'

'I don't understand,' said Br. Seán.

'The spoon is a symbol for me that something better is to come. That is the message of Gospel: a promise to the world of

better things to come. That is the message that I want to take
with me to my grave.'

SPOTTING OPPORTUNITIES

A very religious woman was at home when a storm came and
the river burst its banks. Soon the water was up to the level of
the first storey of her house. A man passed by her house in a
raft and offered to take her to safety. She said, 'No. God will save
me.'

As the water continued to rise the woman waited in her upstairs
bedroom. A man rowed by her window in a boat. He stopped and
offered to rescue her. She replied, 'No thank you. God will save
me.'

The water rose higher and higher. The woman had to climb
on her roof to stay alive. A helicopter passed by and offered to
rescue her. The woman shouted, 'No, God will save me.'

The rain got heavier and heavier and the water got higher
and higher. An hour later the woman drowned.

Some time later, the woman's spirit met with God in the
next world. She was very angry and shouted at Him: 'Why did
you not save me during the flood? I trusted you. I was sure you
would come to my assistance.'

God calmly replied, 'I sent you a raft, a boat and a helicopter.'

IN THE BEGINNING WAS THE WORD

God created the heavens and the earth and everything in them.
Words were His creative agents because words are power. God
spoke: 'Let it be done', and it was done. And everything He
made was good.

The apple of God's eye was the man and woman He created

because He had breathed into them a part of himself, His spirit. The countryside smelled clean and fresh, and the scent of soil mingled with the heavier odour of grass and fresh vegetation. The man and the woman followed a road that took them through a wood, and some of its trees seemed to have been there before time even began, they were so gnarled and ancient. A brook accompanied them most of the way, trickling between its muddy banks with a gentle bubbling sound. Beautiful blackbirds sang from the top branch of the tall oak trees, and a dog barked with pleasure in the distance.

The devil was jealous that God had partners to share His love and vowed to teach Him a lesson. One day when God was chatting with Adam and Eve, the devil sneaked up behind Him and put a bond on His tongue so that He could not speak. God could no longer talk and, because His creative power was in his words, the devil had denied Him that power. It was not raining, but the clouds were low and menacing and it was crystal clear that a deluge was coming. The man and woman were astonished and closed their eyes in apparent despair.

The devil made fun of God and kept Him in captivity for a long time. Every hour the devil would return to taunt Him. Eventually God responded by waving one finger. Intrigued, the devil asked Him if He wanted to say just one word. God nodded a definite *yes*.

The devil thought to himself, 'Sure, one word can do no harm,' and removed the bond. Adam and Eve, pale and heavy-eyed, said nothing. God had a gleam in His eye that said He was looking forward to outwitting his enemies. He spoke one word in a whisper so gentle that the devil could barely hear Him. The word released all the forgiveness that God had been storing in His heart during his period of silence. Dawn came early, with streaks of pale blue sky showing through the clouds.

The devil tugged his cloak around him as if he suddenly found the garden too cold and squawked as icy water seeped into his boots, and then he released a string of vulgar words. His face was a mask of anger, furious that a single word should cause him so much misery. He exaggerated a shiver as he stood alone.

The word was *Jesus*.

PAST SPEAKING TO THE PRESENT

The former Abbot of Glenstal Abbey, Mark Patrick Hederman, is one of the most interesting thinkers on how our past spirituality can speak to our present reality. When I interviewed him in November 2019 he shared the following insights with me:

'What more could one say about *The Rule of Saint Benedict*, which the author also calls "a little rule for beginners"? It concerns the elements of style, but a style of life for those interested in living with and in God. Benedict was also a keen and compassionate observer of human nature. He realised that people are weak, that people fail, and yet he believed that they were able to measure up to this challenge. This is a no-nonsense, unembroidered handbook for those who want to join the rewarding school of the Lord's service. Any unusual calling, whether you choose to be an athlete, an academic or an astronaut, requires training and discipline. Benedict knows that too. But he refuses to lay down anything harsh or burdensome just to impress the monastic weight-watchers. If there is any strictness in his rule it is to correct faults and to safeguard love.

'Benedictine spirituality is a living-out of *The Rule of Saint Benedict*, a little book on how to organise people who want to live together with God written at some time in the sixth century. Not a book at all, but a book about the book of your own life.

It is how to have that script written for you by God, if you are prepared to waive your rights of authorship. *The Rule of Saint Benedict* can make this happen. It is not something to read, it is something to be done. So describing it is like describing how to play Scrabble or Monopoly or snooker, complicated and tedious until you know how to play. Or describing a trellis, a lattice, a runway, anything that exists to allow something else, something other than itself, to happen. It is a structure to promote growth, to put some order into abundance, to help you take off and fly. It is a form which teaches you to do without it; showing that all form is empty.

'Benedict emphasises the importance of both the human person and relationships between persons living together. He has the natural psychologist's sureness of touch when arbitrating between conflicting interests in human affairs. His rule contains directions for all aspects of community life, but there is an inbuilt diffidence and flexibility allowing for adaptation to different countries and climates, and centuries; which it is why it has lasted for over fifteen hundred years. You can say it has carried, almost unconsciously, the wisdom of Christianity throughout the Dark Ages, when anything more articulate or less durable might have perished. It had a seminal influence on European history, providing the sanest and simplest infrastructure for community living, co-operative work, and communal prayer. *The Rule of Benedict* is as genial for what it leaves out as for what it puts in. It is not devotional, decorative or diffuse. It is food for the desert; pemmican rather than puff pastries. It is the lowest common multiple of monasticism and, at the same time, quintessentially distilled wisdom of the mystical East. It combines the genius of Rome for legislation with the Christian flair for personal touch. It has the beauty of a simple, yet effective, metal container, to which it takes time to warm and adjust.

The community which forms this complex tapestry would fray, stretch, tear and break without this delicate container. Poetry, as always, says it more accurately than prose.

'Ausculta is the Latin word for "Listen". And is the first word in the *Rule of Saint Benedict*. Since the sixth century, communities have followed this Rule, as do the Benedictine monks of Glenstal Abbey in Ireland. Ireland is situated in a pivotal position off the mainland of Europe; Glenstal, in southern Ireland, and within easy reach of Shannon airport, is ideally placed as a centre for spiritual revitalisation. Monasteries, like the ancient hill-forts of Celtic Ireland, provide access to the spiritual realm. A monastery is a listening ear for the world around it. As such, the monastery is an essential part of society, providing a place to be in touch with our deepest selves, with nature, and with God.

'Hospitality, an essential feature of the *Rule of Benedict*, is also a hallmark of Celtic culture. After careful consideration, the monks of Glenstal Abbey feel they are being asked by God to listen more intently to the needs of society and have decided to make themselves, their grounds, the ethos and atmosphere of their monastery, more available to people assailed by a world of unprecedented stress. The monks themselves have no great gifts to give away; they offer instead a place and an atmosphere conducive to the discovery of personal value and inner peace.

'Monks are those who take a step away from the world around them. They strive to preserve what is best in the heritage received, while remaining open to what other cultures and traditions offer. They welcome with enthusiasm and discernment the advances of technology and science, and try to weave these into a wider and more ancient understanding of the universe. A daily round of prayer and liturgical celebration combines with work in education, ecumenism, pastoral ministry, counselling, farming, bee-keeping, gardening, woodturning, forestry and silviculture, research, scholarship, writing and the arts.

'Farm and woodland, castle and gardens, inspirational surroundings for monastic life, must be preserved, even when offered to a contemporary world eager for genuine spirituality and inner peace. An architectural strategy has been devised to ensure that monastic life, as it has been lived for centuries, continues undisturbed no matter how many guests or visitors come our way at any given time. The vision of the monastery as a beehive of the invisible, distilling wisdom from many new sources, searching out a new cultural perspective; a new way of hearing, seeing, and being in touch with life. The search is for a fresh articulation of traditional beliefs and values, towards a better quality of life in a new century.

'I do believe that this Church, whatever human beings may do to it, especially those who see themselves as in charge of it, contains everything we need for allowing us to be disciples of Jesus Christ, whom I believe to be the Son of God, the Second Person of the Trinity come on earth. He gave us His Holy Spirit and promised that this Holy Spirit would be with us forever until the end of time, and that not even the gates of hell should prevail against us. That is all that matters to me. I have the Holy Spirit in my heart and that Person will never desert me. The food and drink, which I need for the journey through life, is the Body and Blood of Jesus Christ which he gave to us in the Eucharist at the Last Supper. "Do this in memory of me," he said. It is a deed that we do, not a dogma, or a book, or a set of concepts. Wherever this deed is done, indeed, wherever two or three of us are gathered in His name, He is there with us. We eat His body and drink His blood to give ourselves the blood transfusion which we need to swap our kind of loving for His kind of loving, to transfer from our own human energy to His Divine Energy. And this can be done in many ways. It matters little how we do it; what matters is that the deed is done in memory of Him and that we participate actively as often as we want to have the deepest communion with Him.

'All the rest is secondary: what clothes we wear, what rules we obey, what forms of government and structures of community we adopt. If the whole world were to betray us, the Holy Spirit would never do so. We need to cultivate a direct relationship with the Persons of the Holy Trinity, first person singular, present tense. There should be no intermediaries, no third person, no go-between. Christ gave us the life and love of the Three Persons of the Trinity flowing in our own hearts; we only have to drop down there to bathe ourselves in this supernatural splendour. We don't need anyone else or anything else to access this privilege, which is our birthright since the time we were baptised. Of course, it is a pity beyond all telling that we have been so betrayed by human institutions, but God never relied on any of these to speak directly to His chosen people. All we have to do is answer the phone.

'I believe that everything can change, and should change if necessary, except one thing which is the love of God made present to us in Jesus Christ and the Holy Spirit.

'It is up to us to insist on such changes, but for my part, I do not want to invent a new Church, nor do I feel the need to abandon this one. And this one, for me, means recognising that Judeochristianity is one religion stemming from the revelation of the one God; that the break between Judaism and Christianity is similar to that between Protestantism and Catholicism, namely a family quarrel; that Jews and Christians belong to the Catholicism which stems from the God of Abraham, also recognised by Muslims, and Isaac and Jacob, which in our view reaches its culmination and fulfilment of revelation in Jesus Christ, the Messiah that Judaism has announced through its prophets, who is God incarnate. The Church, the One, Holy, Catholic and Apostolic, must as an organisation, embody the Holy Spirit of Christ. Until it does so, it remains human, fallible and faulty, not yet having reached its full potential.

'I believe in God and I believe that the Holy Spirit is gradually improving the mechanisms which might change the Church from being the fragmented, self-opinionated, thick-headed, sexist, male dominated organisation that cultural forces in our patriarchal world have allowed it to become, so that it may eventually struggle towards being the transparent image of the God it was meant to be serving. I shall work as hard as I can to remove such dross and clean these windows, so that all manner of things may be well, and that all may be one, without that meaning uniform. There are many ways of being Christian and our union is one of love, not of domination.

'I like to think of Glenstal as a spiritual centre which would offer initiation into a way of life which aligns the whole person, body, mind and spirit, with the universe as a whole, with those who are in it, and with the Three Persons of the Trinity who have invited each one of us to share in their life. Taking our cue from Cluny, Glenstal can provide many people with an element and an atmosphere allowing them to breathe spiritually. Again poetry describes this:

> If you came this way in May time, you would find the hedges
> White again, in May, with voluptuary sweetness.
> There are other places
> Which are also the world's end, some at the sea jaws,
> Or over a dark lake, in a desert or a city –
> But this is the nearest, in place and time.

'There are other places, of course. But the Spirit seems to

be saying that, at this moment and as things are, Glenstal is the nearest in place and time. We do have one of the most beautiful places in the world imbued with the mysterious time of liturgy.

'Most people educated in the twentieth century are blind and deaf to the symbolism of liturgy, the "divine beauty" of nature, the language of art. Western European civilisation has long ago sold its birthright for a mess of pottage. Our birthright is the mystery of life hidden in the symbols from the beginning of time: the mess of pottage is a world constructed by scientific technology. Not that science and technology are not wonderful and essential, but without the other dimension they are "a dry weary land without water".

'Monks should provide for a world that has become blind, deaf and dumb to the language of symbolism, the meaning of life.

'Monks must first of all learn for themselves the language of symbolism, the language of liturgy, the language of the saving mysteries of Jesus Christ, made real for us on a daily basis through the power of the Holy Spirit. The *digitus Dei*, or finger of God, as the Holy Spirit is named, spells out "the word" for us as the water of life is poured on the other hand. The Holy Spirit writes on our hands, as blind, deaf and dumb people, also through the medium of sound.

'Glenstal would become like Clonmacnoise in Seamus Heaney's poem. This is a place where the abbot and community help the artist to anchor the altar. The monastery becomes a place where artists can hope to tie whatever kite they happen to be flying to a firm and stable anchor. The monastery as silent hub of that fireworks display which art and culture need to scatter with reckless flamboyancy into the night.

'Such revelation is possible only from the ambience and tranquillity of a monastery where, to quote Alexandr Solzhenitsyn;

people have the time, the atmosphere and the opportunity "to survey, as from a great height, the whole tortuous flow of history; and yet at the same time, like people completely immersed in it, they can see every pebble in its depths." (Solzhenitsyn, *The Gulag Archipelago* 1971:358). Providentially, it seems to me, the Holy Spirit has gathered together in this very beautiful place, the people and the competences, the genius and the generosity, which could allow us to provide a well-organised and effective oasis in an over-expanding spiritual desert.

'There is a place in every person where God touches us and where we are constantly in contact with God. If I can reach this place I can touch God. The Bible gives this interior place the name "heart". At a given moment, a great withdrawal of all other faculties must take place, a sort of fast must be imposed on them. We try to rest before God in reverent and loving attention, while our interior faculties remain empty. We must work to create this emptiness, this space within. This does not normally happen quickly. Perseverance, humility and patience are needed. If I can arrive at a point where I can free myself from every other reality and bring the gaze of my spirit to bear on this point exclusively, I can meet God. Our desire for God leads us toward that reality in ourselves which is the deepest and most divine part of our being. That place where God dwells in me is also the place of prayer.'

THE TWELVE-STEP PROGRAMME

1. Make up your mind to be happy. Learn to find pleasure in simple things.

2. Make the best of your circumstances. No one has everything, and everyone has something of sorrow intermingled with gladness of life. The trick is to make the laughter outweigh the tears.

3. Don't take yourself too seriously. Don't think that somehow you should be protected from misfortune that befalls other people.

4. You can't please everybody. Don't let criticism worry you.

5. Don't let your neighbour set your standards. Be yourself.

6. Do the things you enjoy doing but stay out of debt.

7. Never borrow trouble. Imaginary things are harder to bear than real ones.

8. Since hate poisons the soul, do not cherish jealousy, enmity, grudges. Avoid people who make you unhappy.

9. Have many interests. If you can't travel, read about new places.

10. Don't hold post-mortems. Don't spend your time brooding over sorrows or mistakes. Don't be one who never gets over things.

11. Do what you can for those less fortunate than yourself.

12. Keep busy at something. A busy person never has time to be unhappy.

ROBERT LOUIS STEVENSON, 1850–1894

POETRY
FOR
SPRING

One of the great blessings of my life has been the opportunity to converse with one of Ireland's finest poets, Brendan Kennelly, about the Celtic tradition and its poetry in particular. He told me that 'the Celtic mind did not take kindly to obscurity'. He went on to point out that Celtic poetry had two other prominent characteristics: a great love of nature and a religious intensity. He kindly agreed to share some of his own translations of these poems from the original Gaelic and his own poems, which reflect aspects of the Celtic sensibility for this collection. There could only be one place to start for this purpose.

Begin

Begin again to the summoning birds
to the sight of the light at the window,
begin to the roar of morning traffic
all along Pembroke Road.
Every beginning is a promise
born in light and dying in dark

determination and exaltation of springtime
flowering the way to work.

Begin to the pageant of queuing girls
the arrogant loneliness of swans in the canal
bridges linking the past and future
old friends passing though with us still.

Begin to the loneliness that cannot end
since it perhaps is what makes us begin,
begin to wonder at unknown faces
at crying birds in the sudden rain
at branches stark in the willing sunlight
at seagulls foraging for bread
at couples sharing a sunny secret
alone together while making good.
Though we live in a world that dreams of ending
that always seems about to give in
something that will not acknowledge conclusion
insists that we forever begin.

BRENDAN KENNELLY

Making Waves

I am the wind which breathes upon the sea,
I am the wave of the ocean,
I am the murmur of the billows,
I am the ox of the seven combats,
I am the vulture upon the rocks,
I am the beam of the sun,
I am the fairest of the plants,
I am the wild boar in valour,

I am a salmon in the water,
I am a lake in the plain,
I am a word of science,
I am the point of the lance of battle,
I am the God who created in the head the fire.
Who is who throws light into the meeting of the mountain?
Who announces the age of the moon?
Who teaches the place where couches the son?
(If not I)

POEM BY AMERGIN, A CELTIC DRUID WHO LIVED BEFORE CHRIST;
TRANSLATED BY IRELAND'S FIRST PRESIDENT, DOUGLAS HYDE

Invocation

ETERNAL God omnipotent! The One
Sole Hope of worlds, Author and Guard alone
Of heaven and earth Thou art.

CAELIUS SEDULIUS, DIED CA. 454 AD

Habits

'O Cormac, grandson of Conn,' said Carbery. 'What were
your habits when you were a lad?'
'Not hard to tell,' said Cormac.
I was a listener in woods
I was a gazer at stars
I was blind where secrets were concerned
I was silent in a wilderness
I was talkative among many
I was mild in the mead-hall
I was stern in battle
I was gentle towards allies

I was a physician of the sick
I was weak towards the feeble
I was strong towards the powerful
I was not close lest I should be burdensome
I was not arrogant though I was wise
I was not given to promising though I was strong
I was not venturesome though I was swift
I did not deride the old though I was young
I was not boastful though I was a good fighter
I would not speak about any one in his absence
I would not reproach, but I would praise
I would not ask, but I would give
For it is through these habits that the young become old and
kingly warriors.

CELTIC POEM

All Seeing

With an eye made quiet by the power
Of harmony, and the deep power of joy,
We see into the life of things.

WILLIAM WORDSWORTH

Every Breath You Take

God works where God will . . .
And yet, I raise my hands to God
That I might be held
Just like a feather
On the breath of God
Which has no weight
From its own strength

And lets itself
Be carried to the wind.

HILDEGARD OF BINGEN, 1098–1179

Sweet, Sweet Smile

Go into the world
With a smile on your lips.
Go to spread a little happiness,
Over this valley of tears,
Smiling to everyone, but especially
To sad people,
To those disheartened by life,
To those falling under
The weight of the cross,
Smiling to them with that bright smile
That speaks of God's goodness.

BLESSED URSULA LEDÓCHOWSKA, 1865–1939

Visions

The vision of God which thou dost see
Is my vision's greatest enemy.
Both read their bibles day and night,
But thou read'st black where I read white.

WILLIAM BLAKE

Making a Difference

If you sit down at set of sun
And count the acts that you have done,
And, counting, find

One self-denying deed, one word
That eased the heart of him who heard,
One glance most kind
That fell like sunshine where it went –
Then you may count that day well spent.
But if, through all the livelong day,
You've cheered no heart, by yea or nay –
If, through it all
You've nothing done that you can trace
That brought the sunshine to one face –
No act most small
That helped some soul and nothing cost –
Then count that day as worse than lost.

GEORGE ELIOT, 1819–1880

Care and Share

To let go doesn't mean to stop caring;
It means I can't do it for someone else.
To let go is not to cut myself off . . .
It's the realisation that I can't control another . . .
To let go is not to enable,
but to allow learning from natural consequences.
To let go is to admit powerlessness,
which means the outcome is not in my hands.
To let go is not to try and change or blame another,
I can only change myself.
To let go is not to care for, but to care about.
To let go is not to fix, but to be supportive.
To let go is not to judge,
but to allow another to be a human being.
To let go is not to be in the middle arranging all the outcomes,

but to allow others to affect their own outcomes.
To let go is not to be protective,
It is to permit another to face reality.
To let go is not to deny, but to accept.
To let go is not to nag, scold, or argue,
but to search out my own shortcomings and correct them.
To let go is not to adjust everything to my desires,
but to take each day as it comes and cherish the moment.
To let go is not to criticise and regulate anyone,
but to try to become what I dream I can be.
To let go is not to regret the past,
but to grow and live for the future.
To let go is to fear less and love more.

AUTHOR UNKNOWN

Healthy Living

There is nothing the matter with me.
I'm as healthy as I can be.
I have arthritis in both my knees
And when I talk, I talk with a wheeze.

My pulse is weak, and my blood is thin
But I'm awfully well for the shape I'm in.
Arch supports I have for my feet
Or I wouldn't be able to be on the street.

Sleep is denied me night after night,
But every morning I find I'm all right.
My memory is failing, my head's in a spin
But I'm awfully well for the shape I'm in.

The moral is this, as my tale I unfold,
That for you and me who are growing old,
It's better to say 'I'm fine' with a grin
Than to let folks know the shape we are in.

How do I know that my youth is all spent?
Well, my 'get up and go' just got up and went.
But I really don't mind when I think with a grin
Of all the grand places my 'get up' has been.

AUTHOR UNKNOWN

Come Not

Come not in terror, as the King of Kings;
But kind and good, with healing in thy wings.
Tears for all woes, a heart for every plea;
Come, Friend of sinners, thus abide with me.

HENRY FRANCIS LYTE, 1793–1847

PRAYERS
FOR
SPRING

In Deep

Deep peace of the running wave to you
Deep peace of the flowing air to you
Deep peace of the quiet earth to you
Deep peace of the shining stars to you
Deep peace of the gentle night to you
Moon and stars pour their healing light on you
Deep peace of Christ the light of the world to you
Deep peace of Christ to you.

CELTIC PRAYER

God Bless

God bless Thou Thyself my reaping,
Each ridge, and plain, and field,
Each sickle curved, shapely, hard,
Each ear and handful on the sheaf.

CELTIC BLESSING

Bending the Knee

I am bending my knee
In the eye of the Father who created me,
In the eye of the Son who purchased me
In the eye of the Spirit who cleansed me
In friendship and affection.

CELTIC BLESSING

Help Me if You Can

Dear God, So far today I've done okay.
I haven't gossiped, or lost my temper.
I haven't been grumpy, nasty or selfish.
But in a few more minutes, God,
I'm going to get out of bed,
And that's when I will need your help!
    Amen.

The Fire Inside

Preach the Truth as if you had a million voices.
It is silence that kills the world.
You are rewarded not according to your work or your time
but according to the measure of your love.
A soul cannot live without loving.
It must have something to love,
For it was created to love.
To the servant of God, every place is the right place,
And every time is the right time.
We are of such value to God
That He came to love among us.
We can only respond by loving God for his love.

Be who God meant you to be
And you will set the world on fire.

ST CATHERINE OF SIENA

The Journey of Life

For each of us life is like a journey.
Birth is the beginning of this journey,
and death is not the end but the destination.
It is a journey that takes us from youth to age,
from innocence to awareness,
from ignorance to knowledge,
from foolishness to wisdom,
from weakness to strength and often back again,
from offence to forgiveness,
from loneliness to friendship,
from pain to compassion,
from fear to faith,
from defeat to victory and from victory to defeat,
until, looking backward or ahead,
we see that victory does not lie at some point along the way,
but in having made the journey, stage by stage.

ADAPTED FROM AN OLD HEBREW PRAYER

Why Worry?

Pray, hope and don't worry.
Worry is useless.
God is merciful and will hear your prayer.
    Amen.

PADRE PIO, 1887–1968

Belonging

Christi Simus Non Nostri
(We belong to Christ and not ourselves.)

Illuminations

Jesus, help me to spread your fragrance wherever I am.

Fill my heart with your Spirit and your life.

Penetrate my being and take such hold of me that my life becomes a radiation of your own life.

Give me your light through me and remain in me in such a way that every soul I come into contact with can feel your presence in me.

May people not see me but see you in me.

Remain in me, so that I shine with your light,

And may others be illuminated by my light.

All light will come from you, Oh Jesus.

Not even the smallest ray of light will be mine.

You will illuminate others through me.

Amen.

ST JOHN HENRY NEWMAN

Prayer of Abandonment

Father,
I abandon myself into your hands;
Do with me what you will.
Whatever you may do I thank you;
I'm ready for all, I accept all.

Let only your will be done in me,
And in all your creatures.
I wish no more than this, O Lord.

Into your hands I commend my soul;
I offer it to you
With all the love of my heart.
For I love you, Lord,
And so need to give myself,
To surrender myself into your hands,
Without reserve,
And with boundless confidence,
for you are my father.

CHARLES DE FOUCOULD, 1895–1916

Prayer for the Start of the Week

We pause to pray at the start of this new day and at the beginning of this brand-new week.

O God, I know that I am going to be very busy today.

Help me not to be so busy that I miss the most important things.

Help me not to be too busy to look up and see a glimpse of beauty in your world.

Help me not to be too busy listening to other voices to hear your voice when you speak to me.

Help me not to be too busy to listen to anyone in trouble, and to help anyone who is in difficulty.

Help me not to be too busy to stand still for a moment to think and to remember.

Help me not to be too busy to remember the claims of my home, my parents and my family.

Help me all through today to remember that I must work my hardest, and also to remember that sometimes I must be still.

Amen.

Walk Tall

In beauty may I walk
All day long may I walk
Through returning seasons may I walk
On the trail marked with pollen may I walk
With grasshoppers about my feet may I walk
With dew about my feet may I walk
With beauty may I walk
With beauty behind me may I walk
With beauty above me may I walk
With beauty below me may I walk
With beauty all around me may I walk
In old age wandering on a trail of beauty, lively may I walk
In old age wandering on a trail of beauty, living may I walk
It is finished in beauty
It is finished in beauty.

NAVAJO INDIAN PRAYER

The Fire Inside

Let us ever make it our prayer and our endeavour, that we
may the whole counsel of God, and grow into the measure
of the stature of the fullness of Christ; that all prejudice and
self-confidence, and hollowness and unreality, and positive-
ness, and partisanship, may be put away from us under the
light of Wisdom, and the fire of Faith and Love; till we see
things as God sees them, with the judgement of His Spirit;
and according to the mind of Christ.

ST JOHN HENRY NEWMAN

HUMOUR
FOR
SPRING

Only one God

At a very early age – round about age nine, if I remember rightly – I had to make a big decision: either I was God or there was another. I had to admit after some calculation, that the first scenario was improbable.

MARK PATRICK HEDERMAN

Holy Hell

Fr. Iggy was in a hurry one Saturday and consequently did not give as much attention to the layout of the church noticeboard as normal. The next morning the choir were a bit miffed to see his injunction to 'Come hear our choir' immediately under the title of his sermon 'What Is Hell Like?'

Religious Convictions

Once Fr. Iggy visited prison as a chaplain. He asked one of the prisoners: 'Why are you back here again, Thomas?'

Thomas: 'Because of my belief, Father.'

Fr. Iggy: 'What? How could your belief bring you back to prison?'

Thomas: 'I happened to believe that the policeman had already patrolled his beat past the bank.'

Career Move

'And why did you leave your last job?' Fr. Iggy asked the young applicant for the position of parish secretary.

'It was something the boss said,' came the reply.

'Was he abusive to you?' asked Fr. Iggy in a voice full of concern.

'No, not really.'

'Well then, what did he say?'

'He said: "You're fired."'

Substitute

Fr. Iggy was not always well served by the reports in the parish bulletin:

'A large crowd attended the Palm Sunday service. The donkey failed to arrive for the procession at St Peter's Church, so that the procession was led by Fr. Iggy instead.'

All Ends Up

Then was the excerpt from the magazine article on baptism:

'Fr. Iggy announced last Sunday that he was going to install a second font near the chancel steps, so that he could baptise babies at both ends.'

You've Got a Friend

Fr. Iggy was giving his last sermon in the parish after twenty-five years of sterling service. He worked himself into an emotional frenzy as he said, 'Jesus brought me to this parish, Jesus guided the bishop to pick me to serve here and Jesus helped me to work with you all these years.'

The stifled sounds of sobbing could be heard all over the church.

Fr. Iggy's last words were: 'And now Jesus has called me to serve in another parish.'

Cue the choir.

Fr. Iggy's face turned to shock as they sang: 'What a friend we have in Jesus.'

Good Colour

Fr. Iggy was a workaholic. He did not take a holiday for forty years. Finally the bishop persuaded him to take a break. He went to Lourdes for a week. The weather was absolutely beautiful and Fr. Iggy returned home with a lovely tan. Tragically, the day after he returned from Lourdes, Fr. Iggy died.

When the parishioners came to see him laid out in his coffin Winnie Cooper was very taken by his tanned face and remarked, 'The holiday did him a power of good.'

LETTERS
FOR
SPRING

The Celtic monks were people of the pen, or more accurately the quill. Given that writing was such a central part of the Celtic tradition I thought it would breathe new life into that tradition by inviting some well-known people to write a letter to either their mother or father, given the centrality of the family in the Celtic tradition. In Ireland today we are wonderful at saying how great people were after they died, but the Celts did not wait until people died to say how great they were. Here is another lesson they can teach us.

To begin I invited author and journalist Martina Fitzgerald to write a letter to her mother.

Letter to My Mother

Dear Mum,

I don't think I have said it enough – thank you.

You and Dad worked so hard to ensure all of us had the opportunity to pursue our dreams. I know it was hard especially when you had three children in university at the same time but you made it happen. You never grumbled. I hope I never took it for granted.

Many people say we look alike but, in fairness, Maria got your colouring and brown eyes. I think I inherited something else – your determination and stubbornness – traits that I have come to admire. There are not many people on their way to hospital for a check-up, that would ask the ambulance driver to stop so they could vote. You were so determined. While initially taken aback, I was secretly so proud.

I have always admired your candour – you are a straight-talker and scrupulously fair. You taught us all to pay our bills and not to live beyond our means. You feel strongly about certain things, which we all admire, although we flee the scene when you are watching particular football games.

All of my friends think you are amazing and look great and are so fashionable. I look back at family photographs and I hope I've inherited your genes. It's no wonder that you take particular pride in telling people, often strangers, your age. You enjoy the reaction, although you're not necessarily truthful. You always add an extra year on because you believe it's technically closer to the truth. To my amusement, I have learned that you are not so forthcoming locally, where you keep such matters private.

I will always remember how strong you were when Granny, Dad, Peter and Auntie Bridget were ill. You often said that you'd have liked to have been a nurse – you certainly had the skillset and the patience. You did everything possible for all of them and they knew it.

Mum, I love you and am so proud of you. Myself, Maria, Thomas and Peter really hit the jackpot. Thank you for everything.

Martina

PART TWO
SUMMER

PERHAPS ONE OF THE REASONS WHY St Patrick was such a success as a missionary was that he considered himself a country man and spoke in a country idiom so that his message might be better understood by his audience. Equally he appreciated that to really engage people he could not rely only on words. Patrick understood that people's faith needed to be nurtured on the sensual as well as on the intellectual level.

One of the big buzz words today is 'holistic'. Yet our contemporary Christianity seems to be excessively dependent on the written and spoken word. There has been a marked shift from the experience of authority to the authority of experience. Yet our liturgical practices do not reflect this. Establishing a folk group can be a meaningful experience for many people and can energise a congregation, but it is not always a substitute for experiences of awe and mystery that linger deep in the subconscious.

A SACRAMENTAL UNIVERSE

The invocation of the elements in St Patrick's *Breastplate* reveals a belief in the sacramental universe, a sense of kinship with nature, a humility about the human condition, and a sense of not being alone in the universe. In his *Confession* he wrote:

'After I reached Ireland, well, I pastured the flocks every day and I used to pray many times a day; more and more did my love of God and my fear of him increase, and my faith grew and my spirit was stirred, and as a result I would say up to a hundred prayers in one day, and almost as many at night; I would even stay in the forests and on the mountain and would wake to pray before dawn in all weathers, snow, frost, rain; and felt no harm and there was no listlessness in me – as now I realise, it was because the Spirit was fervent within me.'

This passage clearly illustrates that Patrick's primary place of prayer was in the world of nature. However, Patrick speaks the language of inculturation in the *Confession* most clearly in a passage on the resurrection, which he compares to a form of sun-experience.

'Without any doubt, we shall rise in that day in the brightness of the sun, that is the glory of Jesus Christ, our Redeemer, as sons of the living God, and joint-heirs with Christ, . . . For that sun which we behold, at God's command, raises daily for us – but it shall never reign, nor shall its splendour continue; but all even that worship it, miserable beings, shall wretchedly come to punishment. But we who believe in the true sun, Jesus Christ, will never perish; neither shall he who does his will, but shall continue for ever' – as Christ continues for ever.

Likewise Colum Cille, one of Ireland's three patron saints, is associated with nature as is indicated by his nickname, 'dove of the church', which seems to bridge the gap between Christianity and nature.

HEAVEN AND EARTH

The late Brendan Behan once went into a bookshop and saw a copy of the *Catholic Standard* and remarked: 'Ah here is the news of the next world.' This is a revealing observation highlighting as it does the way in which many people think of the Christian life, to prepare our souls here in this world for the next world. This kind of dualism between heaven and earth or body and spirit is largely alien to Celtic Christianity.

Celtic Christians clung to the tradition of the holiness of nature, which it had subsumed from the pre-Christian Irish tradition. The Celts turned to nature and the elements for their gods. Aedemar, for example, was the Celtic goddess of fire. St Patrick's Irish contemporary, Pelagius, contended that nature was incorruptible and John Scotus Eriugena would later claim that the living body of Christ is in the world and not in the Church, as God is in all things.

One of the distinctive elements of the Celtic tradition is that the goose was the symbol of the Holy Spirit, whereas in the Christian tradition as a whole it was the dove, which was the symbol of the Spirit. The more raucous, wild and persistent goose fitted the Celtic sensibility more readily than the more placid doves – even though there were doves around. Of course, the flight pattern of the geese in their unique V formation would also have appealed to the Celts, each flying in the slipstream of the bird in front. As they fly, they switch positions, and so they take turns in leading and supporting, which is a powerful metaphor of a supportive, nurturing and egalitarian community. In the geese community, each has a role to play and none is more important so there were no hierarchies. So much of contemporary society is about the importance of the individual, but the Celts were attracted to symbols of a sustaining community like the geese. Given their closeness to God, the Celts also gravitated to the idea of a spirit unseen as the wind who spread a message of love.

St Patrick was quick to pick up on this central tenet of the Celtic tradition and to appreciate its fundamental importance for Christianity. He knew intuitively that, for his message to flourish, he needed to achieve a happy marriage between his new religion and the paganism he was hoping to usurp. To do this, he and his followers would have to creatively and subtly

adapt aspects of Christian practice to the conventions of the
Celts. Moreover, they saw that the traditional Christian practices
could only reap the rewards of an injection of the vitality of
the Celtic approach to life. As history shows, particularly in the
context of its mission to Africa, Christianity has a remarkable
facility for cleverly adapting itself to indigenous cultures while
simultaneously clinging on to its essence. St Patrick skilfully
used the Christian message of the God in all things in a way that
resonated deeply with the prejudices of his Celtic audience.

> Our God, God of all men,
> God of heaven and earth, sea and rivers,
> God of sun and moon, of all the stars,
> God of high mountains and of lowly valleys,
> God over heaven, and in heaven, and under heaven.
> He has a dwelling in heaven and earth and sea
> and in all things that are in them.
> He breathes in all things, makes all things live,
>   supports all things . . .
> He lights the sun, makes wells . . .

This passage highlights the presence of a divinity in the world,
eternally co-creating. The paths of nature and spirit kiss, creating
a web of life between people, creation and God. Heaven and
earth forge an intimate alliance. Humankind and creation were
not just God's playthings, but partners in God's creative project.
The theology which underpins Celtic Christianity is emphati-
cally incarnational. Of course, the Bible itself is radically incarnational, when the Word was made flesh and Jesus of Nazareth
came as the human face of God. Early Irish Christianity was
also Trinitarian and this fascinating combination of emphases
had a major influence on the Celtic religious imagination.

The value of the person was seen as inviolable only when the human person was understood as a creature of God. The personal meaning of life could only lie in religious communion with God. The mystery of God was a reality which pervaded all of creaturely life. This worldview was later taken up by Meister Eckhart who believed 'outside God there is nothing but nothing'.

Celtic Christianity was literally down to earth. It had no sense of a rigid dichotomy between the secular and the sacred. The Gaelic language ensured that the most mundane of social intercourse became occasions of prayer. In the Celtic tradition people were blessed every time they say goodbye in the phrase, *Go mbeannaí Dia dhuit* (God bless you). The standard greeting to friend and stranger was *Dia is Muire dhíbh* (God and Mary be with you). What is particularly instructive is that many of these greetings were in the plural as the presence of Christ in the other was also acknowledged.

This sense of God in nature had a deep resonance for Celtic Christians as revealed in the traditional prayer, which is now better known as a hymn.

> *Ag Críost an síol,*
> *Ag Críost an fómhar,*
> *In iothlann Dé*
> *Go dtugtar sinn.*

> Christ is the seed
> And Christ is the Harvest,
> Into God's granary
> May we be drawn.

Much later, Patrick Kavanagh would react against an over-institutionalised religion which failed to see Christ outside the institutional structures. Indeed in style and tone that part of Kavanagh's poetry mirrors a poem written by a Celtic monk in the eighth century.

THE DEER'S CRY

I arise today
Through the strength of heaven
Light of sun,
Radiance of moon,
Splendour of fire,
Speed of lightning,
Swiftness of wind,
Depth of sea
Stability of earth,
Firmness of rock.

Summer for the Celts was a time of joy and fun and time in the sun. It was above all a time for celebration for the wonder all around them. It was a time for celebrating that the world of nature was divine.

WISDOM
FOR
SUMMER

Bread of Heaven

The bread is pure and fresh
The water is cool and clear
Lord of all life be with us
Lord of all life be near.

TRADITIONAL AFRICAN PRAYER

Gardening for all Seasons

The mindful God abhors untimely growth.

JOHANN CHRISTIAN FRIEDRICH HÖLDERLIN, 1770–1843

All for One

The ritual is One.
The food is One.
We who offer the food are One.
The fire of hunger is also One.
All action is One.
We who understand this are One.

TRADITIONAL HINDU BLESSING

Think Positive

Do not overlook tiny good actions, thinking they are of no benefit; even tiny drops of water in the end will fill a huge vessel.

BUDDHA

Let Us Praise

Insults should be written in the sand,
And praises carved in stone.

ARAB PROVERB

The Orchestra

You are the notes, we are the flute
We are the mountain, you are the sounds coming down
We are the pawns and kings and rooks
We set on board: we win or we lose.
We are lions rolling and unrolling on flags.
Your invisible wind carries us through the world.

RUMI, 1207–1273

Tell Me Why?

The one who has a why to live can bear with almost any how.

NIETZSCHE

One Day at a Time

The best thing about the future is that it comes one day at a time.

ABRAHAM LINCOLN

Gentleness

Nothing is so strong as gentleness; nothing so gentle as real strength.

ST FRANCIS DE SALES

Empower

Go with the people
Live with them
Learn from them
Love them
Start with what they know
Build with what they have
But with the best leaders
When the work is done
The task accomplished
The people will say
'We have done this ourselves'.

LAO TZU, CHINA, 601–531 BC

True Measure

Try not to become a man of success, but rather try to become a man of value.

ALBERT EINSTEIN

Love and Affection

You can search throughout the entire universe for someone who is more deserving of your love and affection than you are yourself, and that person is not to be found anywhere. You yourself, as much as anybody in the entire universe deserve your love and affection.

BUDDHA

TALES
FOR
SUMMER

WHOSE HEART IS THE FAIREST?

An t-ualach is mó ar an gcapall is mine.
The heaviest load is on the gentlest horse.

One day Pádraig was standing in the middle of the town proclaiming that he had the most beautiful heart in the whole land.

A large crowd gathered and they all admired his heart for it was perfect. There was not a mark or a flaw in it. Yes, they all agreed it truly was the most beautiful heart they had ever seen.

Pádraig was very proud and boasted more loudly about his beautiful heart.

Suddenly, Proinsas appeared at the front of the crowd and said, 'Why your heart is not nearly as beautiful as mine.'

The crowd and Pádraig looked at Proinsas's heart. It was beating strongly . . . but full of scars. It had places where pieces had been removed and other pieces put in . . . but they didn't fit quite right and there were several jagged edges.

In fact, in some places there were deep gouges where whole pieces were missing. The people stared . . . how could he say his heart is more beautiful? they thought.

Pádraig looked at Proinsas's heart and saw its state and laughed. 'You must be joking,' he said. 'Compare your heart with mine . . . mine is perfect and yours is a mess of scars and tears.'

'Yes,' said Proinsas. 'Yours is perfect looking . . . but I would never trade with you. You see, every scar represents a person to whom I have given my love . . . I tear out a piece of my heart and give it to them . . . and often they give me a piece of their heart which fits into the empty place in my heart . . . but because the pieces aren't exact, I have some rough edges, which I cherish, because they remind me of the love we shared. Sometimes I have given pieces of my heart away . . . and the other person hasn't returned a piece of his heart to me. These are the empty gouges . . . giving love is taking a chance. Although these gouges are painful, they stay open, reminding me of the love I have for these people too . . . and I hope someday they may return and fill the space I have waiting. So now do you see what true beauty is?'

Pádraig stood silently with tears running down his cheeks. He walked up to the Proinsas, reached into his own perfect young and beautiful heart and ripped a piece out. He offered it to Proinsas with trembling hands.

Proinsas took his offering, placed it in his heart and then took a piece from his old scarred heart and placed it in the wound in Pádraig's heart. It fit . . . but not perfectly, as there were some jagged edges.

Pádraig looked at his heart, not perfect anymore but more beautiful than ever, since love from the Proinsas's heart flowed into his. They embraced and walked away side by side.

A REVERSAL OF FORTUNE

Long ago there lived a poor woodcutter named Eoin (the name means 'God is gracious'). Every day he went by the river to the forest with his strong, sharp axe over his shoulder. He was able to buy just enough food for his family by cutting wood.

On his way to the forest, shallow bogs lined the sides of the track, and stunted elder and aspen trees hunched over them, as if attempting to shrink away from the icy winds that often howled in from the flat expanses to the north and east. He had been told that the Celtic wind that shrieked across the hills with such violence every winter came from icy kingdoms above Norway and Sweden, where the land was perpetually frozen and the rays of sun never reached. Reeds and rushes waved and hissed back and forth, and the grey sky that stretched above always seemed much larger here than it did elsewhere. As they walked, more briskly than usual because it was cold, ducks flapped in sudden agitation in the undergrowth, and then flew away with piercing cackles.

The other early risers looked cold and miserable as they trudged along, and seemed to be wearing clothes that had dulled to a shade of drab brown in the wet semi-darkness. Even the cows that were being herded for milking were dirty and bedraggled.

Poor Eoin was sad because although he had enough to buy bread for his family he had no money to buy a turkey or potatoes or ham for the dinner or toys for his seven children or even a small present for his beautiful and kind wife, Winnie, for her birthday on the nineteenth of June.

Then just when he thought his spirits could go no lower, disaster struck. The path by the river was very icy and Eoin slipped and his axe fell into the river.

'What will I do?' the woodcutter cried. 'I've lost my axe! How will I feed my children now?'

Just as he finished, up from the lake rose a beautiful lady. She was the water queen of the river, and came to the surface when she heard his sad voice. 'What is your problem?' she asked in a soft, gentle whisper.

The woodman told her about his situation, and at once she sank beneath the surface, and reappeared in a moment with an axe made of silver.

'Is this your axe?' she asked.

The woodcutter shook his head sadly as he thought of all the things he could buy for his children with such an axe. But the axe wasn't his, so he shook his head, and answered, 'My axe was only made of steel.'

The water queen lay the silver axe on the bank, and sank into the river again. In a moment she rose and showed the woodman another axe. 'Maybe this one is yours?' she asked.

'Oh, no!' the woodcutter replied. 'This one is made of gold. It's much, much more valuable than mine.'

The water queen lay the golden axe on the bank. Once again she sank. Up she rose. This time she held the missing axe.

'Ah, yes. That one is mine.' the woodcutter said.

'It is yours.' said the water queen, 'and so are these other two now. They are gifts from the river, because you have told the truth.'

And that evening Eoin walked home with all three axes on his shoulder, happily thinking of all the good things he could now buy for his family even though the day had grown even darker since they had been in the lake, and black clouds slouched above, moving fast in the rising wind. Rain fell in a persistent, heavy drizzle that quickly soaked through his cloak and boots. He was soon shivering. It was much too cold to travel at the ambling pace he usually favoured.

His house was a tiny cottage with a red-tiled roof and ivy-clad walls. Smoke curled from its chimney, to be whisked away by the wind. From the house next door came the sweet, warm scent of newly baked bread. When he arrived at his front door, and had made his way through the dripping vegetation, he was puffing and panting like a pair of bellows, although it had still not been fast enough to drive the chill from his bones. Shivering, but with a sense of triumph, he knocked on the door. The bright blue eyes of his wife peered out at him. Before he could announce his news, the door had been fully opened, and his children nearly crushed him with their loving embraces.

The following morning, just as the first glimmerings of dawn lightened the sky, Eoin dragged himself from a deep sleep, and washed and shaved in the dim light, muttering under his breath when he could not find a clean shirt. The light danced across the thin green grass in tiny pools of brightness as it filtered through branches that were shorn of their leaves. The village was unusually peaceful.

When his family woke they could not believe their eyes because Eoin had a wonderful feast prepared for them, toys for all the children and a beautiful brooch for Winnie. Seeing the joy and surprise on their faces, tears filled his eyes. He gave them a surreptitious scrub with the back of his hand.

Later that night when the kids were sleeping soundly, Winnie asked Eoin what he had learned from his adventure. He thought for a long while before answering: 'Our life is a book of three chapters: the past, the present, and the yet-to-be. The past is gone, it is stowed away; the present we live with every day; the future is not for us to see, it is locked away and God holds the key.'

SET FREE FOR FREEDOM

> Money can buy . . .
> A bed but no sleep.
> Food but no appetite.

A house but not a home.
Medicine but not health.
Finery but not beauty.
Acquaintances but not friends.
Entertainment but not happiness.
Stop looking for happiness in the things outside of you.
Instead, try looking WITHIN.
What are the best things in YOUR life that come for FREE?

ANON

THE POWER OF LOVE

Although they were brothers, Oisin and Setanta, did not look much alike. However, the tie of common blood was not all that truly linked the two brothers. They both had the same kindness and sensitivity and a warm affection for all people.

Both brothers lived and worked together on the family farm. Oisin was married with five children, but Setanta never married. They shared the workload and what they grew equally, and they divided their profits in two halves.

One day Setanta said to himself: 'You know, it's not fair that we should share the produce equally and all the money too. After all, I'm all by myself. My needs are simple. However, look at my poor brother with a wife and all those kids.' So, in the middle of the night, he took a sack of grain from his barn and sneaked over to the granary behind his brother's house and left it in there.

Meanwhile, unknown to him, Oisin was thinking on similar lines. 'You know, it's not right that we should share our farm produce equally. After all, I'm married and I have five fantastic children who will look after me in my old age. But there is my poor brother with no wife nor family to support him when he gets old.' So that same night he took a bag of grain from his granary, crept over the field between their houses and stored it in his brother's barn.

For the next five years, at the same time every night, the two brothers left a sack of grain in each other's granary. They were both very puzzled as to why their supply did not dwindle. Then one night, Setanta left his home twenty minutes later than normal. He had been delayed because his cow had decided to bring her beautiful healthy young calf into the world. The calf had a red spot above his nose on his white face, so Setanta decided to call him Rudolf.

As Setanta carried the sack of grain, in the darkness of night he bumped into Oisin. Each was startled, but then it slowly dawned on them what had been going on for years and they hugged each other.

Suddenly, the dark sky lit up and a voice came booming down from the sky:

'Here at last is a fitting place where I shall build my temple. For where my children embrace in love, there my presence shall abide for evermore.'

HEAVEN'S GATE

Good King Niall had ruled over the people of Connacht for many years. At the end of his life, Niall felt that he had enough time on earth and it was time to go on to the kingdom where people lived forever. When he had sorted out his affairs, he set off for the high mountain, Mount Heaven. His beautiful wife, went with him and his seven brothers. Very soon, they were joined by a dog which followed quietly behind him.

But the journey was a difficult and painful one. Niall's seven brothers died one by one along the way, and after that his wife.

The king was all alone then, except for the dog, which continued to follow him faithfully up and up the steep, windy road to the Heavenly City.

Finally the two, tired and shattered, stopped before the gates of heaven. Niall bowed humbly there as he asked to be admitted.

Sky and earth were shaken by a great noise as the father of the Gods, arrived to meet and welcome the king to Paradise. But Niall wasn't fully ready.

'Without my wife and my brothers, I do not wish to enter heaven.'

'Have no fear,' the great God answered. 'You shall meet them all in heaven. They came before you and are here in heaven.'

But Niall had another request to make.

'This dog has come all the way with me. He is devoted to me. Surely for his faithfulness I cannot leave him outside! And besides, my heart is full of love for him!'

The great God shook his head and the earth quaked.

'You yourself may come into heaven but you can't bring a dog in here. Cast off the dog. It's no sin.'

'But where would he go? asked the king. 'And who would go with him? He has given up all the pleasures of earth to be my companion. I cannot desert him now.'

The great God was very annoyed by this and asked, 'Are you willing to abandon heaven, then, for this dog's sake?'

Niall replied, 'Great God of all Gods. I have steadily kept this vow – that I will never desert one that is frightened and seeks my protection, one that is homeless, or one that is too weak to protect himself and desires to live. Now I add a fourth. I have promised never to abandon one that is devoted to me. I will not leave my friend.'

Niall reached down to touch the dog and was about to turn sadly away from heaven when suddenly before his eyes a great wonder happened. The faithful dog was changed into the God of Justice.

The God of Justice said, 'You are a good man, King Niall. You have shown loyalty to the faithful and compassion for all creatures. You shall be honoured in heaven for there is no act more highly and rewarded more richly than compassion for the humble.'

So Niall entered heaven where he was reunited with his wife and brothers, and there he enjoyed eternal happiness.

A RUPTURED RELATIONSHIP

Fintan the Frog and Seamus the Snake met as strangers in the forest one day, and played together all day.

'Watch what I can do,' said Fintan the Frog, and he hopped high into the air. 'I'll teach you if you want,' he offered.

So he taught Seamus how to hop, and together they hopped up and down the path through the forest.

'Now watch what I can do' said Seamus, and he crawled on his belly straight up the trunk of a tall tree. 'I'll teach you if you want.'

So he taught Fintan how to slide on his belly and climb trees.

After a while they both grew hungry and decided to go home for lunch, but they promised to meet each other the next day.

'Thanks for teaching me how to hop,' said Seamus.

'Thanks for teaching me how to crawl up trees,' said Fintan.

Then they each went home.

'Look what I can do, mother,' cried Fintan, crawling on his belly.

'Where did you learn how to do that?' his mother asked.

'Seamus the Snake taught me,' he answered. 'We played together in the forest this morning. He's my new friend.'

'Don't you know that the snake family is a bad family?' his

mother asked. 'They have poison in their teeth. Don't ever let me see you crawling on your belly either. It isn't proper.'

Meanwhile Seamus went home and hopped up and down for his mother to see.

'Who taught you to do that?' she asked.

'Fintan Frog,' he said. 'He's my new friend.'

'What foolishness,' said his mother. 'Don't you know that we've been on bad terms with the frog family for longer than we can remember. The next time you play with the frog, catch him and eat him up. And stop that hopping. It isn't our custom.'

So next morning when Fintan met Seamus in the forest, he kept his distance.

'I'm afraid I can't go crawling with you today,' he called, hopping back a hop or two.

Seamus eyed him quietly, remembering what his mother had told him. 'If he gets too close, I'll spring at him and eat him,' he thought.

But then he remembered how much fun they had together, and how nice Fintan had been to teach him how to hop. So he sighed sadly to himself and slid away into the bush. And from that day on, Fintan and Seamus never played together again. But they often sat alone in the sun, each thinking about their one day of friendship.

HOLY MOTHER

Tá Dia láidir is máthair mhaith aige.
God is strong and has a good mother.

Traditionally in Ireland, many people welcomed the fine weather by joining the rush to erect a May altar in honour of Our Lady.

Boxes, tea-chests and all kinds of idle implements were draped with white sheets to make homemade altars. Flowers were piled into jam jars for decorations. The most colourful ceremony of all was the procession from the chapel down to the village. It seemed to be an injunction for the sacred to leave the church and make its home in the ordinary. Every house along the way was decorated with flowers. From an early age we were given a great devotion for the Virgin Mary – intercessor, mother of mercy, star of the sea. To call upon the Father for daily bread and praise the kingdom, the power and the glory, was inspiring and comforting, but we felt a warm glow within us when we spoke phrases like 'fruit of thy womb'.

Mary was an integral part of the fabric of Irish life, even Irish history. One story told was about the Virgin Mary walking by a house in the west of Ireland on a stormy night during the Great Famine. She and the child Jesus had no coat to protect them from the elements. As they passed the house, the woman of the house called them inside and gave Mary a bowl of nettle soup, and an old sack to give extra cover to the child. Mary's final blessing was that the family line would always remain intact. They were one of the few families who survived the Great Hunger. A sign that God's favour rested on them was that their rooster did not crow 'cock-a-doodle-doo', but rather cried out: 'The Virgin's Son is risen.'

All of us who have lost a loved one know what it is like to experience a hidden grieving that rises to grab the heart. We are occasionally ambushed by painful emotions.

Many of us today can identify with the sentiment of Robert Frost in his poem 'Lodged' when he describes flowers lodged – though not dead. Many of us know 'how the flowers felt' because we have experienced what it is like to be pelted with sorrow.

Inevitably, in times of suffering, we experience moments of doubt. This is not unusual. Jesus himself suffered from uncertainty. At the wedding feast of Cana, Jesus initially did not want to perform the miracle of turning water into wine because he did not believe he could. He was only spurred into action when Mary said to him: 'Do you not know yet who you are?'

In times of suffering I find myself thinking of Mary the Mother of God. However, it is not the holy woman whose picture we see on countless Christmas cards. Instead it is the Mary of Michelangelo's statue *Woman and Son*. This is the Pietà, the Mother of Jesus, holding the body of her dead son in her arms. In the Pietà we see great love and strength, but equally a heart-wrenching moment of lamentation and agony at life's capacity for cruelty. This Mary speaks loudly of suffering, of pain, of agony.

While Mary recognised God's love and had hope in the power of God working in her life she had to live with the imperfections of the present. She is united today with all people who suffer by an openness to allowing God to grow in their lives and in their sadness. God grows in them as in Mary – though like a seed in winter, which grows silently, most often in darkness, so that frequently they could not recognise what was happening. Often it was only in retrospect that they could see the signs of the divine presence.

While Mary was honoured with the greatest gift of all she also had her own trials and tribulations. She received the Good News at the Annunciation, but she also had to watch her son suffer in agony on the cross at Calvary. Her gifts were matched by her crosses. In this way she is close to our own lives – which are unique mixtures of joy and sadness.

She wondered and reflected as she nurtured the child growing within her. We often think of Mary as different from ourselves.

But, reflecting on her life, we discover that she herself walked in darkness and uncertainty before us. She herself has known our fears and insecurities. That is why we can turn to her with confidence in our moments of crisis.

This does not mean that all our problems will melt away like snow in the rain. Rather, Mary points us to a new reality, which will give us the strength to face up to the harsh aspects of modern life, to experience and to transmit the touch of God's gentle love. The message of Mary is not that we get a ladder to climb up to heaven – but instead we have joy because God has come down from heaven to raise us up to new heights.

In May we remember Mary. She understands our suffering, but is also a woman of hope. She invites us to place our trust in God, who never leaves us or abandons us. She was open to learning from all her experiences and came to understand that God speaks to us through all the events of our lives, be they good or bad. In this way we can face the future with confidence knowing that God will give us what we need for each day.

MIRACLE CURE

One woman who reached out to Mary in a special way was Athlone woman Marion Carroll. Marion was at death's door when she travelled to Knock in 1989 as a pilgrim. This is her testimony.

When we got to Knock they brought me into the nurse and she settled all the things you do with an invalid. I was too sick to be brought to the Basilica immediately, so I was taken to the rest and care centre. Eventually, just before Mass, we went over to the Basilica and they put me under the statue of Our Lady of Knock and when I looked up at the statue, that's the statue they carry in the procession, I thought she was the most beautiful and friendliest statue I had ever seen in my life.

I had been thinking about dying, about my husband Jimmy, and my children Cora and Anthony. I knew being a young mother that people would give Cora and Anthony an extra bit of love and attention, which people do, but I was worried about Jimmy because I was only three months married when I got sick and Jimmy built his whole life around me. I mean he could have run out on me because all of a sudden he was caught every way, he was caught mentally, physically and financially. He was very quiet, he never went out with the lads, if he wasn't at work he was with me, that's the way we were. If a woman loses her husband everyone is up to her, if a man loses his wife they think after two days he's all right. There's no difference. I knew that when the funeral was over people would think he didn't want anybody or need anybody. I was thinking if Jimmy was the one to die on me how I would feel in myself. There would be part of me gone. When there's part of something gone it's hard to make it whole again. They were the thoughts and feelings that were going around in my heart and mind but I couldn't put them into words I wanted. I wanted another housewife, another woman to talk to me who would understand what was within me and I looked back up at the statue of our Lady and I said to her 'You are a mother too, you know how I feel about leaving my husband and children.'

It wasn't a prayer, it wasn't a statement it was just one woman chatting to another. I then prayed to her to look after Jimmy and the children and to give them the grace to accept my death as the will of God.

The Rosary was recited and Benediction imparted, and when the bishop walked down with the Eucharist during the Blessing of the Sick and came to the front of my stretcher, I heard the words: 'The lame shall walk.' When the ceremonies started my bishop anointed me. After I was anointed I got restless. I can't explain it. It was really my mind that was restless. When it came to the consecration during Mass, I can't really explain this, I wasn't afraid but all of a sudden I wanted someone I knew. I received holy communion after which I got a tremendous pain in both my heels which was very unusual. Then the pain disappeared and so did all the other pains in my body.

After communion there was the Rosary, Benediction and the Blessing of the Sick. It was at that time I got this magnificent feeling – a wonderful sensation like a whispering breeze telling me that I was cured. I got this beautiful, magnificent feeling telling me that if the stretcher was opened I could get up and walk. Being very practical, I laughed it off.

My mind was a tangle of thoughts, orderless, confused, inexpressible. I tried to cop myself on and remind myself that I was going to die. I knew if I said to anybody to open the stretcher that they would get a nurse and I knew the nurse would say, 'No she's too sick, just pacify her.' So I said I would tell nobody and that I would go home and tell Jimmy because he always sorted things out for me. I was last out of the Basilica and I looked up at the statue of Our Lady and I said to her, 'Well, if you did do anything for me in Knock and I didn't tell anybody, maybe by the time I got to Roscommon you might take it back.' I was trying to laugh it off.

My friend Nuala came over to talk to me and I couldn't control myself and I said to her, 'Would you think I was stupid if I said to you that if the stretcher was opened that I could get up and walk?' and she said no, but I knew the poor woman didn't know what to say, so she called a nurse who opened the stretcher and my two legs swung out and I stood up a straight. It was the first time in three years I had been able to do so. I wasn't a bit stiff even after all those years; also I was strapped into the stretcher since a quarter to nine that morning and this was 4.30 p.m. and you know even because of that I would have expected to be stiff. I got a lovely warm feeling and it has stayed with me constantly. I am absolutely convinced it was a miracle. My speech was perfect and my hands and arms were perfect. I was standing unaided on my own two feet.

Taken from *My Miracle Cure* by Marion Carroll as told to John Scally,
published by Black & White Publishing, May 2020.

A DAUGHTER'S LOVE

In one of his recent homilies, Pope Francis asked people to reflect on which figure we would have been at the original Passion. Sadly, many of us today are like the two Marys weeping for a lost loved one. A case in point is a young woman from Clondalkin, Lydia Greene, who is still mourning for her beloved father:

> My dad was diagnosed with cancer. It felt like the end of the world and then they said about an operation and treatment. This was a light at the end of the tunnel for us as a family. The treatment was going well and my dad was able to live a normal life apart from his treatment every couple of weeks. He was even able to go back to work, which he loved so much and it kept him going, but as we all know, nothing lasts forever. The cancer came back and unfortunately no amount of treatment was making him any better.

Sometimes, though, Lydia could not help thinking: Why is God not listening?

'My dad liked his religion and was a great believer in holy water particularly St Albert's water from Whitefriar Street Church. He had so much faith in this holy water. He was full sure that the holy water was going to cure him.'

It was difficult for Lydia to come to terms with her father's suffering.

'As I watched my dad, lying in the hospice bed, still a young man of sixty-one, clinging on to the last bit of life he had in him with both hands. I went out to the oratory and begged God to be merciful and take him. He had suffered enough and my mam and I could no longer watch him like that. We had finally surrendered to God's will. My mam and I were grateful to God that we were there with him holding his hands while he took his last breaths.'

At her darkest hour Lydia saw the light.

'My dad's face changed in front of our very eyes. It was like something you would see in a movie or read in a book. It was incredible. All the pain and suffering was gone from his face and he looked like a very young man again and happy. The bonus was he still had his thick head of jet-black hair even after all the chemotherapy. The nurses even said how handsome he looked. We got the miracle from God, it just wasn't the one we prayed for.

'When we feel like no one up there is listening to us and we see no light at the end of the tunnel we must remember to keep our faith, not to give up on God. God is always willing to listen. We just have to be patient and although sometimes we feel like we have been hard done by, that things don't work out the way we want them to, we need to trust that God has his reasons and he knows the right time for everything. It has gotten me through my darkest moments in the past few months.'

Although the sadness remains, Lydia now has reclaimed her hope.

'Our Lady, Mary, the Mother of God, knows what it is like to suffer just as the parents that lose a child suffer. Jesus's suffering on the cross tells us how much He loves us and how much God loves us. God sent His only son to the earth to suffer for us, for our sins. This shows the lengths God has gone to, to show us He will do whatever it takes to prove His love for us.

'Just as I know God is there to turn to when I need guidance or consolation, I believe so too are our loved ones that are gone to God before us. I believe their spirits are still with us but their souls are gone to God and they will watch over us until it is our turn to join God in the Kingdom of Heaven. I know God has always been there and always will be but I also know my dad is watching over me every step of the way.'

RONAN'S ROVING

Ronan's day began as all his days had begun, meandering through the Irish countryside in search of a breakfast of bountiful blackberries. This was his favourite time of the day, the only pleasure in his poverty-stricken life. Suddenly, he came to an abrupt halt, his attention held by a wooden notice, written in bold handwriting and hanging precariously on a magnificent oak tree.

It was common knowledge throughout the kingdom that the reigning king had no heir and was frantically searching for a successor, as he was now in his eighty-fifth year. The sign on the tree showed that he was trying for a different approach, now every qualified young man should apply for an interview with the king. The qualifications were very specific, love of God and love of neighbour.

Ronan thought long and hard about the notice and, even though he was a very modest young man, considered that he

indeed loved God and his fellow human beings. He decided
there and then that he would go to be interviewed by the king.
However, there was one obstacle which had to be immediately
overcome. He was so poor that he had no clothes which would
be presentable in the king's palace. Worse still, he had no money
to buy the food and clothes he needed. Still, he managed to find
himself enough food and presentable clothes to set off for the
palace. His journey was almost complete when he came upon a
poor beggar sitting feebly on the side of the road. His haunted
eyes, his ashen face, his outstretched arms pleaded for help,
much more loudly than any words ever could have.

Ronan's heart was so moved with tender compassion at
this picture of vulnerability and suffering that he immediately
stripped off his clothes and swapped them for the beggar's rags.
He gave all his food to the beggar without the slightest hesitation.
The beggar smiled in grateful appreciation as Ronan headed off
uncertainly to the king's castle. Ronan felt completely out of
place as he waited what seemed like an eternity to be presented
to the king.

When the moment arrived, his heart was in his mouth as he
bowed before the king. When he raised his eyes, he was shocked
to see the king's face.

'But you . . . you were the poor beggar by the side of the
road.'

'Yes,' answered the king. 'I was that shabby beggar.'

'But, why did you put me through all this?' asked Ronan.

'Because I had to find out if you really do love, if you really
love God and your fellow human beings. I knew that if I came to
you as king, you would have been so dazzled by my crown and
robes that you would have bent over backwards to do anything
I wished, but I would never have known what was really in your
heart. So I came to you as a simple beggar, with no claims on

you except for the love in your heart. Now I know that you truly do love God and your fellow human beings. You shall be the new king.'

CATS

The great Irish poet William Butler Yeats was going home from work one cold winter's evening. Having failed to find a coat hanger that morning, he had casually thrown his overcoat at the foot of the Abbey stage. However, when he went back for it that evening, a little kitten had snuggled up inside the coat and was now fast asleep. Rather than disturb the kitten, it is said that Yeats went backstage and got a scissors and cut the section of his coat that was sheltering the kitten and headed out in the cold night air with a big hole in his coat!

POETRY
FOR
SUMMER

The Good

The good are vulnerable
As any bird in flight,
They do not think of safety,
Are blind to possible extinction
And when most vulnerable
Are most themselves.
The good are real as the sun,
Are best perceived through clouds
Of casual corruption
That cannot kill the luminous sufficiency
That shines on city, sea and wilderness,
Fastidiously revealing
One man to another,
Who yet will not accept
Responsibilities of light.
The good incline to praise,
To have the knack of seeing that
The best is not destroyed
Although forever threatened.
The good go naked in all weathers,

And by their nakedness rebuke
The small protective sanities
That hide men from themselves.
The good are difficult to see
Though open, rare, destructible;
Always, they retain a kind of youth,
The vulnerable grace
Of any bird in flight,
Content to be itself,
Accomplished master and potential victim,
Accepting what the earth or sky intends.
I think that I know one or two
Among my friends.

BRENDAN KENNELLY

O King of Stars!

O King of stars!
Whether my house be dark or bright,
Never shall it be closed against anyone,
Lest Christ close His house against me.
If there be a guest in your house
And you conceal aught from him,
'Tis not the guest that will be without it,
But Jesus, Mary's Son.

THIRTEENTH-CENTURY POEM, TRANSLATED BY KUNO MEYER

Soul Searching

Come, O beautiful soul!
Know, now, that your desire beloved lives hidden within
your heart.

ST JOHN OF THE CROSS

Jesus Christ, the Apple Tree

The tree of life my soul hath seen,
Laden with fruit and always green:
The trees of nature fruitless be
Compared with Christ the apple tree.

Its fruit doth make my soul to thrive,
It keeps my dying faith alive;
Which makes my soul in haste to be
With Jesus Christ the apple tree.

ANONYMOUS AMERICAN HYMN, FOUND IN 1784

Love Story

Oh, when a soul is hid in thee
For what adventure can it yearn
Save love and still more love to learn,
And thus to love increasingly,
So deep does love within it burn?
My God, I pray thee for a love
That yearns until I see thy face,
And builds itself a nest above
Within its true abiding place.

ST TERESA OF ÁVILA

Feast at the Banquet

You who have fasted, rejoice today.
The table is set, approach it without thought of the past;
The fat calf is served, let all eat their fill.
Partake of the Banquet of faith;
Let all drink from the riches of mercy.

FROM THE OFFICE OF MATINS IN THE BYZANTINE RITE

I Believe

I believe – that our background and circumstances may have influenced who we are, but we are responsible for who we become.

I believe – that no matter how good a friend is, they're going to hurt you every once in a while and you must forgive them for that.

I believe – that just because someone doesn't love you the way you want them to doesn't mean they don't love you with all they have.

I believe – that true friendship continues to grow, even over the longest distance. Same goes for true love.

I believe – that it's taking me a long time to become the person I want to be.

I believe – that you should always leave loved ones with loving words. It may be the last time you see them.

I believe – that you can keep going, long after you can't.

I believe – that we are responsible for what we do, no matter how we feel.

I believe – that either you control your attitude or it controls you.

I believe – that heroes are the people who do what has to be done when it needs to be done, regardless of the consequences.

I believe – that money is a lousy way of keeping score.

I believe – that my best friend and I can do anything or nothing and have the best time.

I believe – that sometimes the people you expect to kick you when you're down, will be the ones to help you get back up.

I believe – that sometimes when I'm angry I have the right
to be angry, but that doesn't give me the right to be cruel.

I believe – that maturity has more to do with what types of
experiences you've had and what you've learned from
them and less to do with how many birthdays you've
celebrated.

I believe – that it isn't always enough to be forgiven by
others. Sometimes you have to learn to forgive yourself.

I believe – that no matter how bad your heart is broken the
world doesn't stop for your grief.

I believe – that just because two people argue, it doesn't
mean they don't love each other. And just because they
don't argue, it doesn't mean they do.

I believe – that you shouldn't be so eager to find out a secret.
It could change your life forever.

I believe – that two people can look at the exact same thing
and see something totally different.

I believe – that your life can be changed in a matter of hours
by people who don't even know you.

I believe – that even when you think you have no more to
give, when a friend cries out to you – you will find the
strength to help.

I believe – that credentials on the wall do not make you a
decent human being.

I believe – that the people you care about most in life are
taken from you too soon.

AUTHOR UNKNOWN

I Love You

I love you,
Not only for what you are,
but for what I am when I'm with you.

I love you,
Not only for what you have made of yourself,
But what you are making of me.

I love you for
The part of me that you bring out;
I love you for
putting your hand into my heaped-up heart
And passing over all the foolish weak things
that you can't help dimly seeing there,
And drawing out in the light
All the beautiful belongings
that no one else had looked
Quite far enough to find.

I love you because you
Are helping me to make
Of the lumber of my life
Not a tavern, but a temple;
Out of the works
Of my every day
Not a reproach
But a song.

I love you because you have done
More than any creed
Could have done

To make me good,
And more than any fate
Could have done
To make me happy.

You have done it
Without a touch,
Without a word,
Without a sign.
You have done it by being yourself.
Perhaps that is what
being a friend means, after all.

ADAPTED FROM ELIZABETH BARRETT BROWNING

A Poem for Hard Times

You Still Have Hope
If you can look at the sunset and smile,
then you still have hope.
If you can find beauty in the colours of a small flower,
then you still have hope.
If you can find pleasure in the movement of a butterfly,
then you still have hope.
If the smile of a child can still warm your heart,
then you still have hope.
If you can see the good in other people,
then you still have hope.
If the rain breaking on a roof top can still lull you to sleep,
then you still have hope.
If the sight of a rainbow still makes you stop and stare in
wonder,
then you still have hope.

If the soft fur of a favoured pet still feels pleasant under your
fingertips,
then you still have hope.
If you meet new people with a trace of excitement and
optimism,
then you still have hope.
If you give people the benefit of a doubt,
then you still have hope.
If you still offer your hand in friendship to others that have
touched your life,
then you still have hope.
If receiving an unexpected card
or letter still brings a pleasant surprise,
then you still have hope.
If the suffering of others still fills you with pain and
frustration,
then you still have hope.
If you refuse to let a friendship die,
or accept that it must end,
then you still have hope.
If you look forward to a time or place of quiet and
reflection,
then you still have hope.
If you still buy the ornaments,
put up the Christmas tree or cook the supper,
then you still have hope.
If you can look to the past and smile,
then you still have hope.
If, when faced with the bad,
when told everything is futile,
you can still look up and end the conversation with the
phrase . . . Yeah . . . BUT,

then you still have hope.
Hope is such a marvellous thing.
It bends, it twists, it sometimes hides,
but rarely does it break.
It sustains us when nothing else can.
It gives us reason to continue and courage to move ahead,
when we tell ourselves we'd rather give in.
Hope puts a smile on our face
when the heart cannot manage.
Hope puts our feet on the path
when our eyes cannot see it.
Hope moves us to act
when our souls are confused of the direction.
Hope is a wonderful thing,
something to be cherished and nurtured,
and something that will refresh us in return.
And it can be found in each of us,
and it can bring light into the darkest of places.
NEVER LOSE HOPE!

AUTHOR UNKNOWN

PRAYERS
FOR
SUMMER

Teicht do Róim
Mór saído, becc torbai!
In rí chon-daigi hi fos,
Manim-berre latt, ní fogbal.

Pilgrim, take care your journey's not in vain
A hazard without profit, without gain,
The King you seek you'll find in Rome, 'tis true,
But only if He travels on the way with you.

CELTIC PRAYER

The Difference

I got up early one morning
and rushed right in to the day;
I had so many things to accomplish
that I didn't have time to pray.
Problems just tumbled about me,
and heavier came each task.
'Why doesn't God help me?' I wondered.
He answered, 'You didn't ask.'

I wanted to see joy and beauty,
but the day toiled on, grey and bleak,
I wondered why God didn't show me.
He said, 'But you didn't seek.'
I tried to come into God's presence;
I used all my keys at the lock.
God gently and lovingly chided,
'My child, you didn't knock.'
I woke up early this morning,
and paused before entering the day,
I had so much to accomplish
that I had to take time to pray.

AUTHOR UNKNOWN

A Prayer for Father's Day

God took the strength of a mountain,
The majesty of a tree,
The warmth of a summer sun,
The calm of a quiet sea,
The generous soul of nature,
The comforting arm of night,
The wisdom of ages,
The power of the eagles' flight,
The joy of a spring morning,
The faith of a mustard seed,
And the depth of a family need.
Then God combined these qualities
And there was nothing more to add.
He knew his masterpiece was complete
And so he called it DAD.

AUTHOR UNKNOWN

HUMOUR
FOR
SUMMER

Cardinal Error
Competition comes into all walks of life. Two cardinals were bemoaning the drop of vocations.

One, a Jesuit remarked, 'It will be a shame if in the next fifty years or so if we have no more Jesuits. It would be a tragedy and a huge loss to the Church.'

His colleague, a Benedictine, said, 'Nonsense. The Church managed for fifteen hundred years without any Jesuits. It will do so again. Now if there were to be no more Benedictines that would be a crisis.'

All in the Game
Peter Ustinov remarked once of Pavarotti, 'Luciano is difficult to pass at the net in tennis – even when he is not playing.'

Down to the River
A priest was giving a fire and brimstone sermon on the evils of the demon drink. With great enthusiasm he said, 'If I had all the beer in the world. I'd take it and throw it into the river.'

Then in a tone of intense ferocity he said, 'And if I had all the wine in the world, I'd take it and throw it into the river.'

And then, with even more gusto, he shouted, 'And if I had all the whiskey in the world, I'd take it and throw it into the river.'

He sat down in a state of moral indignation.

The choir leader then stood very cautiously and announced with a smile, 'For our next song, let us sing: "As I went down to the river to pray".'

Self-help

G.K. Chesterton was once asked what book he would most likely take with him if he was forced to live on a desert island. Chesterton replied: 'First and foremost an instruction book on how to build a boat!'

Guess Who Is Coming to Dinner?

These days it sometimes seems that everybody is doing an assertiveness course. When Frank went on his he resolved to change things at home. As soon as he came in the door he told his long-suffering wife Danielle, 'I want dinner on the table each evening when I get home. I want you to run a bath for me every evening and towel me down afterwards. I want my shirt ironed every day and hot breakfast every morning. And do you know, who is going to button up my shirt and tie my tie?'

'Yes,' replied Danielle with a sweet smile. 'The undertaker.'

Keeping the Faith

Liverpool signed Avi Cohen and made him the first Israeli international to play for the Reds. Avi's mother was a devout member of the Jewish faith and was concerned that Avi would lose out on his faith in Liverpool. A few weeks after he arrived in the club she rang her son and said, 'Do you still wear your skull cap?'

Avi: 'No one wears skull caps in Liverpool.'

Mrs Cohen: 'Do you still go the synagogue on the Sabbath?'

Avi: 'How can I? We have a match every Saturday.'

Mrs Cohen [attributed]: 'Tell me, are you still circumcised?'

The Ear of the Beholder

Pastor Fritz read an article to his wife about how many words woman use a day – thirty thousand compared to a man's fifteen thousand words. His wife replied, 'That is because a woman has to say everything twice.'

Pastor Fritz then turned to her and asked: 'What?'

The Dinner

As only he could, Brendan Kennelly imagined in this poem what might have happened if James Joyce had been a guest at a meal of the Holy Family – a Celtic version of the Last Supper.

James Joyce had dinner with the Holy Family
One Saturday evening in Nazareth.
Mary was a good cook, her Virgin soup was delicious,
Joyce lapped it up till he was nearly out of breath.
The Holy Family looked at Joyce who said
Nothing, he was a morose broody class
Of a man, his glasses made him look very sad,
It was next to impossible to get him to talk and
The dinner was uncomfortable as a result.

'How're things in Ireland?' asked Joseph. 'Ugh,' said Joyce.
'What're you writing now?' persisted Joseph. 'I couldn't find
    fault
With your last book. Perfect.'
Joyce seemed to sulk.
'A large work,' he muttered, 'Like the Bible, the sea. My voices.'
'Am I in it?' queried Jesus. 'Yep,' said Joyce. 'Pass the salt.'
'Is it too much to enquire about the role I play?'
Continued Jesus. 'It is,' said Joyce.
Mary changed the subject. 'Are there many grottoes to me
In Ireland?' 'Countless,' replied the hero.
Joyce's short answers were buggering the dinner up.
'The Society of Jesus,' queried Jesus, 'How's it going?'
'Who knows Clongowes?' said Joyce. 'Could I have a cup
Of Bewley's coffee to round off this occasion?'
'Why did you leave Ireland, James?' queried Joseph.
'The Swiss, French, Italians are just as lousy
In their ways.' Joyce pondered. 'Crime,'
He replied, 'Of non-being.' Jesus butted in:
'In that case you must have sinners in plenty.
I think I should visit Ireland, sometime.'
'I wouldn't, if I were you,' said Joyce.
'But you're not me,' said Jesus. 'Though there
Are times when you behave as if you were
The Son of Man Himself. You get in my hair.
James, from time to time, with your pretentious
Posturing, sitting on a cloud, paring your toenails
In an orgy of indifference, pissed on white wine.
Though I readily admit your prose is divine
With touches of Matthew Mark Luke and John,
Why can't you be an honest-to-God
Dubliner, go for a swim in Sandymount, spend

Sunday afternoon in Croke Park or Dayler.
Boast of things you've never done,
Places you've never been,
Have a pint in O'Neill's,
Misjudge the political scene,
Complain about the weather,
Miss mass, go to Knock,
Take a week in Killarney,
Listen to McCormack's records,
Re-learn to mock, jibe, scandalise, sneer, scoff
And talk your head off.
James, you have a block about Ireland,
You're too long on the continent.
In some strange way, James, you are,
If you ask me, bent.'

'But I didn't ask you, Jesus,' replied Joyce,
'It so happens I think things out for myself,
I had to leave Ireland to do this
Because no one in Ireland has a mind of his own,
I know that place to the marrow of its bone
And I insist that people are dominated by henchmen,
Those chaps in black who tell folk what to think.'

'I beg your pardon,' said Jesus 'These men
Are not me.'
'Would you put that in ink?'
Asked Joyce.
'In blood,' Jesus replied.

'This is getting too serious,' Joseph interrupted.

'Shut up, Dad! said Jesus. 'The matter *is* serious.

It's precisely for this kind of crap I came and died.'

'But you're alive and well, son.' Joseph said, 'You're not dead
And we're the Holy Family. That's what they call us.'

'What family is wholly holy?' asked Jesus.
Joseph looked at him, then at the ground, perplexed.
The honest carpenter didn't seem comfortable.

There was nothing he couldn't do with timber.
But his was a different matter.

He said nothing.
Just poured himself another cup of Bewley's coffee.
Mary said, 'Let's finish with a song,
Mr Joyce, I understand that you
Took second place
To Mr McCormack at a Feis.
But that's a long time ago, a long
Time ago.
Though second place is not the place for you
Perhaps you'd give the Holy Family a song.'

Joyce brooded a bit, took a deep breath,
Straightened his glasses gone slightly askew.
Coughed once, then sang *The Rose of Nazareth*.

The Holy Family loved his voice.
It was pure and clear and strong,
The perfect voice of the perfect sinner

And the perfect end to the dinner.

BRENDAN KENNELLY

Born to Run

In our parish in the days before television we weren't very exposed to celebrities. But we did have two of our own – albeit of the minor variety.

Eamon was only a little taller than a brush and as thin as a goose. His grey hair stuck out in little wisps round his forehead and ears. Two pale, green oval eyes stared down over permanently freckled cheeks. In many ways he was a child who had never grown up. He loved a good yarn but was never unduly bothered about trifles like veracity.

Eamon was a greyhound trainer and had a lot of big wins at venues like Shelbourne Park and Harold's Cross. At least once a year a photographer would come to take pictures with Eamon and his dogs for some publication or other. But what really clinched his fame for the locals was that he knew Michael O'Hehir. Any wife or child would have been delighted to receive the type of attention Eamon lavished on his dogs.

Eamon's bachelor son Cillian was the seventh son of a seventh son and had what was known locally as 'the gift'. People came from all over the country for him to lay their hands on them in a desperate hope that he would cure them. I had to visit him once myself in his professional capacity when I fell victim to the highly infectious rural disease – ringworm. My arm was invaded by an unsightly and maddeningly itchy scab. Cillian placed his hand in a bowl of holy water and made the sign of the cross on it. He rubbed some kind of homemade concoction on it. It looked awful and smelled worse. It did, though, take away the itch and stopped me scratching.

It was difficult to understand how Eamon could have sired a son like Cillian. Cillian was a giant of a man – with an astonishing appetite. He had bright blue eyes which looked out with impact-making intelligence, sun-blond hair and his muscles left

women gasping. His young eyes had an apparently indestruct-
ible vitality and he had a face in which even the bones looked
determined. His lips were so thin they hardly existed.

One day Cillian picked potatoes using old socks for gloves. It
was a bitter raw autumn afternoon and although he was wearing
a heavy overcoat, scarf and balaclava, the frost penetrated into
his very bones.

The hard furrows in the fields were as immobile as waves
of corrugated iron, and the few surviving tufts of grass that
remained crackled as his boots hit the hoar frost that coated
them.

When his task was completed, he came to the gap in the
hedge which served as his gate. He crunched his way up the
tangled garden, glanced round at the trees which were now
quite naked and thin, and blew into his hands – stamping his
feet into some semblance of life.

Cillian's eyes lit up when he walked into the house. A huge
plate of meat lay on the kitchen table. The steam rose tantalis-
ingly. Five minutes later Cillian patted his tummy contentedly
having literally licked the plate clean.

A short while later Eamon entered the room. Despite his
whispering voice nobody could have mistaken the undercurrent
of menace as he asked, 'In the name of God what happened to
my plate of dog food?'

Déjà Vu

The early morning air was clear and crisp and all the fields and
hedgerows were covered in a layer of sparkling dew. The sun
filtered through the trees so that I was constantly moving into
patches of gloom and out into sudden patches of sunlight.
I reached the small stream and listened to it gently rippling

beside me. The problems with my grey Morris Minor which had stranded me in the middle of nowhere were momentarily forgotten. It was then that I saw it.

It was like the mother ship was calling me home. In this remote outback of Roscommon stood a mansion: three storeys high with marble pillars and columns. Every detail was uncannily familiar to me – including the ivy on the side wall.

A stockily built man with a head of thick white hair answered the door. He had skin like coarse, wrinkled brown paper and a voice like thunder. Something told me not to ask him if he believed in reincarnation. I meekly explained that my car had broken down and asked if I might use the phone.

'You best come in,' he snapped abruptly.

Nervously I followed him into a dark hallway. It took a few seconds for my eyes to adjust from the brilliant sunshine I had left to the comparative darkness of the house. I could just make out the shape of a few coats on some wooden pegs and two pairs of boots standing below. The flagstoned floor was covered in a faded crimson, green and brown rug.

It was a house of extraordinary contradictions and yet every piece of furniture had its unique memory for me. Ghosts of my past time in this house whispered from every corner. How could some place so alien welcome me like a lost long friend?

The phone call was made in the dining room. It had an embossed ceiling and a carpet in which you could get lost. A helicopter could land safely there. I wondered if it was this sort of building which the cognoscenti referred to as a Victorian Gothic mansion.

I was summoned to the kitchen for a cup of tea in a tone which refuted the possibility of argument. A large black range stood solidly in an alcove in the back wall, a thick dark pipe curving its way upward through the ceiling. Stretched out beneath the side window were a few shelves filled with recipe books, old newspapers and odds and ends and by a front window stood a heavy table and two chairs.

We took our flowery mugs into what my host termed the parlour. Its contents were a large desk, an enormous dark table, a massive wardrobe, an old brown leather chair and a bookcase. Only the most unobservant person would be totally oblivious to the fact that the room was predominantly brown in colour.

Two hours later, after a jovial mechanic had performed minor surgery on my car, I drove home. As I reflected on my adventure it was increasingly obvious to me that in a previous existence I had been a landlord of a great estate.

That night my illusions of grandeur were rudely shattered when my mother informed me that the house in question had been owned by an elderly relative of my father's. On the first Sunday of every month he had brought me to visit him until I was five. In that instant my lineage with the Ascendancy class was obliterated.

Déjà vu is not what it used to be.

Interesting?
Men are like bank accounts with scarcely any money in them. They generate little interest.

A WOMAN

LETTERS
FOR
SUMMER

I invited the noted author and actress Angela Keogh to write a letter to her mother.

Kilkenny and then Carlow

Dear Mam,

From this remove, you in your seventies and me in my forties, it's hard to see the holes we tore in this garment called relationship. We've had the privilege, denied to so many, of living long enough to darn the worst of the damage and create some new attire that no longer has the kind of tautness that can snap at any moment. We are made of softer things now.

Thank you for your care. You were always a practical woman, someone who came to motherhood with years of farming and nursing behind you. Thank you for clothing me (sorry about the rows, especially about the purple boots, the ones you got at the market; on reflection, they were really lovely, and you were right to give Marian the navy ones, after all they were in her size and would have been too big for me). Thanks for the steady routine when you worked split shifts at the hospital, cycling home to cook a dinner and light the fire and then racing back again to work – a place where, unlike home, you cared for those who couldn't do it for themselves.

Thanks for not dividing work according to gender, although little brother Micheál probably regrets this. He'd have been able to put his feet up. There's an apology due, too, for the way I treated my big sister, Teresa, who was often *in loco parentis*. I didn't get the gravity of her job, she being just three years older than me, and I made it hard for her and probably you because of that. (I won't go into the pencil-stabbing or stapling incidents, which by the way were unintentional.) I really should have done more to help.

Thanks for supporting me at rowing regattas. Back then young people were generally left to get on with the business of their own lives; parents were not expected to stand on the bank and I'm grateful for Dad's and your support, it was a tradition you've kept up and continued into the lives of your grandchildren. Your presence, along with my coaches and crew, kept my smoking to a minimum.

Thanks for your unfailing support and constant interest in my life and in the lives of my daughters. It really is a blessing to know that I can talk over problems – especially parenting ones. I'm thinking of the time that Katie was caught sneaking out and was grounded. She was almost stopped from going to the USA with her dad. I think that was the moment I realised that you were far wiser than I had given you credit for. The trip to her aunt was exactly what was needed.

When I went to London to do my nurse training, you were right to have been worried and I'm sorry for the months that I let go by without making contact. I'm sorry, too, that when I did visit you, I spent as much of that time as I could in the pub. It wasn't because I didn't love you, it was because I couldn't break away from alcohol. I was a 1990s raver, a hardcore clubber and it was by the grace of God that life gave me two children that brought my partying days to a halt.

I'm sorry for the pain I caused you when, unmarried, I became pregnant twice in the same year. You were still paralysed with the fear that surrounded pregnancy outside marriage. I know now that the fear was in the very air you breathed growing up in Ireland and it was unavoidable in a strong Catholic household. Thanks for the help you gave me with Katie and Mairenn, I couldn't have managed without you.

The woman who was my mother through the 1980s and 1990s has changed and so have I. I'm no longer the wayward daughter I was back then and I'm delighted and so very grateful that we are still growing together.

In love and admiration,
Angela

PART THREE
AUTUMN

THE FIRST IMPRESSION I HAD AS I stepped off the boat after a short open-boat journey across the lake was of an island that was a mixture of Alcatraz and an abandoned holiday camp. The sun was gleaming off the darkening waters of the lake, a haven of primitive splendour. The south-west wind rushed through the reeds. The sound of the rocks was a sad one, challenging and threatening. This roar in the background came from the constant surging of the water off the rocks and reefs like the roar of distant drums. Lough Derg or St Patrick's Purgatory, a lake in County Donegal, is one of the loneliest places in the world.

The purpose of the journey was to sample the old ascetic rigours of prayer, fast and vigil, the dream of ages. We went barefoot over the island's million stones, did without sleep for twenty-four hours, fasted for three days and recited countless prayers. The diet, or lack of it, of watery tea and unbuttered bread, sharpened the religious appetite. As pilgrims conducted their penitential rounds in bare feet, they underwent a stripping-down in spirit that brought them closer to their Maker.

Historically, Lough Derg has been the Celtic equivalent of the desert. In the western world, deprived of the sandy open spaces of the Sahara, the Celtic monks sought the sea. In biblical times, the desert in scripture was the place of the revelation of God. The elemental experience on Lough Derg was to help pilgrims on this road of faith to go through the desert as the place of struggle and purification.

Light, faint at first, had ripened into the bold yellow of an autumn morning. It was a clear Irish day, white clouds lazy in blue skies, a cool breeze, sunlight on the rolling hills. Although it was late autumn it was unseasonably fine, and springlike. As the cloud shadows racing in the wind flew over my head, trailing ribbons of shade and brightness over the endless blues and brown, I felt an overwhelming sense of aesthetic pleasure, despite my fears for the future. Not for the first time I really appreciated the natural beauty of my environment, particularly the marshy land, with its enchanting blanket of purple heather and bog pools with the black waters rippling and the tufts of rushes bending and swaying in the eternal wind. Lough Derg speaks today of our Celtic past.

INSTANT SUCCESS

The speed at which children of chieftains become monks and nuns is a small indication of how quickly the tentacles of Christianity had spread throughout Ireland. In the early years when Christianity was still in its infancy it did take considerable moral courage for a chieftain to depart from the traditions and customs of his forefathers and allow his daughters to take the veil as Christian virgins. This practice was particularly prevalent among certain families.

Before Patrick arrived there were relatively few Christians in Ireland with no ecclesiastical organisation and no bishop; by his death the Church was solidly entrenched. It is noteworthy that this was accomplished peacefully. There is no evidence of martyrs in early Christian Ireland. Paganism was in a marked decline. Yet some of Patrick's more enthusiastic disciples were prone to exaggerating his successes. He did not achieve instant evangelisation. Chieftains like Diarmait, son of Fergus Cerrbél, king of Tara in the mid sixth century, and Eógan Bél, king of Connacht, were pagan. They were by no means unique. Indeed, long before the term was fashionable, many chieftains were *à la carte* Christians. In the good times they called on the Christian God, but in times of crisis they called on the gods of their ancestors. In later centuries this pattern of 'fair day Christianity' became commonplace in Ireland.

From the outset, Celtic Christianity developed traits of its own. Throughout the continent, the Church was being built up in lands which had once constituted components of the Roman empire, where the culture of territorial divisions was firmly established; for example, the word 'diocese' was inherited from the Roman administrative system. In contrast, territorial divisions were not of primary importance in Ireland where the unit of government was a curious hybrid of kinship groups and ruling families. Irish church organisation adopted a similar structure. Rather than follow the Roman norm and organise the Church on diocesan lines, bishops were attached to particular families.

According to Nennius's eleventh-century *Historia Brittonum* – *History of the Britons* – Patrick ordained 365 bishops. We need to be somewhat suspicious of sources quoted several centuries after Patrick's death, though Tirechan, writing in the eighth century, claims that Patrick consecrated about 450 bishops. Whereas, in the Roman model bishops exercised great power and authority, that was not the case in Ireland because there were so many of them and the small size of their flocks prevented them from acquiring any significant power base.

A consequent major distinction between the Roman model and the Celtic one was that in Ireland the real centres of religious importance were monasteries rather than episcopal sees under the jurisdiction of a bishop. These monasteries were not compact groups of stone buildings. Instead they were effectively tiny towns, mapped out in streets, with a small stone church as the focal point. Large numbers of monks lived and worked and prayed together under the control of the abbot, who was normally elected from among the family of the founder.

SIGN LANGUAGE

Perhaps one of the reasons why Patrick was such a success as a missionary was that he considered himself a country man and spoke in a country idiom so that his message might be better understood by his audience. Equally he appreciated that to really engage people he could not rely only on words. Patrick used the shamrock with its three leaves springing from one stem to show that God was Tri-une; that is, a three-personed God with life and love expressed by Father, Son and Spirit bound together. Patrick had a keen appreciation of the importance of symbols to Christian catechesis.

Of course he was not unique in this. For instance, in one of Patrick Kavanagh's poems, 'The Great Hunger', there is a beautifully economic and evocative portrayal of the centrality of the Eucharist in the Christian life where he argues that 'in a crumb of bread' we discover the 'whole mystery'.

It is noteworthy that Kavanagh's star is rising internationally. In 2010 Russell Crowe quoted his poem 'Sanctity' – in which he describes the intense heartbreak of being a lover who has the singular talent of repelling all women and to be a poet without knowing the trade – in his BAFTA acceptance speech. In 2015, Barack Obama quoted 'let grief be a fallen leaf' from one of Kavanagh's most famous poems 'Raglan Road' when he delivered the eulogy at the funeral of Joe Biden's son, Beau. Kavanagh recognised that symbols give us our identity and self-image; they are our way of explaining ourselves to ourselves and to others. Symbols determine the kind of history we tell and retell.

The masterstroke of using the shamrock showed how Patrick appreciated that people's faith needed to be nurtured on the sensual as well as on the intellectual level. Have we forgotten this tenet of Celtic Christianity? In our haste to rid ourselves of some of the baggage of the pre-Vatican II Church, have we gone too far and too easily got rid of our sense of ritual and too readily dumped our symbols? In our search for relevance and accessibility have we sacrificed our sense of mystery? Is this too high a price to pay? Do we live in an age of imaginative emptiness?

O LORD, IT'S HARD TO BE HUMBLE

Thanks to writers like Frank McCourt we are all au fait with the literary memoir. Fifteen hundred years before *Angela's Ashes*, St Patrick produced an autobiographical work called *Confessions*. Patrick was the first to admit that it is not a work of great literary merit. 'Anyone can see from the style of my writing how little training in the use of words I got.' The book is a happy one, a celebration of a mind and soul journeying to God.

As is the fashion today, Patrick describes himself 'warts and all'. When he writes, he opens with incredible honesty and humility: 'I am Patrick, a sinner, the most unlearned of men, the lowliest of all the faithful, utterly worthless in the eyes of many.'

The Ireland of Patrick was a very stratified and paternalistic society. There were a lot of slaves. Patrick, though, acted in a deeply countercultural way by treating slaves as equals. He had no time for people who acted sanctimoniously or who loved pomp; he felt that humility was the bedrock of the Christian Church. Down through the years this kind of humility was often lost as the Christian Churches became shackled with the trappings of institutionalism. In the light of many recent traumas and scandals, the Christian Church needs to rediscover Patrick's sense of humility.

For this reason, Patrick's writings ought to be required reading for all those in charge of the Christian Church in Ireland today.

In the Celtic tradition, autumn is the season of the harvest. It often started with great hunger as people relied on berries and fruit until the crops were brought home. Then came the first fruits of the harvest and a time of plenty as the good earth yielded its bountiful treasures in the form of new corn and new potatoes as darkness was overtaking the earth.

The primacy of the harvest was one of the reasons why the Celts had such reverence for the aged: they were an invaluable resource because of their wisdom. Nothing is of more value in the Celtic tradition than wisdom.

WISDOM
FOR
AUTUMN

Mistaken

The only real mistake is the one from which we learn nothing.

HENRY FORD

Life Lessons

It is relatively easy to list what needs to be taught. What requires the greatest consideration is the means by which it is taught, so that teachers enjoy their work while they teach. The better they succeed in this the more attractive they will be.

ST AUGUSTINE

Mind Blowing

The value of a college education is not the learning of many facts but the training of the mind to think.

ALBERT EINSTEIN

Lifelong Learning

As long as I am a good teacher, I will continue being a student.

ST AUGUSTINE

Functionality

The function of education is to teach one to think intensively and to think critically. Intelligence plus character – that is the goal of true education.

MARTIN LUTHER KING, JR.

Answer Me

The wise man doesn't give the right answers, he poses the right questions.

CLAUDE LÉVI-STRAUSS

Food for Thought

In the same way that you choose what you eat, choose carefully what you teach. What you say is food for those who listen.

ST AUGUSTINE

All Things New

The principal goal of education in the schools should be creating men and women who are capable of doing new things, not simply repeating what other generations have done.

JEAN PIAGET

Managing Your Life

See everything
Overlook a great deal.
Improve a little.

POPE JOHN XXIII

Friendship

One's sorrow is nothing, but the sorrow one has caused to others makes bitter the bread in the mouth.

PAUL CLAUDEL

A Friend in Need

All sufferers have one refuge, a good friend, to whom they can lay bare their griefs and know they will not smile.

MENANDER, 342 BC–291 BC

Heart-warming

Friendship is a word the very sight of which in print makes the heart warm.

AUGUSTINE BIRRELL, 1850–1933

I'll Be There for You

A friend is the one who comes in when the whole world has gone out.

SPANISH PROVERB

Honours Uneven

It is in the character of very few to honour without envy a friend who has prospered.

AESCHYLUS

Wicked

The slanderous tongue kills three: the slandered, the slanderer and they who listen to the slander.

THE TALMUD

How

Children must be taught how to think, not what to think.

MARGARET MEAD

The Best Teacher

Time, as it grows old, teaches all things.

AESCHYLUS

TALES
FOR
AUTUMN

THE CHOSEN ONE

Everyone in the town gathered for a big meeting in the town square. People were very angry because there was so much cruelty in the town and everyone seemed to have forgotten how to be good, kind, generous, honest and helpful. The meeting went on for hours and hours because everyone was blaming everyone else for all their problems. Eventually someone suggested, 'Why not ask the Wise Woman of the Woods what we should do?'

It was agreed that the oldest man in the town should go and speak to her. He found the Wise Woman of the Woods and explained why everyone in the town was so unhappy and not getting on with each other. He asked her what they should do. She said, 'You must all open your eyes.'

The old man was shocked and puzzled and so he asked, 'What do you mean by that?'

The Wise Woman of the Woods replied, 'One of the people living in your town is the Chosen One in disguise and you are blind to this.'

As the old man went back to the town his heart beat fast at the thought that the Chosen One was right there in their town. How is it they had all failed to recognise him, or was it a her? And who could it be? Freddie the fireman? Harriet the hairdresser? Sarah the policewoman? Bertie the bank manager? No, not he; he had too many bad sides to him. But then the Wise Woman of the Woods had said the Chosen One was in disguise. Could those bad sides be the disguise? Come to think of it, everyone in the town had bad sides. And one of them had to be the Chosen One!

When he got back to the town he called everyone together one more time and told them what he had discovered. They looked at one another in disbelief. The Chosen One? Here? Incredible! But here in disguise. So, maybe. What if it was so-and-so? Or the other one over there? Or even . . .

One thing was certain: if the Chosen One was there in disguise it was not likely that they would recognise her or him. So they started to treat everyone with respect and kindness. 'You never know,' they said to themselves when they dealt with one another, 'maybe this is the one.'

The result of this was that the atmosphere in the town changed at once. Everyone was kind, patient and good to each other. Soon people came to live in the town from far and near because people knew this was the best way to live.

FROM SIGHT TO INSIGHT

My name is Saoirse.

This is the story of a day in my life.

The park bench was deserted as I sat down to read beneath the long, straggly branches of an old willow tree. Disillusioned by life, with good reason to frown, for the world was intent on dragging me down.

And if that weren't enough to ruin my day, a young boy out of breath approached me, all tired from play.

He stood right before me with his head tilted down and said with great excitement, 'Look what I found!'

In his hand was a flower, and what a pitiful sight, with its petals all worn, not enough rain, or too little light. Wanting him to take his dead flower and go off to play, I faked a small smile and then shifted away. But instead of retreating he sat next to my side and placed the flower to his nose and declared with overacted surprise, 'It sure smells pretty and it's beautiful, too. That's why I picked it; here, it's for you.'

The weed before me was dying or dead. Not vibrant of colours, orange, yellow or red. But I knew I must take it, or he might never leave. So I reached for the flower, and replied, 'Just what I need.' But instead of him placing the flower in my hand, he held it mid-air without reason or plan. It was then that I noticed for the very first time that weed-toting boy could not see: he was blind.

I heard my voice quiver, tears shone like the sun as I thanked him for picking the very best one. *You're welcome*, he smiled, and then ran off to play, unaware of the impact he'd had on my day. I sat there and wondered how he managed to see a self-pitying woman beneath an old willow tree. How did he know of my self-indulged plight?

Perhaps from his heart, he'd been blessed with true sight. Through the eyes of a blind child, at last I could see the problem was not with the world; the problem was me. And for all of those times I myself had been blind, I vowed to see the beauty in life, and appreciate every second that's mine. And then I held that wilted flower up to my nose and breathed in the fragrance of a beautiful rose. I smiled as I watched that young boy, another weed in his hand about to change the life of an unsuspecting old woman.

AUTHOR UNKNOWN

SEPTEMBER BLUES

As a boy, summer was the season for mushrooms. I woke up early in the mornings during early autumn to go out mushroom-picking under the warm glow of the rising sun before gathering cows for the milking. I learned quickly that most valuable skill for any practitioner of my new profession – how to tell a field which would yield mushrooms from one which would not. Now and then I would reach treasure island – a seemingly limitless, just-popped bunch of pure white mushrooms lovingly caressing the green grass. Summer was above all, though, magical because of the freedom that came with the school holidays.

As a result, the month I hated the most was September because it signalled the dreaded return to school. With the benefit of hindsight, though, I know that I was incredibly lucky because I had a wonderful teacher. One particular incident will live forever in my memory.

The afternoon remained beautifully raw, with a flawless blue sky offering sunlight as pale as malt whiskey – though much less warming. As she rang the bell to summon us back into class, Katy Dobey's lilac corduroys and clumpy shoes made a bold fashion statement. She normally wore an ensemble that could have been looted from a jumble sale by someone with a severe visual impairment. The wind, having tried unsuccessfully to scrape the light make-up from her blue-green eyes, concentrated on blowing the short brown hair into thick bunches about a face that mirrored the liveliness and contained strength of her nature. She was slim, but not at all frail, with square, capable hands adorned with a wedding ring as broad as a bangle.

Inside the cramped classroom, anticipation mingled with apprehension as she stated that she had an announcement for us. A lengthy theatrical pause ensued as she sat in an ordinary armchair, which enclosed her like a small cave. Katy Dobey's statements were sometimes as enigmatic as the Dead Sea Scrolls. A chorus of groans greeted the news that we were to have our annual visit from the community doctor. A large frown crossed Katy Dobey's forehead. Her demeanour was almost always friendly to the point of fervour, but in rare moments, especially if she suspected she was being taken for less than she was, a glacial sternness came over her features and only the resolute hung around to debate. Then her thick-lensed glasses steamed up as she wagged her finger. All thoughts of dissent were suspended and we meekly responded as one, 'Yes, Miss.' The width of her smile echoed the generosity of her nature.

Privately we were aghast. Dr Stewart was a short, stocky man whose pugnacious features and brisk, assertive gestures might mark him as a former professional boxer. He usually looked about as cheerful as a man trying to get a cyanide capsule out from behind his teeth. When he formed a set of opinions he was slow to rearrange them. He was to visit us to check our eyesight and hearing.

Almost as one we turned around to look at Stephen. His thin-framed glasses under the high waves of strawberry-blond hair, partially concealed his shrewd, rather pouchy face. Nonetheless it was clear that his normally boyishly pleasant expression was a study in anxiety.

Stephen had been in a car accident six months previously. His face had been disfigured, though the scars were fading. Looking back into the blank spaces of memory, we were unpardonably cruel in the comments we made about them. Stephen's self-confidence had taken a battering. He also suffered from intermittent hearing loss.

Katy Dobey decided to give all of our hearing a little test. She asked us individually to put our right hand up to our right ear and to repeat back a sentence she dictated to us. There was a collective intake of breath when it came to Stephen's turn.

He was obsessed with butterflies. The fascination arrived like talking, too early to remember. I would have bet my last thrupenny bit that Katy Dobey would have asked him something about butterflies – but not for the first time our teacher fanned the flames of imagination and surprised me.

Stephen's face lightened like a cloudless dawn as he confidently repeated Katy Dobey's sentence, 'I wish you were my little boy.'

TRAVEL COMPANIONS

Once upon a time Truth and Falsehood met each other on the road.

'Good afternoon,' said Truth.

'Good afternoon,' replied Falsehood. 'And how are you doing these days?'

'Not very well at all, I'm afraid,' sighed Truth. 'The times are tough for a fellow like me, you know.'

'Yes, I can see that,' said Falsehood, glancing up and down at Truth's ragged clothes. 'You look like you haven't had anything to eat for ages.'

'To be honest, I haven't,' said Truth. 'No one seems to want to employ me these days. Wherever I go, most people ignore me or mock me. It's getting discouraging. I'm beginning to ask myself, why I do it.'

'And why the devil do you? Come with me, and I'll show you how to get along. There's no reason in the world why you can't stuff yourself with as much as you want to eat, like me, and dress in the finest clothes, like me. But you must promise not to say a word against me while we're together.'

So Truth promised and agreed to go along with Falsehood for

a while, not because he liked his company so much, but because he was so hungry he thought he'd faint soon if he didn't get something into his stomach. They walked down the road until they came to a city, and Falsehood at once led the way to the very best table at the restaurant.

'Waiter, bring us your best food and your finest wine.' All afternoon they ate and drank. At last, when they could hold no more, Falsehood began banging his fist on the table and calling for the manager, who came running at once.

'What the devil kind of place is this?' Falsehood snapped. 'I gave that waiter a gold piece nearly an hour ago, and he still hasn't brought our change.'

The manager summoned the waiter, who said he'd never even seen a penny out of the gentleman.

'What?' Falsehood shouted, so that everyone in the place turned and looked. 'I can't believe this place! Innocent, law-abiding citizens come into eat, and you rob them of their hard-earned cash. You're a gang of thieves and liars. You may have fooled me once, but you'll never see me again. Here.' He threw a gold piece at the manager. 'Now this time bring me my change.'

But the manager, fearing his restaurant's reputation would suffer, refused to take the gold piece, and instead brought Falsehood change for the first gold piece he claimed to have spent. Then he took the waiter aside and called him a thief, and said that he was going to fire him. And as much as the waiter protested that he'd never collected a cent from the man, the manager refused to believe him.

'Oh Truth, where have you hidden yourself?' the waiter sighed. 'Have you now deserted even us hard-working souls?'

'No, I'm here,' Truth groaned to himself. 'But my judgement gave way to my hunger, and now I can't speak up without breaking my promise to Falsehood.'

As soon as they were on the street, Falsehood gave a great laugh and slapped Truth on the back. 'You see how the world works?' he cried. 'I managed it all quite well, don't you think?'

But Truth slipped from his side.

'I'd rather starve than live as you do,' he said.

And so Truth and Falsehood went their separate ways, and never travelled together again.

EIGHT LEVELS OF CHARITY

Level 8 – The donor is pained by the act of giving.

Level 7 – The donor gives less than he should but does so cheerfully.

Level 6 – The donor gives after being solicited.

Level 5 – The donor gives without being solicited.

Level 4 – The recipient knows the donor but the donor does not know the recipient.

Level 3 – The donor knows the recipient but the recipient does not know the donor.

Level 2 – Neither the donor nor the recipient knows the other.

Level 1 – The donor gives the recipient the wherewithal to become self-supporting.

MAIMONIDES, D. 1204

POETRY
FOR
AUTUMN

The Habit of Redemption

I have felt the world shrivel to days
Beckoning me
Into a hell of indifference

Until I found
The habit of redemption
Living in my mind.

It breathed in the morning
As I wrote a letter
To a woman in mourning

For her dead brother
He was sixty-six
And rare.

His days touched by imagination.
He died in October
Tending his garden.

It reached the deepest part of me
When the middle-aged man
Raking leaves turned quickly

And said 'how are you?'
Autumn died at his feet
But the day was new.

I would say nothing about all this,
Never bother to mention
The moment's metamorphosis

Were it not that hell gapes
At every step.
What I am given is not a means of escape

But of confrontation,
The truest education
That I know.

Moment that is all moments
Be with me when I grasp
A little of the meaning of transience,

A hint of the infernal night.
Come in the shape of the blade of grass
Stuck to the side of my boot

Or a kind word from stranger or friend
Or a yellow shedding from an old tree
That will not bend.

BRENDAN KENNELLY

Success

In Memory of Christina Schmidt

Success is speaking words of praise,
In cheering other people's ways.
In doing just the best you can,
With every task and every plan.
It's silence when your speech would hurt,
Politeness when your neighbour's curt.
It's deafness when the scandal flows,
And sympathy with others' woes.
It's loyalty when duty calls,
It's courage when disaster falls.
It's patience when the hours are long,
It's found in laughter and in song.
It's in the silent time of prayer,
In happiness and in despair.
In all of life and nothing less,
We find the thing we call success.

AUTHOR UNKNOWN

The Spirit Level

Let nothing disturb you
Let nothing frighten you
All things are passing
God never changes
Patience obtains all things
She who possesses God lacks nothing
God alone suffices.

ST TERESA OF AVILA

PRAYERS
FOR
AUTUMN

Pathways

God before me, God behind me,
God above me, God below me,
I on the path of God,
God upon my track.

CELTIC BLESSING

Each Thing

Each thing I have received,
From Thee it came,
Each thing for which I hope,
From Thy love it will come,
Each thing I enjoy is of Thy bounty,
Each thing I ask comes of Thy disposing.

CELTIC PRAYER

A Prayer for the Start of the School Year

Back in the days of Celtic Christianity, Ireland was known
as 'the land of saints and scholars'. Education then was the

silver bullet. For many it still is today. Hence the importance of this prayer.

The Good Lord was creating teachers. It was His sixth day of 'overtime' and He knew that this was a tremendous responsibility for teachers would touch the lives of so many impressionable young children. An angel appeared to Him and said, 'You are taking a long time to figure this one out.'

'Yes,' said the Lord, 'but have you read the specs on this order?'

TEACHER:

. . . must stand above all students, yet be on their level.

. . . must be able to do 180 things not connected with the subject being taught.

. . . must run on coffee and leftovers.

. . . must communicate vital knowledge to all students daily and be right most of the time.

. . . must have more time for others than for herself/himself.

. . . must have a smile that can endure through pay cuts, problematic children and worried parents.

. . . must go on teaching when parents question every move and others are not supportive.

. . . must have six pairs of hands.

'Six pairs of hands,' said the angel, 'that's impossible.'

'Well,' said the Lord, 'it is not the hands that are the problem. It is the three pairs of eyes that are presenting the most difficulty!'

The angel looked incredulous. 'Three pairs of eyes . . . on a standard model?'

The Lord nodded His head. 'One pair can see a student for what he is and not what others have labelled him as.

Another pair of eyes is in the back of the teacher's head to see what should not be seen, but what must be known. The eyes in the front are only to look at the child as he/she "acts out" in order to reflect, "I understand and I still believe in you," without so much as saying a word to the child.'

'Lord,' said the angel, 'this is a very large project and I think you should work on it tomorrow.'

'I can't,' said the Lord, 'for I have come very close to creating something much like Myself. I have one that comes to work when he/she is sick . . . teaches a class of children that do not want to learn . . . has a special place in his/her heart for children who are not his/her own . . . understands the struggles of those who have difficulty . . . never takes the students for granted . . .'

The angel looked closely at the model the Lord was creating. 'It is too soft-hearted,' said the angel.

'Yes,' said the Lord, 'but also tough. You cannot imagine what this teacher can endure or do, if necessary.'

'Can this teacher think?' asked the angel.

'Not only think,' said the Lord, 'but reason and compromise.'

The angel came closer to have a better look at the model and ran his finger over the teacher's cheek.

'Well, Lord,' said the angel, 'your job looks fine but there is a leak. I told you that you were putting too much into this model. You cannot imagine the stress that will be placed upon the teacher.'

The Lord moved in closer and lifted the drop of moisture from the teacher's cheek. It shone and glistened in the light.

'It is not a leak,' He said. 'It is a tear.'

'A tear? What is that?' asked the angel. 'What is a tear for?'

The Lord replied with great thought, 'It is for the joy and

pride of seeing a child accomplish even the smallest task. It is for the loneliness of children who have a hard time to fit in and it is for compassion for the feelings of their parents. It comes from the pain of not being able to reach some children and the disappointment those children feel in themselves. It comes often when a teacher has been with a class for a year and must say goodbye to those students and get ready to welcome a new class.'

'My,' said the angel. 'The tear thing is a great idea . . . You are a genius!'

The Lord looked sombre. 'I didn't put it there.'

AUTHOR UNKNOWN

A Student's Prayer

Creator of all things, true source of light and wisdom, origin of all being, graciously let a ray of your light penetrate the darkness of my understanding. Take from me the double darkness in which I have been born, an obscurity of sin and ignorance. Give me a keen understanding, a retentive memory, and the ability to grasp things correctly and fundamentally. Grant me the talent of being exact in my explanations and the ability to express myself with thoroughness and charm. Point out the beginning, direct the progress, and help in the completion. I ask this through Christ our Lord. Amen.

THOMAS AQUINAS, 1225–1274

Prayer of Thanks

Every now and then, I stop and think of you, God. Maybe it's because I feel guilty for not making enough contact but I want you to know that I really haven't forgotten you.

There are times when life is going well and I really want to praise and thank you for those times. Even when things are not going well, I pray for a plan and I know you are always prepared to listen to me. You know my needs, my joys, my pain and my struggles. You understand exactly what is going on for me. All others struggle to fully understand but not you. So I thank you God for being my guiding light that will never burn out. Although I may not always show it, I am grateful, grateful for all you have given to me, my family, my friends, my blessings, everything. Sometimes I simply forget how lucky I am and how grateful I should be. I just get carried away with life and forget. But not today and all I want to say is thank you for everything.

HUMOUR
FOR
AUTUMN

The Devil's Beatitudes
If the devil were to write his beatitudes, they might be of this nature.

1. Blessed are those who are too tired, too busy, too distracted to spend an hour once a week with their fellow Christians – they are my best workers.

2. Blessed are those Christians who wait to be asked and expect to be thanked – I can use them.

3. Blessed are the touchy who stop going to church – they are my missionaries.

4. Blessed are the troublemakers – they shall be called my children.

5. Blessed are the complainers – I'm all ears to them.

6. Blessed are those who are bored with the minister's mannerisms and mistakes – for they get nothing out of his sermons.

7. Blessed is the church member who expects to be invited to their own church – for they are a part of the problem instead of the solution.

8. Blessed are those who gossip – for they shall cause strife and divisions that please me.

9. Blessed are those who are easily offended – for they will soon get angry and quit.

10. Blessed are those who do not give their offering to carry on God's work – for they are my helpers.

11. Blessed is the one who professes to love God but hates their brother and sister – for they shall be with me forever.

12. Blessed are you who, when you read this, think it is about other people and not yourself – I've got you too!

If

If you can start the day without caffeine,

If you can get going without pep pills,

If you can always be cheerful, ignoring aches and pains,

If you can resist complaining and boring people with your troubles,

If you can eat the same food every day and be grateful for it,

If you can understand when your loved ones are too busy to give you any time,

If you can overlook when those you love take it out on you when, through no fault of yours, something goes wrong,

If you can take criticism and blame without resentment,

If you can ignore a friend's limited education and never correct them,

If you can resist treating a rich friend better than a poor friend,

If you can face the world without lies and deceit,

If you can conquer tension without medical help,

If you can relax without liquor,

If you can sleep without the aid of drugs,

If you can say honestly that deep in your heart you have no prejudice against creed, colour, religion or politics,

Then, my friend, you are almost as good as your dog!

AUTHOR UNKNOWN

Frankly Speaking

Frank Duff was the founder of the Legion of Mary. He once organised a silent retreat for the members in Mount Mellary. One of the members was in the refectory for the evening meal and was surprised to see a picture hanging on the wall of Mary Magdalene wearing a low-cut dress. He could not speak so he wrote a message to Frank saying that he was distressed by this image and was concerned that would be detrimental to his moral wellbeing. The message was passed all the way up to Frank.

The following morning when the writer of the note arrived for breakfast he found a second note from Frank which read as follows: 'After a lengthy discussion with the abbot we have found the solution to your problem. Please move to the other side of the table.'

You Light Up My Life

A man was married to his wife for forty years and was devoted to her. When she died he wrote on her tombstone: 'The light of my life has gone out.' Within a year he was married to another woman.

A week later some graffiti was added to the tombstone: 'But he struck another match.'

Walking on Sunshine

'Save us from sorrow-filled saints.' This was the motto of St Teresa of Avila. One day she was out travelling to a monastery on a donkey when she fell off and landed in the mud. She shouted to God, 'How could you let this happen to me?'

God replied, 'This is how I treat my friends.'

St Teresa responded, 'If that is how you treat your friends it is no wonder you have so few of them.'

Morning Has Broken

Old age is golden, I've heard it said;
But sometimes I wonder as I get into bed
With my ears in the drawer, my teeth in a cup,
My eyes on the table until I wake up.

Ere sleep overtakes me, I say to myself,
'Is there anything else I could lay on the shelf?'
When I was young my slippers were red,
I could kick my heels over my head

When I was older my slippers were blue,
But I still could dance the whole night through.
Now I am old, my slippers are black,
I walk to the store and puff my way back.

I get up each morning and dust off my wits
And pick up the paper and read the obits.
If my name is still missing, I know I'm not dead
So I fix me some breakfast and go back to bed.

AUTHOR UNKNOWN

Talk Is Cheap

I love to talk about nothing, it is the only thing I know anything about.

OSCAR WILDE

LETTERS
FOR
AUTUMN

Family ties were crucially important to the Celts. I thought it would make for a nice symmetry to invite a husband and wife to contribute letters, so here we follow Angela's letter in the previous section with a letter from her husband, John MacKenna, to his late mother.

Letter to My Mother

Dear Una,

Last night I had a strange but comforting dream. I rarely dream about you now, not like I did in the weeks and months after you died, but last night you were there. And the unusual thing about it was that, although I was in my fifties in the dream, you were a woman in her forties, as though, year by year since your death you had grown younger.

Anyway, in this dream, you were sitting on the wall of the cemetery at Coltstown, outside Castledermot. It was an evening in early summer and the trees that skirt that sleeping ground were in full leaf, the cherry blossoms hanging in fists from the branches near the road and you were reading a book of poetry and swinging your legs, more relaxed than I ever remember seeing you in life.

And then word came, don't ask me how – on the wind, perhaps. Word that your eldest son had died, word winging its way across the Atlantic from the sunny heart of Carolina. And, in the dream, you left your book on the cemetery wall and walked up between the stones to the plot where you and Jack are buried. He was setting a table for tea, it was right there on the site of your grave and you told him about your son's death and he put his arm around your shoulder and then he said: 'Will I set another place, for Jarlath, at the table?' You nodded.

When I woke, I felt a surge of reassurance and warmth, a surge of gratitude to you for bringing that hopeful feeling and I was reminded – and sometimes at this remove I need reminding – of the warmth of your welcome for our friends when we brought them home; of your love of books; of your concern for others; of the fact that so rarely in life did you allow yourself to sit and swing your legs on some low wall and let the world go by. Instead you were scrimping and saving to get us through school or college, to put us on the road to somewhere rather than nowhere.

I was gladdened by that dream and by the thought of you and my father and brother sharing a quiet meal on a summer evening while all around you the birds sang and the cherry blossom hung in the still air, waiting, like the rest of us, for the time when we will fall.

As always – thank you for being there to say that everything will be alright.

John

PART FOUR
WINTER

ALTHOUGH THE SYSTEM OF ECCLESIASTICAL government Patrick introduced into Ireland would have been the episcopal one he grew up with, Ireland quickly departed from the European norm by having a significant number of monasteries. The fledgling Irish Church adapted to the particular needs of the local community rather than imposing its institutions from above. Less than a hundred years after Patrick's death new monasteries had eclipsed the older Patrician foundations as the key religious and education centres. In Armagh, for example, which claimed a unique position with Patrick, the abbot of Armagh had as a subordinate member of his community a bishop – whose function was to administer the sacraments for which episcopal orders were necessary.

Many of the founders of Irish monasteries had been moulded by outside influences. St Enda had been trained under Ninian in 'the White House' (because of the exceptionally bright sheen on the walls) or Candida Casa in Galloway. Although St Enda's monastery in Aran, noted for its school of asceticism, was very influential, St Finnian of Clonard soon surpassed it. Finnian was heavily influenced by the Welsh reformers, Cadoc and Gildas, and placed a new emphasis on sacred study as an integral part of the monastic life. He earned the nickname the 'teacher of the saints of Ireland' and his twelve famous disciples were known as 'the twelve apostles of Ireland'. Each in turn founded their own monastery, i.e. Colum Cille in Durrow, Derry and Iona; Ciarán in Clonmacnoise; Brendan in Clonfert; Molaisse in Devenish; Cainnech in Aghaboe; Mobhi in Glasnevin.

As would be expected, monasteries which shared the one founder tended to have close ties. To us today, the high numbers of monasteries at the time is not that remarkable, but what is surprising is that whereas today the diocesan clergy happily co-exist with the religious orders; in early Christian Ireland, the monks effectively replaced dioceses altogether.

An additional feature which gave Irish monasteries a distinctively Celtic texture was that in many of them they choose their abbots from the founder's family. Accordingly, ten of the first twelve abbots of Iona, came from the Cenél Conaill from which Colum Cille descended. This trend had the effect of consolidating the power base of the ruling families in their local area.

The early Irish monks were a formative influence on Irish cultural and religious identity. Architecturally, they have bequeathed a magnificent legacy to the Irish nations, as is evident from even a cursory glance at Clonmacnoise or Glendalough. This was one of those very rare times when Ireland exerted a real formative influence on European civilisation as many people came to study here from Europe.

Over the last thousand years Irish history has been scarred by division and conflict, but the monastic tradition is part of our shared history as Christians on the island of Ireland before the divisions set in. In Nendrum, Strangford Lough, County Down, there is a monastic site which was neglected for most of the Middle Ages. It was only discovered in relatively modern times. Whereas monastic sites in Clonmacnoise developed through the centuries, Nendrum still remains virtually as it was. The outline of the old monastic settlement, the old monk's grave and even the pathway to the grave remains and none of this has been overlaid with subsequent development and civilisation. This is part of the history of the whole island.

There were great differences in the types of monastic settlement. Glendalough called itself a city while others were very small. Some were comprised of men, some of women and some were, in contemporary parlance, co-educational. Some were very important as centres of learning. Some were important centres of local devotion.

The monastic sites were normally surrounded by a ráth, an enclosing circular bank with a ditch outside it. Within this enclosure were the main buildings of the monastery; i.e. the church, the monks' cells, the guest-house, the refectory and the schools. In the early years, the churches tended to be made of hewn oak planks and a roofed thatch of rushes. As a consequence of the lack of timber on the islands off the west coast, the monastic buildings were constructed of stone. Gradually this became the norm on the mainland also. To the contemporary eye, the monastic buildings, particularly the churches, were very small. Even when the monasteries grew in size, the monks tended to build several small churches rather than one large one. The monks were self-sufficient. They adhered to a very strict regime and did severe penance for even the tiniest offence. Columbanus summed up the daily life of the monk:

'Pray daily, fast daily, study daily, work daily.'

SENSE AND SENSIBILITY

The monasteries were simultaneously centres of learning and piety. Novices were taught how to read and write Latin. Their chief textbook was the Bible, particularly the Psalms, which they learned by heart. Latin grammar was another area of special study, though Greek received less attention. In addition they learned the commentaries of the Fathers of the Church, the lives of the saints, the works of the Christian authors and even some of the classic authors like Virgil, Horace and Ovid. Individual monks such as Columbanus, who studied at Bangor in the sixth century, show a great familiarity with Latin authors like Virgil and Horace. As a result of the strong cultural connections between Ireland and Spain in the sixth and seventh centuries, Spanish writings like those of Isidore of Seville were read in Ireland and subsequently brought by Irish monks to central Europe. The monks were the first chroniclers of local history, as can be seen in the various annals they compiled.

The copying of manuscripts, particularly of the gospel texts, was an important duty for the monks. The copyists worked in the *scriptorium* or writing room of the monastery. The monks wrote on vellum, the skins of calves which were cured, pared, rubbed and made suitable for writing on. The completed texts were preserved in leather satchels and hung on the walls of the *scriptorium*.

At the top of the academic hierarchy was the scribe. The first two abbots of Iona, Colum Cille and Baíthín, pioneered the use of scribal art, which subsequently evolved into illuminative elements, which represent the high point of Irish monasticism. Colum Cille's own hand is said to be responsible for the *Cathach*, a fragmentary copy of the psalms. Written about 600 AD, it has features which later became commonplace in Hiberno-Saxon manuscripts. In it the scribe provides headings with a series of decorated initials which diminish in size until they are interwoven into the body of the text. This can also be seen in manuscripts from Bobbio Abbey, Italy. While the *Cathach* manuscript had some ornamentation, as time passed the decoration and illumination of these texts became ever more stylish and captivating.

As was the case during the Renaissance in Italy, as the church began to acquire more power and wealth, it became a great patron of the arts, particularly in the area of metalwork. The relics of the saints and the priceless texts of the monasteries were enclosed in reliquaries and shrines of the finest metalwork. Two of the great achievements in this era were the Tara Brooch and the Ardagh Chalice. Both are distinguished by their delicate workmanship and their intricate spirals. The Tara Brooch is made of cast bronze and lavishly ornamented with interlacing animal patterns. Dating from about 700 AD, it was discovered on the seashore, near Drogheda. The Ardagh Chalice, a large silver chalice, decorated with gold, glass and enamel, dates from around 750 AD and was found at Ardagh, Co Limerick.

The animal patterns furnish us with a revealing insight into the spirituality of the monks. They were very close to nature and have bequeathed a vast canon of tales and legends about their love of animals, which have engrained themselves in the popular mind. One story relates how three monks who were going on a pilgrimage to an isolated island, vowing to take nothing with them and to eat nothing only water cress. However, out of compassion for a fellow monk, they took his cat along. Once on the island the cat provided the monks with fresh salmon to eat every day. This tale shows the close bond between monks and animals. Even though legends like these are very romanticised, they show the close connection between the monks and the natural world as a common part of God's creation. Their belief system was such that a monk should love God above all, and their neighbours as themselves. They saw God in the little, everyday things of life particularly in nature.

In the pre-Christian era the *file* was an esteemed member of the community because of his learning. These men passed on their poems through the oral tradition. The coming of Christianity to Ireland slowly changed that. As the poets became Christian, they learned the art of writing from the monks and they wrote down their traditional knowledge. This made for a fascinating cross-fertilisation of Irish and Latin learning. St Colum Cille was a poet and is traditionally referred to as the protector of poets.

Discipline was very strict in Irish monastic life. It is interesting to note that in the rule of Columbanus corporal punishment was introduced, even though it was not part of Irish civil law at the time. Slaps with a leather strap could vary from six to one hundred strokes. Other forms of punishment included extra silence, fasting on bread and water, expulsion and exile. When Irish monks went abroad, the severity of some of the punishments did not nestle comfortably with the continental temperament and were quietly shelved.

This excerpt from a seventh-century sermon captures the spirit of mortification of the time:

'It is right that every one of us should suffer with his fellow in hardship, and in his poverty and in his infirmity.' We see from those words that fellow suffering is counted as a kind of cross.

Service was very prominent from the earliest days of the Irish monastic tradition. In later centuries, it was arguably a contributory factor in the failure of the Reformation to take off in Ireland, because the monks were catering for the material needs of the marginalised as much as the spiritual needs.

The Irish embraced the monastic ideal with enthusiasm. Lands were granted to the monasteries and they grew in number and in power. Many monasteries founded daughter-houses throughout Ireland and in Britain and throughout the continent.

English scholars arrived in their droves to study in the famous Irish schools and the great historian, the Venerable Bede (672–735), said they were received kindly by their Irish hosts, often given board and lodgings without charge, and a free education too. Bede has provided us with much information about the

Irish monks in England, but we have less detailed sources about the works of the Irish monks on the continent.

The monks visited these places and brought and received new perspectives. This included their tradition of a festival of Samhain, which was critically important as it signified the end of one year and the beginning of the next. It should be noted, though, that the Irish at this time, like the Welsh, did not consider themselves Celts. That description was used about them by the Romans and the Greeks.

The Celts believed that the soul did not die but lived on, and for that reason they did not fear death. They had a number of traditions. One was of the *moruadh* who were mermaids or sirens who lured people to their death. The Celts considered their gods not as remote entities living in a far-off heaven, but as magic people who lived in a hill or underground and who would contact mortals if they wished. Later this pagan cult of the dead would be Christianised.

Rudyard Kipling was the youngest winner of the Nobel Prize for Literature. The second youngest was the French philosopher, Albert Camus (1913–1960). Among his most famous quotes is perhaps, 'In the depth of winter, I finally learned that within me there lay an invincible summer.' These words are classic Celtic wisdom – though the Celts would have discarded the 'finally' – because conclusions were not ends but prisms to new beginnings. Nothing really ended but was merely re-invented in the rhythm of the never-ending cycle of the seasons.

In winter, the Celts closed a door on the past and opened a door to the future. While there is a sadness in letting go of the past, this is subsumed by a joy because the dark days of winter are lit up by light dappled in shadow from the sacred, opening us to the deeper mystery of life. The dark days bring greater opportunities to be attuned to our interior lives.

WISDOM
FOR
WINTER

In Loving Memory

Those whom we have loved and lost are no longer where they were before. They are now wherever we are.

ST JOHN CHRYSOSTOM, D. 407 AD

Be Not Afraid

I do not fear that I may have to die. I fear that I have never lived.

ST JOHN HENRY NEWMAN

The Eternal City

Our dead are never dead to us unless we have forgotten them.

GEORGE ELIOT

Matter of Fact

It matters not how a man dies, but how he lives.

SAMUEL JOHNSON, 1709–1784

Happy Days

As a well-spent day brings happy sleep, so life well-used brings happy death.

LEONARDO DA VINCI, 1452–1519

Keys of the Kingdom

The will to win, the desire to succeed, the urge to reach your full potential . . . these are the keys that will unlock the door to personal excellence.

CONFUCIUS, 551–479 BC

People Listening Without Hearing

To listen well, is as powerful a means of influence as to talk well and is essential to all true conversation.

CHINESE PROVERB

Home, Sweet Home

A house is built of logs and stone,
Of piles and post and piers:
A home is built of loving deeds,
That stand a thousand years.

VICTOR HUGO

True Love Ways

The supreme happiness in life is the conviction that we are loved.

VICTOR HUGO

Starry, Starry Night

For my part I know nothing with any certainty,
But the sight of the stars makes me dream.

VINCENT VAN GOGH, 1853–1890

The Road of Life

The journey is the reward.

TAO WISDOM

Artistic Merit

The greatest artist of all is Christ, who doesn't work with canvas
but rather with human flesh.

VINCENT VAN GOGH

Will to Power

I will be truthful
I will suffer no injustice
I will be free from fear
I will not use force
I will be of good will to all.

MAHATMA GANDHI

Everything Goes

Everything is yours; do with it what you will.
Give me only your love and grace.
That is enough for me.

ST IGNATIUS OF LOYOLA, 1491–1556

River Runs

God is a great underground river that no one
Can dam up and no one can stop

MEISTER ECKHART

Joy

Give me a sense of humour
Give me the grace to see a joke
To get some pleasure out of life
And pass it on to other folk.

ANON

Equality

When you are accustomed to privilege, equality feels like
oppression.

ANON

Sun Set

The sun will set without thy assistance.

THE TALMUD

Time Well Spent

Prolong not the past
Invite not the future
Alter not your innate wakefulness
Don't fear appearances
There is nothing more than this.

BUDDHA

Small is Beautiful

Do not overlook tiny good actions, thinking they are of no benefit; even tiny drops of water in the end will fill a huge vessel.

BUDDHA

Leadership

A leader is a man who has the ability to get other people to do what they don't want to do and like it.

HARRY S. TRUMAN, 1884–1972

Sleeping Beauty

Even in our sleep, pain which cannot forget
falls drop by drop upon the heart
until, in our own despair, against our will,
comes wisdom through the awful grace of God.

AESCHYLUS, 525–456 BC

Happy Hour

Happiness is a choice that requires effort at times.

AESCHYLUS

Fortune Favours the Brave

Wisdom comes through suffering.
Trouble, with its memories of pain,
Drips in our hearts as we try to sleep,
So men against their will
Learn to practise moderation.
Favours come to us from gods.

AESCHYLUS

Simply the Best

His resolve is not to seem, but to be, the best.

AESCHYLUS

On My Oath

It's not the oath that makes us believe the man, but the man the oath.

AESCHYLUS

Weighty Words

The reward of suffering is experience.
Words are doctors for the diseased temper.

AESCHYLUS

A Worthy Undertaking

Let us endeavour so to live that when we come to die even the undertaker will be sorry.

MARK TWAIN, 1835–1910

How Deep is Your Love?

All that we love deeply becomes a part of us.

HELEN KELLER, 1880–1968

TALES
FOR
WINTER

TWIN TRACKS

The Bard was sitting by the side of the road when a traveller came along. The traveller stopped and said, 'I'm on my way to the big city. Tell me what the people are like there.'

The Bard replied, 'You tell me first where you're from and what the people are like there, and I'll tell you what they are like in the city.'

Quick as a flash the traveller responded, 'I come from the tiny town of Eire Og and they are all cheats and liars.'

The Bard sighed sadly and said, 'Alas, those are exactly the same sort of people you'll find in the big city.'

Not long after a second traveller came along the road. He also said to the Bard, 'I'm on my way to the big city. Tell me what the people are like there.'

The Bard replied, 'You tell me first where you're from and what the people are like there, and I'll tell you what they are like in the city.'

The second journeyman responded, 'I come from the tiny town of Eire Og and they are all honest and honourable people.'

The Bard beamed a wonderful smile and replied, 'Good news, my friend, those are exactly the same sort of people you'll find in the big city.'

THE LEAP OF FAITH

The Mother Superior was very sad. Her convent was in a bad way and was literally falling apart. There was barely enough money to feed her community let alone for any repairs. All year her fellow nuns had been saying to her, 'We'll have to leave.' The Mother Superior always replied, 'Have no fear. God will provide.' But as the winter dawned and with the rain coming through the holes in the roof and the wind howling through many of the many gaps in the walls she had a change of heart. It seemed cruel to her to put her older nuns in particular through such hardship.

That night she had a strange dream. She had a vision of walking to the big city and finding a large chest of treasure in the garden with the giant tree. Each night for the next week she had the same dream.

The Mother Superior was not the sort of woman to believe in foolish dreams but in her desperation she decided she would walk to the big city to search for the treasure. The long journey took three days. She spent the nights in lonely stables. If a stable was good enough for the baby Jesus, it was certainly good enough for her.

Finally she reached her destination. Somebody pointed her in the direction of the big tree. Even from a distance she could see that it was exactly like in her dream. A tremor of excitement raced through her body. Maybe her dream would come true after all.

Her joy vanished as she got near the tree. There was no garden, just a big concrete square. She sat on the bench feeling very foolish. Her disappointment became too much and she started to cry. A tall man sat down beside her. He spoke very softly and he was a great listener, so to her surprise the Mother Superior heard herself telling the story. The man said, 'That's very strange. Last night I had a dream that I would discover treasure beside a wishing well.' The nice man insisted on taking the nun into a local inn for a meal. Shortly afterwards, feeling a little more refreshed, she began the long walk home.

Snow was falling lightly when she returned cold and wet to the convent late on in the morning.

She went straight out into the back garden. *It couldn't possibly be*, she thought to herself as she looked at the old wishing well in the corner.

To the amazement of the other nuns, she started digging beside the well. Three hours later, as darkness fell, she had found nothing. The only spot left was under the statue of the baby Jesus. It broke her heart to have to break the statue, but she felt she had no other choice. Ten minutes later she shrieked for joy as she opened a huge treasure chest full of gold coins.

That night, as she read her Bible, the Mother Superior smiled to herself as she read, 'God so loved the world that he sent his only son.'

HELLO, DARKNESS, MY OLD FRIEND

Grace could think of nothing only heaven. It was more real to her than America, Scotland and even London. Strangely she had, or thought she had, a very clear notion of Australia. She laboured under the illusion that she had been there two years earlier, having driven there on what seemed an interminably long journey from her family home outside Roscommon. In actual fact, she had only been as far as Sligo.

Her thoughts on heaven were prompted by her unfamiliar setting. She was in her neighbours', the Atkinsons', house. The cherubic Patricia, the oldest of the family, was trying to cheer her up by reading stories and letting her play with all the toys they owned. Two days earlier, Grace's life had been thrown into chaos when she learned that her 35-year-old father, Iarlaith O'Kelly, and her 27-year-old mother, Aoife, had had their lives stolen from them.

Some places and days are unforgettable. Although Grace was only eight years old at the time, 27 October 1984 would be forever engraved in her mind. The day began brightly. It was Saturday. She was happy because there was no school. Her parents were taking her infant brother, Bryan, into town to buy some clothes. Grace was attending a birthday party for her schoolfriend, Simone Atkinson, when she heard a horrible sound. It was like nothing she had ever heard before: primeval and demoniac, part scream, part sob, part gurgled cry. It chilled her to the bone. The only thing that was clearly evident was unimaginable pain. The whole nightmarish thirty seconds would stay frozen like a freeze-frame in her mind. It would come back to haunt her in subsequent years with monotonous regularity.

The howl came from a tear-stained neighbour, Martha Atkinson, her mother's best friend. It was left to her husband, Paul, to tell Grace in a clear, matter-of-fact voice: 'Your Mammy and Daddy are dead and your little brother, Bryan, is in hospital. Their car was smashed to pieces by a drunk driver.'

Grace did not cry. She always felt guilty about that afterwards. She could say nothing as if she had been afflicted by dumbness. It was her first introduction to death. She could not grasp the fact that all the most important people in her life could cease to exist without warning and that she would never lay eyes on them again except in a coffin.

The rest of the day is blurred like a badly faded photocopy. Grace was dispatched to cousins for the day while arrangements were made to contact all her relatives. Memories of her father flooded her brain. He was slim, soft-spoken, with thinning blond hair. He stood six-foot-three in his bare feet and seemed to be able to lift anything. He possessed a decency and warmth that overshadowed his great physical powers.

In the springtime, she walked with him as he moved the horse to another part of the farm. The horse needed the minimum of direction as if on automatic pilot. His hooves smoothly and tenderly penetrated the skin of earth, throwing the sod sweetly to the right and then crashing onto a big stone. The horse made his own music with his panted breathing and occasional snorting. It was rough ground and very hard on Grace's little legs. It was with great relief she saw that their destination was reached. She was so tired that her father had to carry her home, though that was nothing for his big hands.

She remembered the day her daddy sent for the vet to have a look at the horse when he was limping. The vet was a giant of a man who almost dwarfed her father, who she had always thought was the tallest man in Ireland. She suspected that the vet would easily be capable of blocking out all light from a distance of fifty yards. He had hefty shoulders and an enormous bulk around the midriff that must have seen him clock up twenty stone on the weighing scales. It was said that he was 'fond of sup', which was code speak for the fact that he was a heavy drinker. He dispatched pints, small ones, large ones and brandies with seemingly reckless abandon. Invariably he wore a grey suit which must have been at least two sizes too small for him. On the surface he was a gregarious man and very likeable, but the more she got to know him Grace sensed he was either desperately unhappy or intensely lonely, if not both. He skilfully diagnosed the horse's problem within moments. The weather was unsettled and Grace and her father returned home teeming wet and miserable without having made much inroads into their work. She supposed her father must have found her company of sorts because he could not but be tired of her constant barrage of questions. If so he disguised it skilfully.

Another clear memory of her father was the day of the big snow. It was during the lambing season when she went out with her father to look after the sheep. The chill of the late afternoon made Grace shiver as she pulled her heavy coat around her. The winter that year had been cold and stormy. The gales began in late November, seeming to follow each other, with brief interludes, until the end of the following April.

'You can tell what a winter will be like by the weather on the first of November,' her father had always said. Grace would put that theory to the test every year after he died. As a rule of thumb it was pretty good. There was a lull that day in the winter-long storm. The sky was blue, but there were battalions of black clouds on the horizon westward which were irrefutable evidence that snow was on its way. The low sun seemed to shiver in the raging northern wind. It was an admission of defeat. Normally, on a winter afternoon with darkness due and snow clouds threatening, Grace would have not been allowed out. This was no day to leave lambing ewes to the elements.

'God, it's cold. That cold could kill any baby lamb. Nature is cruel,' said her father uncomfortably, as if his teeth were chattering in the icy air. The wind-chill factor must have been in operation. There were a dozen ruins scattered here and there around the fields. The sheep sheltered behind those walls in bad weather, as it often was at that time of the year. If young lambs survive in the cold, it is the old wisdom of their mothers that preserves them by finding a snug place for them to shelter.

They searched long and hard before they found the final ewe. She was hiding under a furze bush. Thankfully Grace's father had the foresight to bring a flashlamp with him. By then the snow clouds had come in from the west and before they knew it they were enveloped in a blizzard. Grace wanted to take shelter like the flock, behind some wall. Her father answered her plea with a hard look, and silence. He would not allow them to be exiled by the snow and took her up in his arms as if she was a precious jewel and ploughed an uneven furrow through the already-ankle-deep snow. Grace had never known such cold. Although the north wind nearly cut him in two, her father was happy to feel it. It meant the snow clouds would be kept on the move. The warm house awaited them like a sanctuary. Thankfully the snow had stopped. The air was quiet again, though another battalion of blue-black clouds were looming ominously on the western horizon. There would be more snow within the hour. The outside light looked more festive and welcoming than a tinsel-coloured Christmas tree in a window.

As they stumbled in the door she saw her mother putting on her wellingtons to head out to find them. She whisked Grace out of her father's arms and deposited her in front of the range where she began to rub her daughter vigorously to get her circulation going again. The relief on her face and in her voice that they were both safe was palpable. There was a mountain of snowflakes on their clothes and wellingtons. A pool of water formed on the floor as the moisture condensed.

Grace heard herself saying, 'I love you, Daddy.' He was surprised but pleased. Grace was not sure which of the three were the happiest. There was the special atmosphere normally only achieved on Christmas night. Looking back, Grace was glad that none of them knew then how few happy family gatherings lay in store for them.

Another day Grace's mother slipped a bar of Cadbury's plain chocolate into the bag. It was an exceptionally hot day and the sun beat down mercilessly. A slight wind made it ideal drying weather. Grace could not resist the temptation to have a square while she watched her father working. The one square quickly became two and before she knew it she had it all eaten. When her daddy came along, he knew by her guilty face that she had been up to mischief again. Then his eye caught the empty chocolate paper: 'You scoffed it all and left none for me.'

He said the words slowly and softly. They were little more than a whisper, a comment rather than a complaint or condemnation. Grace had never felt such a despicable pig. The memory of that incident would come back to haunt her many times during the weekend he died and for years afterwards.

The innocence of small children cast a magical spell over Grace's father. He had wanted a large family. When pressed further he said he wanted his own football team. Nevertheless, neither he nor his wife had planned to have a child so early in their marriage. As staunch Catholics they were to find that the natural methods of family planning as demanded by the Pope left a lot to be desired in terms of reliability if not in theology. Grace, born eleven months after her parents' marriage, was a child of Vatican roulette.

Although he was a humourist who laughed at life, Iarlaith was a very spiritual person who was always conscious, or so it seemed, of another dimension. His wife was never sure if his macabre sense of humour was tongue-in-cheek or genuine. He had a fund of unusual sayings:

'Conversation at meals, like television on a honeymoon, is not necessary.'

'A big house is like a fat man, hard to get around.'

'Misfortune is the kind of fortune that never misses.'

'The truth is a mixture of desirability and appearance.'

'A camel is a horse designed by a committee.'

Aoife never knew where he got them from or when he would pepper his conversations with them. What she was sure of was that he was a disaster when it came to money. Despite working incredible hours, he was incurring major losses in his small hardware business. Food was put on the table every day because of the work she herself did on the family farm.

Mothering is a complex business. The problems are exacerbated when the one person has to be in many respects both mother and father. It was like landing on an alien planet to begin again a new life, with a new language and culture; experiencing deprivations; struggling to survive materially, spiritually and emotionally. The deprivations of Aoife's life were also agricultural. There was a tremendous and largely hidden toll to working out in the fields, in all kinds of weather, with little machinery, from dawn to dusk. To be strong and capable was inadequate. She had to be resourceful if the family were to have any kind of future. The practical needs of collective survival dictated that Aoife could not wallow in a dull fog of self-pity. Grace saw her in three roles.

There was the provider, often so immersed in the daily farm work and the business of putting bread on the table that Grace hardly saw her for the whole day.

There was the mother, putting on a show for her in public and sparing her husband and daughter her private torment, anxious to give the right impression, deflecting attention from the enormity of the family's financial problems to the trivial, using humour to avoid the pain, hiding her feelings even from herself. She continually saved the day with her warmth and optimism, displaying that maternal ability to avoid total despair by smoothing things over, not making a fuss, keeping the peace, preserving the family unit at great personal cost to herself.

And, thirdly, there was the woman: the moments when the mask slipped, and the heartache and struggle became too much.

Aoife was always up an hour before the rest of the family. There she was a full-time farmer, trotting off to work in the fields, occasionally staying up half the night with a sick calf or lamb, doing the washing, matching socks, remembering birthdays, checking homework, peeling potatoes, cleaning shoes, telling bedtime stories and finding the cough medicine in the middle of the night. Some women had it all, but she had to do it all. Then there were the million questions she was bombarded with by Grace:

'Who made God?'

'Where's my teddy?'

'Can we buy ice cream on Sunday?'

'Is London bigger than Ireland?'

'How can a man talk inside the radio?'

'How do you spell fantastic?'

'What's the difference between a goose and a gander?'

As she grew older Grace suspected that her mother must fantasise about a second home, a tiny cottage by the sea, or even a treehouse, where there was room just for her, furnished with a rocking chair, a few books and a radio, no other voices, no other clutter, but space for relaxing and thinking. She must have pined for a little time in the day that was really hers: a little escape which would refresh and rejuvenate her.

The first thing her mother asked Grace one morning was:

'Did you sleep well?'

'Okay.'

She sensed Grace's low spirits immediately.

'Cheer up, Grace. It's not long until Christmas. Do you know what we will do tonight? You can write to Santa Claus and I will post it tomorrow.'

Grace's spirits revived immediately. That was her mother's great gift. She always seemed to know exactly what to say and when to say it. She always seemed to hit the right note. You could not ask more from a mother than that.

There were so many things for her mother to do that the only quality time she had with Grace was when she put her to bed. She watched her daughter kneel down and say her prayers. Afterwards, she would lay her down in the one bed and tell her a story. Aoife had inherited the art of storytelling from her father. Great storyteller that she was, she could switch at once from gravity to gaiety. Her changes in mood were like the changes of running water. Born into a miners' family in a remote valley in Wales, she grew up in a culture pre-eminently oral and aural. She was sensitive to language at its rhetorical best, harnessing its layers of potentialities. She had a magical way of making the stories come alive.

Grace learned more about the difference between right and wrong from listening to her mother's stories than she ever learned at school. They were decisive for her understanding of a wide variety of concepts from honesty and justice to beauty and God. Her stories were the highlight of Grace's day, more because she had her mother's undivided attention than anything else. They always engaged her totally, because her mother could read reality in a special way and enhance it; by eliciting signs of richness and satisfaction in the mundane events of life.

Grace always suspected that her mother enjoyed the stories as much as she did. All her worries were put away on the shelf. She would always try to enter the spirit of the narrative, by varying the pitch and speed of her voice to suit the mood, by gesture and by dramatic pauses. The stories were born in the womb of creative love. Baby Bryan became an unwitting prop for the account of Sleeping Beauty. He had fallen asleep and her mother rounded off the story by kissing him tenderly on the cheek. This little gesture connected all with the story.

Aoife O'Kelly would have been a brilliant teacher. Although

she generally told the standard children's stories like Little Red Riding Hood and the Five Pigs there were times when she was more ambitious and went for stories with a little moral. Grace's favourite was the one about the warrior who was wounded by a poisoned arrow. Instead of pulling it from his side without delay, he spent his time wondering who shot it at him, what sort of feathers were on the flights, and what type of wood the arrow had been made from. While he wasted all his precious time wondering about these trivial questions the poison was spreading through his body. After telling the story her mother asked Grace a number of questions, skilfully encouraging her to unravel the moral of the story.

Such was the power of her narratives that they touched Grace on the sensual level. She was enchanted by the scent of the pine air in the mountain freshness of the breeze. Her brows almost salted with sweat under the glare of the afternoon sun. She savoured the tranquillity of unspoilt places. She feasted her eyes imaginatively on the plunging shadows where rock faces glistened with springs, the skylight on the hazy blue ocean lovingly caressing the leaf-dappled shoreline and the archipelagos of light in the radiant night sky. The mood was often celebratory, though at times a gesture of defiance, a defence mechanism when the pressures of a life of poverty, material and emotional, threatened to become overwhelming. Her mother mixed a glowing passion for life with her tender evocation of the problems of the world such as war.

There were only ten or twelve stories in her repertoire, but Grace never got weary of listening to them over and over again until she knew them all off by heart in every detail. Each time she added a new piece of background information, Grace would repeat it continually in her mind, until it was as much her story as her mother's.

Grace was always fascinated by her mother's hands. They were working implements, unused to revelling in fancy, sweet-smelling creams; coarse, calloused and crinkled, with badly clipped nails that rarely sensed the glamour-touch of expensive varnish. Normally their only decoration was a layer of dirt or clay. Yet Grace always thought of them as innately beautiful. They were so gentle when necessary, removing splinters when she tried unsuccessfully at five years of age to launch a career for herself as a carpenter, bathing cuts when she hurt herself playing, creatively weaving pretty pictures on her schoolbooks. They were clumsy with a needle and thread, much happier milking a cow or mending fences. Grace admired their strength and seldom felt their anger. Most of the times Aoife was angry had to do with money. At least the swirling tide of history had liberated her from that nightmare.

On the third day, they were buried. The weather was unseasonably cold, more like the middle of January than late October. The penetrating cold offered an unpleasant contrast with the seasonal yellowness, retiring with russet stealth in autumn. The frozen clay seemed to resent the willing shovels. Tradition in the locality dictated that the nearest neighbours on the prompting of the bereaved dig the grave and later fill the clay over the coffin with a sense of privilege and decorum. Grace's parents were laid to rest in an austere ceremony punctuated by the clods of earth shovelled on to the grave by the men present. There was a finality about the proceeding that indicated an instinctive acceptance of death that rose from the filled grave and the tap-tap-tap as the back of the spade shaped the remaining mound of fresh clay.

The funeral was a very moving occasion. Grace's grief, though intensely personal, was generously shared. The local community, as always, responded magnificently in times of adversity. Everyone rallied around. Every seat in the house was crammed with relatives and neighbours, all with mournful faces. Many were weeping. They had good reason to. All the children from Grace's school attended and made a guard of honour outside the church.

The priest, Fr. Gearoid, had found it difficult to preach the funeral homily. Saying 'the few words' seemed so inadequate. He scoured his own personal store of stories to find a new way of saying old things. Crucifixion and resurrection do not find ready echoes in the life of an eight-year-old schoolgirl. It was difficult to achieve the correct balance between eulogy and explication, the pitfall mawkishly sentimental or playing safe with a bland reference to a piece from the Bible. The priest freely admitted that he had no answers to the questions that must have been racing through the congregation's minds. Although it seemed that she was only half-hearing his sermon through a dull fog of self-pity Grace remembered his words because he spoke with extraordinary beauty and lyricism.

'Only a God who had been crucified though totally innocent of all that he was accused of, and who suffered death as a true man, could understand what the O'Kelly family went through. Like Jesus himself, Grace has been stripped of everything that gives life meaning. Iarlaith and Aoife have carried their own cross, had their own Good Friday experience, now they are ready for their Easter Sunday. They have walked with Jesus to Calvary and beyond. In their battered bodies, God's grace has shone like a diamond. For all the darkness of their last few moments on earth they have been children of God's delight and light. We are not here this morning to be sad. Rather we are here to make an act of faith in Iarlaith and Aoife's life, what they lived and died for. But our essential purpose is to make an act of faith in their resurrection.'

It started to rain heavily as both corpses were taken out of the church. Nature seemed to be grieving for two of its own. As the final shovelfuls of clay were thrown on the grave, the rain stopped suddenly. The sun came out of hiding like a scene from an autumnal-hued photograph. The symbol surely was the reality. Grace's parents had risen with the Son.

ONLY A WINTER'S TALE

Simon was a small, slight man. In many ways he was a child who had never grown up. He had three daughters: Maxi, Dick and Twink. He loved a good yarn but was never unduly bothered about trifles like veracity. At heart, though, he was a good man. That was why he gave his niece, Sr. Rita, a parrot for her birthday.

If Sr. Rita had been given her choice that was not the gift she would have chosen, because a convent was not the ideal home for a bird who talked. Her initial instinct was quickly proved to be correct. The bane of her life was the Reverend Mother, who seemed to go out of her way to make Sr. Rita's life a misery. After one particularly humiliating chastisement in front of the entire community, when she got back to the sanctuary of her room, she shouted out in sheer frustration, 'I hope Reverend Mother dies.'

She burst into tears because she had never felt so low. Her only consolation was that things could not possibly get any worse.

She was wrong.

From his new home in the corner of his room her parrot exclaimed, 'I hope Reverend Mother dies. I hope Reverend Mother dies.'

For the next week Sr. Rita's nerves were fraught with

tension because the parrot would not stop repeating that sentence.

Eventually she could take no more and she went to the only person she could think of to help her, Fr. Tom, the local parish priest. He nodded with an expression that exuded kindness and sympathy as he listened to her predicament. At first he frowned because of his bemusement at the situation. Then he smiled in triumph at the end of her story as he announced without preamble, 'I have the perfect solution. I will take your parrot off you and put him alongside my parrot who is incredibly pious and that will put an end to your problems.'

The next day, Sr. Rita, surging to her feet with a grin of happy anticipation, moved her parrot into the parochial house and the two parrots struck up an immediate rapport and they all lived happily ever after.

Well, they did until the next Christmas morning.

As was her tradition, the Reverend Mother called over to Fr. Tom to give him his Christmas present, a large bottle of Irish whiskey, after morning Mass.

As soon as she went into the living room, Sr. Rita's parrot said, 'I hope Reverend Mother dies. I hope Reverend Mother dies.'

Fr. Tom froze.

There was a pregnant pause.

Then the other parrot piped up, 'Lord, graciously hear us.'

THANK YOU FOR THE MUSIC

Now thank we all our God
With hearts and hands and voices.
Who wondrous things hath done,

In whom this world rejoices;
Who from our mothers' arms
Hath blessed us on our way
With countless gifts of love
And still is ours today.

These are the opening words of a well-known hymn. It was written in 1636 by Martin Rinkart (1586–1649), who was a German Lutheran clergyman, during the Thirty Years War, which claimed eight million fatalities. Eilenburg, his hometown, was invaded and occupied by different armies. The local people sheltered war refugees. The town was ravaged by disease and it lost most of its young male population through violence and a severe plague.

Martin Rinkart presided over fifty funerals a day. He buried over four thousand people, including his wife. When harsh taxes were imposed, he was able to persuade the occupiers to reduce them. In the midst of all this bedlam, he composed this hymn of thanksgiving to God.

Martin Rinkart doesn't promise that we will be without troubles. He encourages thankfulness, faith and courage in the face of adversity.

At the end of the Thirty Years War, when the peace treaty in Westphalia was signed, this hymn was sung.

NUN DANKET ALLE GOTT
NOW THANK WE ALL OUR GOD

THE WOUND THAT NEVER HEALS
Grief is the price we pay for love.

The greater the love – the worse the pain.

In the face of intense despair, Gerard Manley Hopkins described in *Dark Sonnets* his sense of 'Pitched past pitch of grief'. Many people share Hopkins' deep despair when they get news of a bereavement.

In the immense panorama of futility that follows a serious act of tragedy the O'Kelly family, united in grief, struggled to comprehend the incomprehensible. With an inarticulacy born out of shock, sorrow and incomprehension what William Butler Yeats described as 'a pity beyond all telling', things which normally connected for a time no longer did. In the dark days that followed, nothing connected with nothing. A vein of grief ran through their lives. This catastrophe was their stations of the cross. They wondered why God could allow the premature sacrifice of such wealth. Life is full of riddles that only the dead can answer.

The life of the dead is placed in the memories of the living. The love we feel in life keeps people alive beyond their time. Anyone who has given love will always live on in another's heart. All the extended family are the curators of the loved one's memory.

One of the phrases I learned in school was: *sunt lacrimae rerum*. There are tears in the nature of things. The month of November is the month the Church remembers all of those we have lost. It is indeed right and fitting that it should do, as in the days, weeks and months of darkness after a bereavement the wounds are often difficult to heal. It is painful for our shroud of suffering to be replaced by the translucent beauty of the Lord who rose from the tomb on Easter Sunday. We live through what Emily Dickinson refers to as 'The Hour of Lead' – a process of mourning that results in a final relinquishing, and an essential thaw.

The message of the Christian story leads us to accept

disappointment and loss, but we never lose hope. Storms make the oak grow deeper roots. The *Rule of Saint Benedict*, the ancient guide to the monastic life, includes the exhortation to 'keep death before one's eyes daily'. To some that may sound morbid, but to Christians in times of tragedy it is a reminder that we come into this world without fear and that our passing allows us to return without fear as well, crossing over knowing that union with God is our first and final home.

In November, the Church recognises that people are all the work of His hand, and that He is shaping us each day like the potter shapes the clay. This is so that we can begin to see that we are the work of the one who is the Life Giver and the Light Giver and begin to feel a new sense of our worth and value in life and death. Our loving God is the potter who will shape us to His image.

Only those who believe in the invisible can do the impossible. By the standards of the world, Jesus was at his most useless on the cross, but it was there that He achieved his greatest glory. The Christian experience is shaped by a particular death, the death of Jesus; His living and dying and rising are the energies that shape our identity. In our suffering we will discover that darkness is the shadow of God's outstretched hand and that a loving God has lowered an arm for us to rest on.

SPEAKING IN DEATH

One young woman who knows all about suffering is Emma Spence. She shared her story with me:

He was all that we want our sporting heroes to be. Nevin Spence was a talented centre with the Ulster rugby team. At just twenty-two years of age he was on the cusp of making the Irish team. The rugby world was his oyster. But, on 15 September 2012, tragedy struck and he lost his life.

In the worst farming accident in over twenty years in Ulster, Nevin was taken from the family he adored in an attempt to rescue a beloved dog after it had fallen into a slurry tank on the family farm in Hillsborough, County Down. His father Noel (aged fifty-eight), and his brother Graham (thirty), also died while trying to rescue each other from a slurry tank. Such were the bonds of family love that Nevin's sister Emma also courageously put her life on the line in an effort to rescue her father and brothers before being overcome by the poisonous fumes and waking up in the recovery position.

Members of the Ulster rugby team carried Nevin's coffin into and out of the church. The then Irish rugby coach, Declan Kidney, and Tyrone Gaelic football manager, Mickey Harte, were among other well-known sporting faces amid more than two thousand people who attended the men's funerals.

Emma pays an emotional tribute to the three men. 'Dad was the one you probably saw taking up half the Drumlough Road with the tractor. He is the one that greeted you with a thump on the arm. He is the one who christened you with a new nickname no matter who you were. To me he was the one sitting at the kitchen table with his coffee made in only Mum's best china cup listening to my every worry and telling me the truth whether I wanted to hear it or not,' she remembers with a tremor in her voice.

Graham was 'driven by the thought of improving farming' and was 'unashamedly Nevin's biggest fan. He was a gentle giant who doted on his two children. He is the one who came alive when he talked about farming. To me, he is the one who protected me as I grew up. To me, he is looking at me when I look at Nathan and I look at Georgia.'

She sums all three up: 'They were hard-working men. They were not perfect but they were genuine. They were best friends. They were godly men – they didn't talk about God, they just did God. They were just ordinary – but God made them extraordinary.'

Many tributes were paid to Nevin after he died. The Ulster physio remarked, 'I have no son but if I did I would want him to be like Nevin and have his values.'

The impression of meeting Emma and her sister Laura is of a shaft of light illuminating the darkness of a family tragedy – two noble natures standing up for people they serve and love. Preserving that cherished image remains important for those who see it at first hand. Their testimonies of faith strike not so much a note of hope as a symphony.

The memory of magical childhood moments with her father and brothers lingers for life in Emma's mind and those who grew up with her, leaving a warm afterglow to light up numerous conversations years later. She remains fiercely proud of her brother's achievements on and off the rugby field. 'He was humble. Often I was congratulated on Nevin's achievement and, to hide my confusion, I accepted the praise for him, then headed home to ask at the dinner table, "So, Nev, I didn't get the paper today, what have you done?" The answer would be: "Nothing, I don't know," only to find he had been selected to train in the Ireland camp, or won young player of the year! Nevin didn't see these things as important; instead, he reflected what Mother Teresa said, "Be faithful in small things because it is in them your strength lies."'

Nevin will always live on in Emma's heart. She says, 'As my mum put it when he was alive and repeats it even more in the past six years, "Nevin was special." Maybe what was even more special was if you had the chance to encounter him in your life.'

Whoever said time heals all wounds has not met the Spence family. 'My dad and Graham worked the farm and were passionate about it, and while Nevin may have been a full-time rugby player, he loved the farming just as much,' Emma says. 'At night-time here he milked the cows and the joke was that his best workouts would be standing out in the yard.'

Emma started to see the farm anew, looking at it from the point of view of her dad and brothers. An artist by profession, Emma has literally drawn on her family's farm for inspiration for her paintings. 'To most people, looking at something like hedges, they would see only weeds, but I was stopping to look at them and recognising the beauty in them, which is why I wanted to paint them,' she laughs. But there were, and still are, plenty of down times as well. 'I remember the first spring after the accident,' Emma recalls. 'It had always been a happy time, seeing the cows going out into the fields after the winter. But that first spring tore me apart because Dad, Graham and Nevin weren't there.

'Now, with the passage of time, I think of the joy that the boys got from something like that. It still hurts, but I am trying to accept that this is life. I'm not saying I have it all sorted out now, because I think we are all still in the grieving process with the enormity of all that has happened. But I suppose we have no other choice but to try and cope with it and live with it.'

Years on Emma's sadness at what she has lost is balanced to some extent by her gratitude for what she had. 'Nevin's masseur used a verse from the Bible to sum him up. Colossians 3:23 says, "Whatever you do, work at it with all your heart, as working for the Lord not for human masters." Nevin's commitment to his faith reflected in his life. This was the core of Nevin's life, which mirrored the person he was. He has left a lasting impression on those who knew him. I have heard it said Nevin along with his brother and father have spoken more in death than in life.'

POETRY
FOR
WINTER

St Brigid's Prayer

I'd love to give a lake of beer to God
I'd love the Heavenly
Host to be tippling there
For all eternity.

I'd love the men of Heaven to live with me,
To dance and sing.
If they wanted, I'd put at their disposal
Vats of suffering.

White cups of love I'd give them
With a heart and a half
Sweet pitchers of mercy I'd offer
To every man.

I'd make Heaven a cheerful spot
Because the happy heart is true,
I'd make the men contented for their own sake.
I'd like Jesus to love me too.

I'd like the people of Heaven to gather
From all the parishes around.
I'd give a special welcome to the women,
The three Marys of great renown.

I'd sit with the men, the women and God
There by the lake of beer.
We'd be drinking good health forever
And every drop would be a prayer.

TRANSLATED BY BRENDAN KENNELLY

Surprise Visitor

I dreamt death came the other night
And Heaven's gate swung wide.
An angel with a halo bright
Ushered me inside.
And there! To my astonishment
Stood folks I'd judged and labelled
As 'quite unfit', 'of little worth',
And 'spiritually disabled'.
Indignant words rose to my lips
But never were set free,
For every face showed stunned surprise –
Not one expected me!

ANONYMOUS

Walking out of History

I'll walk, but not in old heroic traces
And not in paths of high morality,
And not among the half-distinguished faces,

The clouded forms of long-past history.

I'll walk where my own nature would be leading –
It vexes me to choose another guide –
where the grey flocks in ferny glens are feeding,
where the wild wind blows on the mountain side.

What have these lonely mountains worth revealing?
More glory and more grief than I can tell:
The earth that wakes one human heart to feeling
Can centre both the worlds of heaven and hell.

EMILY BRONTË, 1818–1848

Beyond the Doom

It were my soul's desire
To imitate my King,
It were my soul's desire
His ceaseless praise to sing.
It were my soul's desire
When heaven's gate is won
To find my soul's desire
Clear shining like the sun.
Grant, Lord, my soul's desire,
Deep waves of cleansing sighs;
Grant, Lord, my soul's desire
From earthly cares to rise.
This still my soul's desire
Whatever life afford –
To gain my soul's desire
And see Thy face, O Lord.

TENTH-CENTURY POEM

The Song the Devil Sang to St Moling

Pure gold, bright sky about the sun,
A silver goblet filled with wine,
An angel wise is everyone
That still hath done God's will divine.
A caught bird fluttering in the snare,
A leaky ship that wild winds shake,
A wineglass drained, a rotten tree –
Even such they be that God's law break.
A breathing branch that flowers in spring,
A vessel brimmed with honey sweet,
A precious ruby beyond price –
Such he that follows Christ's own feet.
A hollow nut that none desire,
A savour foul, a rotten wood,
A flowerless Crabtree growing wild,
Are those defiled that Christ withstood.
The man that does Christ's heavenly will,
He is the sun that warms the year,
God's image through his heart doth pass,
He is a glass of crystal clear.
A racehorse straining for the goal,
Heaven is the mark for which he tries;
That chariot driven by a king,
A precious thing shall be his prize.
A sun that warms all Heaven round,
God loves him more than things of price:
A noble temple and divine,
A golden shrine of sacrifice.
An altar with the wine outpoured
Where sweet choirs sing in linen stoled,
A chalice with God's blood therein
Of findruine or precious gold.

EIGHT-CENTURY POEM

I Can't Remember!

Just a line to say I'm living,
that I'm not among the dead,
though I'm getting more forgetful
and mixed up in the head.

I got used to my arthritis,
to my dentures I'm resigned,
I can manage my bifocals
but God I miss my mind,

For sometimes I can't remember,
when I stand at the foot of the stairs,
if I must go up for something,
or have just come down from there.

And before the fridge so often,
my poor mind is filled with doubt,
have I just put food away,
or have I come to take some out?

And there's the time when it is dark
with my nightcap on my head,
I don't know if I'm retiring,
or just getting out of bed.

So if it's my turn to write to you,
there's no need for getting sore,
I may think that I have written
and don't want to be a bore.

So, remember that I love you
and wish that you were near

but now it's nearly mail time
so I must say good-bye dear,

There I stand beside the mailbox
with a face so very red,
instead of mailing you my letter,
I opened it instead!

AUTHOR UNKNOWN

Poet's Corner

The late Michael Hartnett (1941–1999) was one of Ireland's greatest poets. One of his passions was for the poetry of St John of the Cross (1542–1591). Michael spoke to me about this interest:

'I am fascinated by Christianity and the figure of Christ. I constantly marvel at the fact that those who are followers of Christianity believe that even before we were born and long after we die, there is at work a provident, gracious God who has created us and loves us and wants us to share in God's own life. This view shapes the Christian's moral life by enabling them to live in faith, in hope and in love. Accordingly, Christianity issues us with an invitation into the heart of what it is to be human. I love the idea of the divinisation being most tellingly revealed by our humanisation.

'Of course, as someone who has spent a lifetime studying, in various ways, words, I particularly admire the statement in the Gospel: "In the beginning was the Word and the Word was with God and the Word was with God."

'I love the idea of a religion that is based on love which is best summed up in the quotation from St Paul, "To live through love in God's presence." Every day I open the papers and I read stories about the absence of love in the world and it depresses me.

'Love of God is expressed not only in prayer and Sunday worship, but must permeate every aspect of our lives. The Bible has no ambiguities on one issue: you cannot love God unless you love your neighbour. The Old Testament prophets were scathing in their criticism of those who sought to appease God by prayers and sacrifices while oppressing the powerless. Jesus told us that all the law and the prophets are summarised in the commandment to love God and thy neighbour. No words are minced when we are told: "Whoever claims to love God but hates his brother or sister is a liar." All love invites love. God calls us to love.

'I am enthralled by the compassion of God and Jesus to people. There are days when I'm very far away from this, but I'm always inspired by the image of Jesus in the Gospels. He was someone who brought the compassion of God to people, someone who didn't judge or condemn. He was someone who was with people wherever they were, especially those who found themselves on the margins of society. That is why I really admire people like Sr. Stanislaus Kennedy because of the work she does with people who are unable to help themselves. One of the things that really interests me is the nature of goodness.'

In John's vision, Christ is the archetype towards whom and in the likeness of whom all have been created. In Christ, the mystery of God is revealed. Paradoxically, the mystery is very simple to grasp – love. One of his most enduring legacies is a picture. He inspired Salvador Dalí to paint a picture which he entitled: *Christ of St John of the Cross*. The painting, which hangs in Kelvingrove Art Gallery and Museum, Glasgow, depicts Christ elevated on the cross and leaning forward in love over the world.

In the final stanza of his poem *El Pastorcico* ('The Humble Shepherd') St John of the Cross wrote:

> At last he did what he alone could do:
> mounting a tree, he stretched his arms out wide
> and there remained in love until he died,
> his heart by a deep wound of love pierced through.

A Common Misunderstanding

Michael continues:

'One of his best-known poems is invariably always mis-named as "The Dark Night" or "The Dark Night of the Soul". In fact, he never used either term in his poetry. However, he did write a massive commentary on this relatively short poem entitled *The Dark Night of the Soul*. This *opus magnus* gave a critique of the poem, drawing heavily on the scriptures and the teachings of the Fathers of the Church.

'Ironically, the poem goes much closer to describing the mystical intuition, which prompted it than the lengthy exposé in the commentary. In his critique he was attempting the impossible – to explain the mystic state in prose. The commentary only provides the faintest of echoes whereas the poem offers loud echoes. The poem keeps the original inspiration intact. In marked contrast, the more assiduously he sought to explain it the more complexity it developed. It became clouded like an onion in a layer of words. In the midst of the weighty analysis, the essence was dissipated like a flower which begins to wither and loses its perfume.

'The poem describes how the human heart made for God can become imprisoned by its own perverse desire for trying to find God in possessing things. The journey or pilgrimage of faith requires that we must liberate ourselves from the shackles of our false gods and take sanctuary in the triune God. Again there is a twofold movement – we become free with and for the hidden God.

> 'In darkness, hid from sight
> I went by secret ladder and sure –
> – Ah, grace of sheer delight! –
> so softly veiled by night,
> hushed now my house, in darkness and secure.'

Oh, Happy Day

'The poem is a happy one, a state of mind and soul where the human person has mystical union with God,' Michael says.

'However, before moving into the light, there is a period of total negation and darkness. Here he is close to themes in Eastern philosophy, the journey to union is a process: before attaining the zenith one must descend to the nadir. This journey of escape from what is not of God, from what is false, is a positive adventure of faith. It is also a gift of a loving God who takes the first step and waits patiently, silently, almost shyly for the human response:

> 'Hidden in that glad night,
> regarding nothing as I stole away,
> no one to see my flight,
> no other guide or light
> save one that in my heart burned bright as day.

'For John, life is a vocation, a call to seek this shy God. The value of the person is seen as inviolable only when the human person is seen as a creature of God. The personal meaning of life can only lie in religious communion with God. The mystery of God is a reality which pervades all of our creaturely life. The poem is a celebration of the love of God. Yet this love is ambiguous, a strange mixture of passionate intensity and painful discomfort, of closeness and distance. The poem is a fascinating dialectic of ignorance and enlightenment, silence and conversation:

> 'Flame, white-hot and compelling,
> yet tender past all telling,
> reaching the secret centre of my soul!
> Burn that is for healing!
> Wound of delight past feeling!
> Willing, you give me life for death's distress.'

PRAYERS
FOR
WINTER

The Hidden Presence

In memory of the much-loved and much-missed Mary Lawler

How do I find You, God?
God is Love.
If you have ever loved,
If you have ever been loved,
You have experienced God
from Within and Without

God is Truth.
If you have ever told the truth,
If you have ever discovered Truth,
You have experienced God
from Within and Without

God is Beauty.
If you have ever helped to create something beautiful,
If you have ever witnessed beauty in any of its myriad
    forms,

You have experienced God
from Within and Without

God is Good.
If you have ever done or thought something good,
If you have ever recognised goodness in or through another,
You have experienced God
from Within and Without

All of those experiences, those gifts,
of Love, Truth, Beauty and Goodness
were directly from God through you or to you.
Glad to Meet You, God.
Let us be friends.

Prayer for Solutions

Creator God, Lord of times and seasons,
May we look for you not just as the fixer,
but as the friend in whose company we are happy to spend
time.
May we enjoy the gifts you give us every day and not worry
about what's missing.
Teach us to live with grateful hearts
the good moments that make us smile,
the shared moments that make us glad we are alive,
the quiet moments that offer us peace.
Nourish our faltering faith so that we may have the courage
and humility
to entrust everything to you who know us better than we
know ourselves
and who still love us without ceasing.
        Amen.

Seeking

Grant me, O Lord, an ever-watchful heart that no alien
thought can lure away from You; a noble heart that no base
love can sully; an upright heart that no perverse intention
can lead astray; an invincible heart that no distress can
overcome; an unfettered heart that no impetuous desires
can enchain.

O Lord my God, also bestow upon me understanding to
know You, zeal to seek You, wisdom to find You, a life that
is pleasing to You, unshakable perseverance, and a hope that
will one day take hold of You.

May I do penance here below and patiently bear your
chastisements. May I also receive the benefits of your grace,
in order to taste your heavenly joys and contemplate your
glory.

Amen.

THOMAS AQUINAS

Lead, Kindly Light

Lead, kindly Light, amid the encircling gloom,
Lead thou me on:
The night is dark, and I am far from home,
Lead thou me on.
Keep thou my feet; I do not ask to see
The distant scene; one step enough for me.

ST JOHN HENRY NEWMAN

A Prayer for New Parents

From the moment you hold your baby in your arms,
you will never be the same.

You might long for the person you were before,
When you have freedom and time,
And nothing in particular to worry about.
You will know tiredness like you never knew it before,
And days will run into days that are exactly the same,
Full of feedings and burping,
Nappy changes and crying,
Whining and fighting,
Naps or a lack of naps,
It might seem like a never-ending cycle.
But don't forget . . .
There is a last time for everything.
There will come a time when you will feed
your baby for the very last time.
They will fall asleep on you after a long day
And it will be the last time you ever hold your sleeping child.
One day you will carry them on your hip then set them
    down,
And never pick them up that way again.
You will scrub their hair in the bath one night
And from that day on they will want to bathe alone.
They will hold your hand to cross the road,
Then never reach for it again.
They will creep into your room at midnight for cuddles,
And it will be the last night you ever wake to this.
One afternoon you will sing 'The Wheels on the Bus'
and do all the actions,
Then never sing them that song again.
They will kiss you goodbye at the school gate,
The next day they will ask to walk to the gate alone.
You will read a final bedtime story and wipe your last dirty
    face.

They will run to you with arms raised for the very last time.
The thing is, you won't even know it's the last time
Until there are no more times.
And even then, it will take you a while to realise.
So while you are living in these times,
remember there are only so many of them
and when they are gone, you will yearn for just one more
    day of them.
For one last time.

AUTHOR UNKNOWN

Embrace Me

Bestow upon me, O Lord my God, an understanding that
knows thee, wisdom in finding thee, a way of life that is
pleasing to thee, perseverance that faithfully waits for thee,
and confidence that I shall embrace thee at the last.

THOMAS AQUINAS

I Said a Prayer for You Today

I said a prayer for you today
And know God must have heard.
I felt the answer in my heart
Although He spoke no word.

I didn't ask for wealth or fame
(I knew you wouldn't mind).
I asked Him to send treasures
Of a far more lasting kind.

I asked that He'd be near you
At the start of each new day;

To grant you health and blessings
And friends to share your way.

I asked for happiness for you
In all things great and small.
But it was for His loving care
I prayed the most of all.

AUTHOR UNKNOWN

A Prayer for Healing

Lord, You invite all who are burdened to come to You.
Allow Your healing Hand to heal me.
Touch my soul with Your compassion for others.
Touch my heart with Your courage and infinite Love for all.
Touch my mind with Your Wisdom, that my mouth may
always proclaim Your praise.
Teach me to reach out to You in all my needs, and help me
to lead others to You by my example.
Most loving Heart of Jesus, bring me health in body and
spirit that I may serve You with all my strength.
Touch gently this life which you have created, now and
forever.
    Amen.

Lord Have Mercy

Go ndéana Dia trócaire ar a n-anamacha dílse.
May God have mercy on all we have loved and lost.

Short Prayer

O compassionate Heart of Jesus, I place all my trust in you
Carry, please carry me O Lord today.

HUMOUR
FOR
WINTER

The Canon

Canon Murphy presided over the funeral Mass of a fellow canon. It was an awesome, if chaotic, sight. The spectacle of a bishop and a multitude of priests, crammed together like bees in a hive behind the altar, made a lasting impression on the faithful. Never have so few stood in so little for so long. One of the priests had forgotten his vestments. As he was only five-foot-one, an old, frilly white alb was found for him. He looked like a cross between an altar boy and Tom Thumb.

The first problem was caused by the microphone. It seemed to have taken on a life of its own and emitted various crackling sounds at the most solemn moments. Such was the disturbance that one of the priests turned it off. This brought hazards of its own. The celebrants had to rely on vocal projection. While this was fine for the bishop, it was less so for Monsignor Rodgers who always spoke as if he was suffering from a bout of tonsillitis. Those priests whose vocal ranges were somewhere in between seemed to think that they were obliged to break the sound barrier by shouting, rather than reciting, their modest contribution to the liturgical celebration.

The second problem was that everybody assumed that

somebody else was organising the ceremony, so that nobody knew who was doing what or what was supposed to be happening. A priest would stand up to intone some prayer and just as abruptly sit down on discovering that at least one other colleague had beaten him to it. There were protracted pauses as everybody looked to the bishop to see what would happen.

Of course, there was the choir. For reasons best known to himself, the late canon had taken a particular aversion to the choir, with the result that they were normally only to be heard on Midnight Mass and Christmas Day. In the light of the musical talent which was evident on those occasions, the canon's decision to employ their services so sparingly looked more and more judicious. Neither the organ nor the organist were in the first flush of youth nor even in the second. The combination of two idiosyncratic performances made for interesting – if not elegant – listening. The choir predictably lived down to expectations. Even by their own standards, they were abysmal. The problem was exacerbated by the fact that the assembled clergy seemed to have formed a rival choral group, apparently singing the same hymns at a different speed to a different arrangement and musical notation.

The last straw was the prayers of the faithful, which Monsignor Rodgers had arranged beforehand. Gerry 'The Hop' McCarthy, the canon's right-hand man in the parish, had been asked to say one of the prayers as a recognition of his loyal service and friendship to our late pastor. In a trembling voice he mumbled something indistinguishable – even to those in the front row. He gained confidence though with each word – only to make an embarrassing *faux pas* just when his voice was clearly audible – by praying for the canon's 'immorality' rather than 'immortality'.

Love Hurts

One day Fr. Dan's car broke down on the way to a wedding ceremony and he was an hour late on arrival. The wedding party was beginning to panic when he arrived, his face taut with worry; he was so embarrassed seeing the distress in everybody's expressions that he never forgot the incident. The groom was a teacher. His name was Tomás and he was a tall, fair, amiable and placid fellow, seldom roused to anger, even when he had the most cheeky and disruptive pupils in his care like Ciaran, who was short, dark and sly, and of course the red-haired Peadar, who was one of the laziest lads he had ever encountered.

The wedding took place on a glorious summer afternoon, with fluffy white clouds flecking an impossibly blue sky, trees whispering softly in a gentle breeze, and the lazy sound of bees humming among the hedgerows. Cows lowed contentedly in the distance, and the air was rich with the scent of ripe corn and scythed grass.

There had been a fierce heatwave earlier that year, followed by torrential rains that had devastated farmland all over the country. Fortune had smiled on this area, though: its crops had survived the treacherous weather, and the harvest was expected to be excellent. It was already evident that the local farmers would not go short of bread that winter, and the fat sheep and cattle dotting the surrounding hills indicated they would not be short of meat, either.

But the father of the bride saw none of this plenty: his mind was on another matter entirely. His only daughter was a slim, elegant woman who took considerable pride in her appearance. She loved clothes, and spent a lot of her father's money ensuring she was never less than perfectly attired, from her always fashionable hat to her stylish designer-brand shoes. Her weakness for finery exasperated her father, who was always reminding her that while he was not a poor farmer, he was not exactly wealthy, either, and that he had a duty to her seven brothers to use the profits from the family farm more wisely than frittering them away on extravagancies. His face went white with anger when he thought of all the money his daughter had cost him. The one bright note on his horizon was that from now on Tomás would have to foot his daughter's bills. Her trusting husband would get an introduction into 'for richer or poor poorer' much sooner than he ever could have envisaged.

Twenty years later, Fr. Dan met Tomás at a function in a local hotel for a fundraiser for the St Vincent de Paul. There was a rainy spirit in the air, too; spiteful little droplets carried in a bitter wind that stung where they hit.

As soon as he got inside the door after seeing an elderly woman staggering in, puffing like a pair of bellows, he greeted the organiser and mumbled, 'I am sorry for being late,' in the automatic way that suggested these were words uttered on far too regular a basis.

He could not help but overhear snippets of conversation as he wove though the tables. As he slumped gratefully into a chair in the corner of the reception room in the hotel and secretly wished he was at home in front of the fire watching *Match of the Day* his sharp expression softened as he saw Tomás for the first time in years. He beckoned the teacher over and shook his hand and smiled as he said: 'I'm so sorry about that horrible fright I gave you on your wedding day.'

'So am I,' said the man, so venomously that Father Dan was repelled by the malice that blazed from his face. In truth Tomás did not look well. His face was pale, and his eyes were watery. He smiled, although it was not a pleasant expression. Tomás sat heavily on a nearby chair, and Father Dan saw the colour drain from his face. He appeared to be on the verge of exhaustion as he said with real feeling. 'I've still got her!'

Go with the Crowd

Claude Stevens won the silver medal at the discus at the Montreal Disabled Athletes Olympics in the 1970s. Claude was a merchant seaman for twenty years until he fell off the hold of a ship and was paralysed from the chest down. He was renowned for his sense of humour. One of his favourite stories was of the wheelchair athlete who flew to Lourdes for a cure, but he was so exhausted when he got there that they were afraid to take him out of the wheelchair to immerse him in the pool, as is the traditional practice for pilgrims, for fear he might collapse. Instead they put him, wheelchair and all, into the sacred pool. Then another of the great Lourdes miracles took place. The man was not cured but when he came out the wheelchair had a new set of tyres!

Gratitude

I am an atheist, thank God.

For God's Sake

If I had served God as diligently as I have done the King, he would not have given me my grey hairs.

CARDINAL WOLSEY, 1473–1530

LETTERS
FOR
WINTER

A Letter to My Father

I invited Fr. Colm McGlynn to write a letter to his father. He shared this poem in response.

Holding His Hand

Today we took a gentle stroll
From Rathfarnham Shopping Centre
To the post box in Templeogue village

And Dad, in his 83rd year,
Became so jaded
I had to hold his hand

Tears welled up in my heart
At this role reversal:

The man who held
My hand as a boy
Now in need of mine.

A Prayer from a Father

During the Vietnam War, an American soldier wrote a letter to his son, in which he seeks to give good advice about how to live a good life. The soldier died in action and the letter remained unfinished.

My dearest Phil,

In the last few months everything has become very clear to me. I have discovered the difference between the important and the trivial. Here is what I ask of you:

Worry about courage
Worry about goodness
Worry about family
Worry about friendship
Worry about honour
Worry about getting a good education
Worry about living a good life
Worry about making a difference
Worry about understanding people

Above all worry that you are making the best of your life and if you are bringing pain to another.

Don't worry about popular opinion
Don't worry about setbacks
Don't worry about the past
Don't worry about the future
Don't worry about growing up
Don't worry about anybody getting ahead of you
Don't worry about triumph
Don't worry about failure unless it comes through your own fault . . .

With a Little Comfort from Your Friends

In 1513, an Italian artist, Fra Giovanni Giocondo, wrote a letter to a friend who was in crisis. This is what he wrote:

I salute you. I am your friend and my love for you goes deep. There is nothing I can give you which you have not got; but there is much, very much, that while I cannot give you, you can take. No heaven can come to us unless our hearts find rest in it today. Take heaven! No peace lies in the future which is not hidden in this present little instant.

Take peace! The gloom of the world is but a shadow. Behind it, yet within reach, is joy. There is radiance and glory in the darkness, could we but see. And to see, we have only to look. I beseech you to look! . . .

And so, my dear friend, I greet you. Not quite as the world sends greetings, but with profound esteem and with the prayer that for you, now and forever, the day breaks, and the shadows fall.

PART FIVE
CHRISTMAS

THE EARLY CELTS DID NOT CELEBRATE Christmas because they did not know about it. However, in the darkest days of winter, the Celts felt the need to party and bring joy to the Celtic world.

The winter solstice is, with the summer solstice, the oldest seasonal festival known to humanity. The Celts did not take the return of the sun for granted, especially as they were much more at the mercy of severe winter weather than we are today. For farming folk, whose survival depended mostly on crops, the return of the sun was literally a matter of life or death.

Newgrange (Brú na Bóinne) is a mighty Neolithic passage tomb and temple structure in the valley of the Boyne River. Its age is estimated at 5,200 years, give or take, making Newgrange older than the Pyramids of Gizeh and Stonehenge. Newgrange is aligned towards the sunrise of the winter solstice. When the sun reaches a certain angle, the light shines through a special window along a passage and at the end of the passage falls onto a big stone, which bears the carving of a three-fold spiral. The event lasts approximately fifteen minutes, during which the light is wandering across the floor of the passage and the stone at its end. This has been interpreted as the insertion of a ray of light by the Sun God into the womb of Mother Earth, to bring about the creation of new life in spring.

On the morning of the winter solstice, the Celts woke early, long before the first faint vestiges of light illuminated the specklings of frost on the hard ground. Sometimes as they were compelled to watch the world take shape despite their haste. The faint horizontal threads of clouds grew a fiercer red against the still grey sky, the streaks intensifying to scarlet and to orange and to gold, until the whole sky was a breathtaking symphony of colour. The stars were like holes in the celestial carpet, which allowed the eternal light to shine through.

A hoar frost lay on the fields and the hedgerows were hung with the lace trimmings of what seemed to be a thousand spiders' webs. In the distance cattle were huddling under creeping hedges, staring vacantly up at the emerging slate-grey sky with their stoic eyes, as they contemplated their own dinner. The trees seemed to be standing and shivering together, hugging bare limbs and grumbling about the cold. On this day more than any other they marvelled at the hand of the gods in the countryside.

What were the celebrations of the winter solstice in pre-Christian times have today metamorphosed into Christmas. There was no need for a giant leap to facilitate this takeover. In the Christian mythology, Jesus Christ is 'the Light of the World' and it is no accident that today we celebrate the birth of Jesus at the time of the winter solstice. Initially the birth of Christ was probably celebrated in the spring, but later moved close to the winter solstice, partly because the early Church was unable to stop the winter solstice celebrations. Christianity wanted to superimpose its own faith message on to the celebration. There also seemed to be a natural synergy and symbolism with fitting the birth of the light into the days of greatest darkness.

There were some changes on the way. The Celts were great fans of mistletoe, but they believed that it was a cure for illness rather than a pathway to a cherished romantic encounter.

EVERGREEN

In the Celtic tradition, homes were decorated with evergreen branches. The green served as a reminder of the promise that nature will be green again in springtime and life will return to farms. In the Irish tradition, a house decorated with greeneries is expected to offer a place of rest to nature spirits fleeing from cold and darkness. Another seasonal prop to reinforce the theme of light breaking through the darkness is the generous use of candles.

The Celts loved to sing. Some old customs can momentarily transfigure our existence and let the eternal shine through. One such custom is the singing of carols. They strike us as simple ways of expressing those parts of Christianity that ordinary people find most interesting, not the parts that people ought to find most interesting. They are memorable because they are so tangible. They celebrate things that we can touch and see and warm to: a mother and a baby, though curiously not a father, or at least not a 'real' father, a stable, donkeys, shepherds, straw and hay.

Before Christmas a great clean-up begins and every room in the house is turned upside down and inside out as if very special visitors were coming. Everything is dusted, swept, scrubbed, scoured or polished, curtains are washed, and every place looks at its very best by the end.

For Christians today, Christmas is a reminder of a wonderful message – God has transformed our brokenness by taking it on. There is also a very keen awareness of the pastoral dimension of Christmas. Every year they remember those who are bruised and broken, melancholic or moody. They pray for those who in a peculiar way both look forward to the season of 'good cheer' and dread it, and for those who are impatient for the magic that never comes for them but that all the preparations promise. Christmas is above all, for them, a time to be lonely.

In times of emigration they remember those with families scattered all over the world; England, Australia, America and Canada. Some feel exile, home-sickness, longing and hoped-for returns that would never materialise, and are trapped in a prison of memories. Their pain is the piercing grief of never being able to return to the way things used to be.

They also recall the elderly people who live alone and whose loneliness becomes more intense and shrill with each passing Christmas – at times ascending to a chilling crescendo. Every year their longing for warmth and affection becomes more desperate. They are other silent victims of a vast and concealed cancer of loneliness. Christmas is little more than a painful reminder of missed chances for lasting happiness.

Traditionally in rural Ireland in dark's dull density, the curtains were stripped off the windows and a single candle was put to burn in each sill until the morning. When the Rosary was said, the children were dispatched to an early night in bed, no dissenting voice was raised. Across the fields, the houses glittered, the light from their candles like jewelled pin-points in the darkness. The back door remained unlocked whatever the weather, so that there was no danger of Mary and Joseph going astray in their search for a resting place.

THE IRELAND OF THE WELCOMES

Christians continue in the Irish tradition of monastic hospitality where the marginalised were welcomed. Hospitality was often very much in the tradition of the story of the widow's mite. Although they had very little to offer, they gave generously, sharing the view of St Francis of Assisi: it is in giving that we receive.

The tradition of the 'Ireland of the Welcomes' can be traced back to pre-Christian times. Under the Brehon Laws, to refuse hospitality was not simply impolite, it was considered an offence. The arrival of Christianity gave a new impetus to this tradition. In the Judgement Gospel (Matthew 25), hospitality is seen as an integral part of the Christian life: 'I was a stranger and you welcomed me.' Hospitality was actually institutionalised in the Irish monasteries with each having its own *Teach Aíochta* (House of Hospitality). The monks supplied food, drink and overnight accommodation to all passers-by without seeking any financial donation.

St Brendan was one person particularly associated with hospitality. He was born in 483 or 484 AD. He was fostered by the famous St Ita, who had a special gift with children, from the age of two until five, in Killkeedy near Newcastle West in county Limerick. St Ita was known as 'the foster mother of the saints of Ireland'. Brendan is reported to have asked her the three things that God especially loved.

She replied: 'God loves a true faith in Him with a pure heart; a simple life with a religious spirit; and open-handedness inspired by charity.'

In the Celtic tradition, the guest was always Christ and hospitality was offered to Christ in the other. One story which illustrates this is told about St Crónán. He had an unexpected visit from a neighbouring abbot and a big number of his monks. While they were eating at table, a young novice caused a bit of a stir by saying aloud, 'It seems there will be no vespers said here this evening.'

After a short, awkward silence St Crónán responded, 'Brother, in the guest is received Christ. Therefore at the coming of Christ we ought to feast and rejoice. But if you had not said that, the angels of God themselves would have prayed on our behalf here this night.'

THE GOD WHO DANCES

St Brigid's monastery in Kildare was known as the City of the Poor, on foot of its reputation for hospitality, compassion and generosity. These were genuinely inclusive communities.

Brigid is the perfect example of Irish hospitality: she can (by a miracle) milk her cows three times in one day to provide a meal for visitors. Brigid celebrated the God who dances. She was no killjoy as we saw earlier, going so far as to describe heaven as a great lake of beer. According to the conventional belief at the time, St Brigid had no interest in material things because her focus was solely on God.

St Brigid was able to see Christ in other people. A famous story told about her illustrates this:

Once Brigid had embarked on a long journey and she stopped to rest by the wayside. A wealthy woman heard that she was in the locality and brought her a beautiful basket of apples. As soon as the apples appeared, a group of people came by and begged for food. Immediately Brigid gave them the apples. Her benefactor was aghast and barked disdainfully, 'I brought those apples for you, not for them.'

Quick as a flash Brigid replied, 'What's mine is theirs.'

Thomas Merton said: 'With those for whom there is no room is Jesus.' This understanding is based on the fact that, especially at Christmas, with those for whom there is no one to share their rooms is Jesus. The sad reality is that life is difficult for many people. The message of Christmas is that Christ is made flesh not in the unreal beauty of the Christmas card, but in the real mess that is our world. For those of us who claim to be Christian, Christ is made flesh in our neighbours.

GLAD TIDINGS

On Christmas morning there is a special feeling. Children – who the night before were bursting with impatience, and had resolved to stay awake all night, to sneak a peep through the bannister, to catch a glimpse of Santa's red cloak – prepare to worship. Then, when sleep had defeated them, they rushed downstairs, drawn as if by a magnet to the place under the Christmas tree, where hopefully Santa Claus had neatly piled their presents. Competition is intense as to who was to be the first to make the discovery, to shriek out: 'He came, He came!' – the excitement transmitting like electricity; their shining faces a fitting reward to the idea of Santa. Then the presents are pulled out and examined with squeaks of delight and excitement, muffled as far as possible to let any sleeping parents have a snooze.

This is a time of mystery and that spirit is carried into the seasonal worship.

In churches, the pungent scent of greenery mingles with the waxy smell of burning candles. The final candle in the advent wreath is lit ceremoniously. So many images of Christ are etched in light, the silver of frost and moonlight, the shining Star of Bethlehem guarding the Magi and the radiance of the lighted candles. The candles quietly complement the elation of the Gospel.

The priests also read the nativity story of how the angel spoke to the shepherds on the hillside and reported that: 'They went in haste and found Mary and Joseph.' Looking back now, they wonder if that was the first Christmas rush!

In the congregation, many are enthralled by the idea of angels.

The pictures they have of angels are of creatures robed in white with outspread wings, kindly smiles and celestial vision. Angels are always good but essentially heavenly. The worshippers like them because they form a tenuous connection between the unseen worlds and signify the greatest of mysteries, human-kind's passage through time.

When the liturgy is finished, the congregation head home to prepare roaring fires which will provide leaping flames, dancing shadows and a rosy glow. After Christmas celebrations, the atmosphere is as Dickensian as Scrooge after the ghosts.

In the German theologian Karl Rahner's magical phrase, Christmas is a time when 'grace is in the air'. Christmas Day is the best reminder that the eternal life began in a stable in Bethlehem.

Christianity today continues to draw heavily on the Celtic battle between darkness and light. The *First Sermon for Advent* of St Bernard of Clairvaux captures this insight incisively:

'Truly the day was already far spent and the evening drawing near; the sun of justice was already beginning to set, and its rays now gave diminished light and warmth to the earth. The light of the knowledge of God had grown feeble, and as sin increased, charity grew cold. Angels no longer appeared to men, no prophet raised his voice; it seemed as though, overcome by the great hardness and obstinacy of men, they had ceased to intervene in human affairs. Then it was that the Son of God said: "Here am I."'

Christmas is a time for what T.S. Eliot calls 'moments in and out of time'. Patrick Kavanagh describes the frost on Christmas morning in the Monaghan of his childhood: 'And the frost of Bethlehem made it twinkle.' The Jesus of history is born in a stable so it is appropriate that, for Kavanagh, 'Christ comes in a January flower.'

For the Celts, this was a time of threshold, an in-between place; it is an invitation to enter, to start again, to reflect on which way to go. Christmas is a threshold to merrymaking, but also to an awareness that life is a continuous cycle of birth and death to rebirth. For the Celts understood that we are all part of a web of life.

WISDOM
FOR
CHRISTMAS

Childlike
For it is good to be children sometimes, and never better than at
Christmas, when its mighty Founder was a child himself.

CHARLES DICKENS, 1812–1870

A Stable Diet
Once in our world, a stable had something in it that was bigger
than our whole world.

C.S. LEWIS, 1898–1963

Stargazing
A little child, a shining star, a stable rude, a the door ajar. Yet in
that place, so crude, forlorn, the Hope of the whole world was
born.

ANON

Lambs and Wisdom
The simple shepherds heard the voice of an angel and found

their lamb; the wise men saw the light of a star and found their wisdom.

ARCHBISHOP FULTON SHEEN, 1895–1979

Free Love

Love feels no burden, thinks nothing of trouble, attempts what is above its strength, pleads no excuse of impossibility; for it thinks all things lawful for itself, and all things possible.

THOMAS À KEMPIS, 1380–1471

Light a Candle

Thousands of candles can be lighted by a single candle, and the life of the candle will not be shortened. Happiness never decreases by being shared.

BUDDHA

The Quality of Mercy

For mercy has a human heart
Pity a human face:
And Love, the human form divine,
And Peace, the Human dress.

WILLIAM BLAKE, 1757–1827

The Spirit Level

Forget my bones
Keep my spirit.

ST KIERNAN FIFTH-CENTURY IRISH SAINT

Lighten the Load

To gladden the heart of a human being
To feed the hungry
To help the afflicted
To lighten the sorrow of the sorrowful
To remove the wrongs of the injured
That person is the most beloved of God
Who does most good to God's creatures.

PROPHET MUHAMMAD

Honest to God

God has no religion.

MAHATMA GANDHI

Admiration

God's admiration for us is infinitely greater than anything we can conjure up for him.

ST FRANCIS OF ASSISI

Mission Impossible

Start by doing what's necessary; then do what's possible; and suddenly you are doing the impossible.

ST FRANCIS OF ASSISI

Bless You

May the Lord bless you and keep you
May He show His face to you.
And have mercy on you.

May He turn His countenance to you
And give you peace.

ST FRANCIS OF ASSISI

Troubled Times

Great troubles come
From not knowing what is enough
Great conflict arises
From wanting too much
When we know when enough is enough
There will always be enough.

LAO TZU, 604–531 BC

The Prince

As dear unto God is the poor peasant as the mighty prince.

PLATO

Stand to Attention

It had long since come to my attention that people of accomplishment rarely sat back and let things happen to them. They went out and happened to things.

LEONARDO DA VINCI

Right Relationship

Health is the greatest gift,
Contentment the greatest wealth
Faithfulness the best relationship.

BUDDHA

In the Mess

Spirituality is not to be learned by flight from the world, or by running away from things, or by turning solitary and going apart from the world. Rather, we must learn to penetrate things and find God there.

MEISTER ECKHART

TALES
FOR
CHRISTMAS

The following collection of short stories invites us to stand
still for a while and to ponder the true meaning of Christmas
before we rush off to do our Christmas shopping. What is
the real meaning of Christmas? Every year, priests, teachers
and theologians struggle to answer this perennial question.
These heart-warming and uplifting stories hint at elements of
the answer. They seek to capture the imagination of all those
who are young at heart and to unmask the reality of Christmas
beyond the tinsel and the turkey. They strive to help us escape
for a while from the frenetic activity of Christmas today, to bring
us back to the celebration of the birth, in a field, of the son of
a poor carpenter who came to reveal the true meaning of life.

Santa Claus is a person of utterly selfless generosity, who
gives without expecting anything in return, except the satisfaction of knowing that he has given happiness to the children of
this world. Santa never judges anyone; even those children who
were bold do not get rejected, but they too receive their gifts
from him.

He inspires a group of little followers who work all year to
get the presents ready so that children everywhere can laugh
on Christmas day; they have committed themselves to the same

selfless generosity as Santa himself. Even Rudolf and the other animals give him their undivided loyalty and do his bidding. Santa's little community is focused on bringing happiness to others.

To many, Santa – in his various incarnations – is the spirit of Christmas, as every child knows. Christmas without Santa would be a Christmas without magic. And Christmas without magic would be a Christmas without meaning. The stories in this section talk of the magic that is Christmas and the smiles of the children when the magic happens.

But for some, Christmas is a time of misery and struggle. Those who are lonely experience their aloneness more acutely at Christmas time, as they think of happy families opening their presents on Christmas morning. Some parents struggle, and end up drowned in debt, to try and bring a smile to the faces of their children on Christmas morning. Christmas is a very busy time for services such as Childline, as children seek someone to whom they can express their unhappiness. The stories in this section also hint at the misery that is Christmas for some and the heroic struggles of some parents to make the magic happen for their children, against all the odds. This collection captures the whole reality of Christmas, both the wonder of Christmas and the injustice in our world that condemns so many to poverty – material and emotional.

THE MAN WITH THE TURNED-DOWN WELLINGTONS

Mickey Dan had the type of exuberant nasal hair from which it is difficult to tear one's gaze. The fact that he was so tall and thin, complemented by a severely lined face and enormous eyelashes, gave him the air of an ancient ascetic.

To say he was not the sort of man to make friends easily

would be the understatement of the century. He was someone who seldom smiled. In fact, he seemed to have an ever-present scowl. Patsy Freyne said of him: 'He has the sort of face that would make milk turn sour.'

Most people in the parish, though, referred to him in a more benign fashion as, 'the man with the turned-down wellingtons', because of his distinctive fashion statement with his footwear of choice. Not even the most senior citizen in the village could remember a time that Mickey Dan did not wear green turned-down wellingtons.

Every Friday he cycled on his Raleigh bike to the post office to collect his pension, in his belted coat, cap on the side of his head, shovel tied on the bar of the bike and a well-worn biscuit tin neatly tied with old twine on the carrier behind him. Then he went on to Monika Herok's shop where each week he religiously bought a side of bacon, two batch loaves, a half-pound of butter, two pound of sausages; rolls of black and white pudding and his treat of choice: a packet of Kimberley biscuits. All were packed untidily on the back of the bicycle as he headed for home. On the way he never spoke to or smiled at anyone. He could peel an orange in his pocket.

When the parish council decided they would erect a Christmas tree and put up Christmas lights outside the shops, everyone was very enthusiastic except for Mickey Dan, who merely rolled his eyes when he heard the news.

With the new tree and new lights there was a real buzz in the parish about Christmas. Inspired by this development, Helmut Sundermann, the parish priest, had spent the afternoon in the churchyard giving it its annual Christmas tidy-up, even though it had been another cold, gloomy day, with clouds thick and heavy overhead. It had been windy too, and autumn leaves swirled around until they made soggy piles in corners. He had breathed in deeply, relishing the clean scent of damp vegetation. The only fly in the ointment was when he whipped around in alarm as he heard a sound close behind him, but it was only the parish secretary. This was a man who prided himself on his stealth, and he was always sneaking up on people with the clear intention of making them jump out of their skin.

The town's forefathers had chosen an idyllic spot for their community. It was just south-west of the castle, on what was effectively an island with two arms of the river sweeping around it. It boasted a range of impressive new and old buildings, along with gardens and an orchard, although it was the church that most caught the eye. This was a wonderful creation of soft grey stone, with tiers of large windows to let in the light. Stone seats were provided for restful reposes in the adjacent park during summer, while a tinkling fountain offered an attractive centrepiece.

The cool air had smelled of wet soil and coming spring blossom, and was damp from a recent shower. A blackbird trilled a final song from the roof of the church, clear and sweet, while Helmut Sundermann sang lustily in his kitchen. Other than that, the evening was still, and he was aware of a growing sense of peace. He breathed in deeply, enjoying the sweet scents of the fading day.

The yard was full of his predecessors' tombs, and was a dark, silent, intimate place. Inside the church, an elderly nun had been praying, although her nodding head and bowed shoulders suggested that her sleepless night was beginning to catch up with her. She turned at the sound of footsteps and heaved herself to her feet, yawning hugely as she did so.

At the back of the church there had been a man so still and poised that he might have been a statute, but then he sneezed, and spoiled his attitude of elegant piety by wiping his nose on his overcoat. He sneezed again, sniffed loudly, and this time it was his sleeve that cleaned his running nose.

The rain had passed, and the day had turned pretty, with fluffy white clouds dotting a bright blue sky and a warm sun drawing steam from the wet ground. The appetising scent of frying eggs wafted from within the home of the parish's most beautiful woman, Judith McAdam. Handel's *Messiah* blasted uplifting tones from the old radio in the parochial house.

Then disaster. Two weeks before Christmas, there was a huge storm which blew a huge hole in the roof of the church. The poor parish priest was so upset by this development that he had a mini-stroke. For the first time ever, there was no Mass in the parish on Sunday.

A week passed. There was a lot of talking, speculation and complaining, but nobody did anything. For the second Sunday in a row there was no parish Mass during a lazy wind that did not go around anyone – it just went through people.

At this stage, an air of crisis had fallen in every corner of the community. The social high point of the year was in the parish hall after Midnight Mass when everyone gathered for mince pies and punch and, to finish, a hush descended when the choir sang 'And So This Is Christmas' – though it was universally recognised that this year nothing was going to match Lisa Dobey's wedding on the eighth of June. But if there was no Midnight Mass, there would be no parish social. And if there was no parish social would it really be Christmas? Of course would it be Christmas even without Midnight Mass when there was not enough space in the church to roll a sweet in anybody's mouth. But what was the alternative? There was just two days left to the big day.

On the twenty-third, at a quarter past ten, Mickey Dan pulled up outside the church with his Massey Ferguson 35 tractor, which to put it at its very kindest, had seen better days. His big trailer, though, was filled with all kinds of building materials. Slowly and methodically, Mickey Dan began to unpack the trailer and to erect a simple scaffolding on the side of the church. News of this sensational development spread like wildfire through the parish. By lunchtime, Mickey Dan was up on the roof. The sound of his hammer in action spread a strange music around the church. The village gossips went into a state of frenzy.

Paddy Joe Burke suddenly shut down his barber shop and speedily strode to the church with a hammer in his hand and he joined Mickey Dan on the roof. The two men nodded to each other, but not a word passed between them. Within minutes the terrifically talented teacher, Noel McManamly, emerged to complete the parish's answer to the Holy Trinity. Within the hour every able-bodied man in the parish had gathered at the church. They all worked like men possessed but still nobody said anything.

A few hours later, the two kindest women in the parish, Patricia Seery and Trish O'Brien, came with flasks of hot chicken soup and trays of sandwiches. Mickey Dan said a quiet word of thanks to the two women and all the men followed suit.

After twenty minutes for silent but restorative refreshments, Mickey Dan led the troop of men back to work. As they climbed back up the scaffolding, Mickey Dan asked Paddy Joe if he remembered the county final they had won together. All the men were shocked to hear Mickey Dan speak in this way. The older men remembered that he had been a brilliant footballer in his youth. He had even been spoken of as 'the new Dermot Earley'. When he was just nineteen he sustained a serious injury on the playing fields, but there was no money to give him the treatment he required to restore his silken skills. Within moments, the church roof was a hive of activity and conversation.

As somebody shared the story of the time when a stray

cat broke into Tony Lee's shed on Christmas Eve and ate his lovely goose hanging on the back door, Mickey Dan burst into laughter. Like a volcano that had been waiting to erupt for years, his laughter seemed to go on and on like a transatlantic ocean-liner.

Just as darkness fell, the roof was finally finished. With all hands on deck, the scaffolding was soon dismantled and carefully placed back on the trailer. Then Mickey Dan did the unthinkable. He gave Paddy Joe a hug. Soon all the men in the parish were hugging each other without embarrassment.

On a car radio the velvety voice of David Essex was crooning about a winter's tale.

At Midnight Mass, everyone's favourite priest Fr. John unexpectedly did the honours. The parish church had been packed to overflowing and the atmosphere was slightly tense, as people jockeyed for the best places. The Reverend Mother's face was pale and waxy. She spoke in a voice that a peculiarly booming quality. She was clutching her arm almost desperately, but she was more interested in nodding greetings to the people she knew as she came out of the church. Sr. Mary, though, had that special knack of making everyone feel better about themselves as she shook everyone's hand.

The clear consensus was that it was the nicest Mass ever. Then it was time for the Christmas fundraiser: for Deirdre Lynch's wonderful 'Not So Different' charity which was bigger and better than ever, not least because Yvonne O'Rourke had a slice of her celebrated Christmas cake for everyone. She could do a miracle with marzipan and icing. As a consequence, each mouthful tasted like the eighth wonder of the world.

As always, Mickey Dan was the last to enter the parish hall. But this time was different. Everyone gave him a standing ovation. Somebody shouted out that Mickey Dan had had a lovely singing voice in school. A hush descended when he was prevailed on to sing. The entire gathering stood in wonder as he sang a rendition of 'When a Child Is Born' that even Johnny Mathis himself would have been proud of. The applause for him afterwards was louder than for the winner of the Eurovision Song Contest.

That was the last time anyone ever described him as 'the man with the turned-down wellingtons'. That night Mickey Dan cycled home happily whistling, 'Will Ye Go, Lassie, Go?'

From that day to his last day, Mickey was known as 'the man who saved Christmas'.

THE LITTLE DRUMMER BOY

Once upon a time about two thousand years ago there was a couple who were very much in love. The man's name was Joseph and his wife was Mary.

They travelled from Nazareth to Bethlehem for the census. It was a difficult journey made all the more challenging because Mary was nine months pregnant and was due to give birth at any moment. When they got to Bethlehem, there was no room for them in the inn so they had to seek shelter in a damp, dusty street corner. It was not long before Mary fell into a deep sleep. Joseph took the opportunity to slip out into the night air. On the way to the stable he had noticed Bethlehem's only shop. It was run by Katy Kindheart, who was known as the kindest woman in the kingdom. When Katy heard that Mary and Joseph had no room in the inn she offered them her stable.

Shortly after they got to the stable, Mary started moaning. A few minutes later, Mary's boy child was born and they called him Jesus.

An angel appeared from heaven and announced the birth of

the baby with soft, sweet music that somehow could be heard throughout the whole kingdom.

Within minutes, shepherds and their wives came and brought beautiful gifts to the new baby. It was around then that Katy Kindheart decided to visit the stable. By now it was hard to see her way. Not a star was to be seen. It was bitterly cold. Only a purring cat shattered the spell of silence. Katy's breath was coming out on to the cold air like puffs of steam from a kettle.

Even before she got to the door, Katy could hear the new baby crying. She saw a few men rushing in before them in a state of great excitement. Some of them were carrying armfuls of nice, clean straw.

Katy walked in and peeped out from behind one of the big men to see Mary holding her new baby and no woman could look happier. A lot of happy visitors were circling the happy couple like a swarm of bees. Outside, children's screams pierced the air. The late-comers frantically scampered up to the door, slipping red-faced into a corner at the back, briefly disturbing the hushed stillness. Men in heavy cloaks shuffled nervously, whispering about the price of sheep over the talk about the new baby. Women in their best coats held their heads high.

Katy heard one of the shepherds whispering: 'Then it is true. About an hour ago, an angel appeared to us as we sat around our campfire. We were tired from looking after our sheep all day and very cold, so we had been drinking whiskey to keep us warm. The first thing the angel said was: "Be not afraid." But we were terrified! Really, I mean it. We were sacred out of our wits!

'Then the angel said a second time: "Be not afraid." And once again we were terrified! The angel went on to say: "Tonight a child is born who will save the world." Just when we thought things could get no stranger, the angel started singing: "Glory to God in the highest and peace to all people on earth. Listen now and hear what I have to say. All children will live for evermore because of Christmas Day.'''

Katy was joined by her tiny son, Luke, with his drum and he said to Mary: 'I would love to offer the Christ child gold and silver but my simple gift is my music. This is all I can give you.'

He played a piece so beautiful that a hush descended in the stable. Luke's drum gave the sweetest music that Joseph and Mary had ever heard.

The baby Jesus gave his first ever smile to Luke. Then he reached out his tiny hand and touched the drum.

THE FIRST CHRISTMAS MIRACLE

Once upon a time, about two thousand years ago, there lived a boy called Tadhg. One morning he had been moving home a big bowl of water. It was much too heavy really, for a boy like himself, but he always did what he was told. He had almost made the mile and a half home when he lost his balance and the bowl crashed on to the ground, smashing into a hundred tiny pieces. He knew immediately that this meant big, big trouble from his father.

Tadhg decided he would run away. He ran and ran until he got very tired. By now, it was very dark. He reached the local small town of Bethlehem which, unusually, was full with people. Tadhg was scared by all the noise and started to cry. A kindly old shopkeeper saw him and gave him some apples and oranges. Tadhg was overjoyed and went to find a quiet place to enjoy this feast.

Just as he was sitting down outside a stable, he heard some shadowy figures come out from the darkness. Tadhg was upset when he heard the woman moaning in pain and holding her stomach. *That poor creature must be very hungry*, thought Tadhg.

Without thinking he brought over all the apples and oranges to the couple. They thanked him warmly and then the man helped the woman into the stable and lay her down on a bed of straw.

Suddenly Tadhg felt a great sense of peace sweep over him and he decided he would return home. He was halfway home when he met three beautiful women, with dark skin and wavy air, in magnificent robes on camels. They were carrying what looked like very expensive presents.

'Young boy do you know where the new king was born tonight?' one asked.

'I'm afraid I know nothing about that, ladies, but there was a lot going on in Bethlehem this evening.'

'Please tell us what you saw,' said one of the women. 'My name is Ruth, by the way, and this is Roberta and Rachel.'

While Tadhg told them everything that had happened to him, the three women listened very carefully. When he had finished Ruth asked, 'I know you are very tired, but would you be kind enough to take us to see that woman in the stable?'

Quick as a flash, Ruth stretched out her long arm and pulled Tadhg up beside her on her camel. Even before they got to the door, Tadhg could hear a baby crying. *Where did that baby come from?* he thought to himself.

Then the three women presented gifts to Mary.

Roberta went first and she gave the new mother a basket of lovely soaps and oils and face-cloths, as well as the tiniest clothes anybody had ever seen in Bethlehem.

Next came Rachel and she presented Mary with a beautiful silk nightdress and dressing-gown.

Finally, Ruth opened the wrapping paper off a bulky object. Mary's eyes nearly fell out of her head when Ruth calmly put a magnificent crib on the strawy floor and placed the baby in it and wrapped his blanket around him.

Tadhg felt bad that he had no gift for the baby. He quietly slipped outside. Young though he was, he knew that it was not the value of the gift that matters, but the spirit in which it is given. He went out to the woods and got a tiny holly tree and dug it up with his hands. It was a poor little thing without a single berry on it, but Tadhg carried the offering to the stable. When he walked back in, the shepherds started laughing at his miserable-looking plant.

Tadhg knelt down before the baby's crib and, in a shaking voice, he said, 'Dear little child, I'm sorry I could not give a beautiful present. The little holly tree was the best I could find, and I give it to you. I always give of my best.'

As soon as Tadhg had finished speaking, a great hush fell upon the stable, for a wonderful thing had happened before their eyes. The colourless little holly tree had become covered with a mass of glowing red berries. It was the first Christmas miracle.

CHRISTMAS GUESTS

Niamh's Christmas dinner was a very simple one of eggs, hot cocoa, biscuits and butter.

Tears came to her eyes, not for the first time that day, as she thought of her late husband. How quickly those marvellous months melted away when they were so happily married.

Niamh woke from her afternoon slumber with a start. A crashing sound boomed through the still air. Somebody was knocking at the door. Niamh's heartbeat accelerated; nobody ever came to see her anymore, but last night she had the strangest dream that the Lord himself would visit her on His birthday. Niamh herself had been born on Christmas day seventy years ago. Her face fell when she saw a shabby old beggar standing on the doorstep. *What a foolish old woman I am becoming* she thought to herself. The stranger's clothes were ragged and threadbare and his shoes were badly worn out. Niamh brought him inside, sat him beside the fire, gave him a mug of steaming tea and went off to look for her late husband's old coat and boots. They fitted the stranger perfectly. With tears in his eyes, the old man bade farewell.

Niamh started to tidy up. Within moments, through the clear frosty air, there came a faint knock. This time it was a bent old woman. She had curly white hair, a very haggard face, brown eyes and a sad smile. 'Could you give me some money and God bless you, ma'am?'

Niamh shook her head regretfully. 'Come in anyway!'

The old woman sat beside the fire while Niamh made her some hot tomato soup and gave her two slices of brown bread. The woman looked at the 'feast' with delight and savoured every mouthful. Then after a short chat, she left warm and contented.

Niamh thought how strange it was that she should be visited by two strangers in such a remote place. An hour and a half later, there was another knock. This time it was a beautiful, slim, pale-faced young woman. 'I'm really sorry to trouble you but would you mind if I came in and sat down for a few minutes because I think I have twisted my ankle?' she asked. Niamh bathed the ankle and bandaged it expertly to prevent any swelling. The young woman thanked her sincerely and Niamh walked her to the door and they exchanged goodbyes.

Niamh shut the door and went back inside. What an extraordinary Christmas day it had been! Suddenly she walked over to the mantelpiece and picked up an old book. It was covered in a sheet of dust. After a short search, she found the lines she was looking for:

For I was a stranger and you gave me welcome,
I was naked and you gave me clothes,
I was hungry and thirsty and you gave me food and
    drink,
I was in pain and you gave me comfort.

A sudden twinkle came back into Niamh's eyes. Dreams come true after all!

So This Is Christmas

At school we learned many favourite Christmas stories. One was the story of how Christmas brought a stop to war when the fierce and bloody First World War came to a halt on the day of Christ's birth in one corner of the Western Front. The Germans waved and called out; speaking in simple French, holding out cigars, they asked for English jam in return. 'Stille Nacht' and 'Silent Night' rang out on different sides.

Adam's Christmas Prayer

It was Christmas Eve and Adam Golden knelt down at the side of his bed to say his prayers. After he said his normal prayers, he added one of his own. 'Please God, make Christmas come for Daddy this year.'

Adam was five years old. He loved his father very much, because he was such a good man. He was also very kind and gentle. One day he brought Adam for a walk in the country. Suddenly Adam shouted, 'Daddy, Daddy, stop! stop! There's a kitten back there on the side of the road!'

Mr Golden said, 'So, there's a kitten on the side of the road. We're out for a walk.'

'But, Daddy, you must stop and pick it up.'

'I don't have to stop and pick it up.'

'But, Daddy, if you don't it will die.'

'Well, then it will have to die. We don't have room for another animal. We already have a dog at our house and a cow in our barn. No more animals.'

'But, Daddy, are you just going to let it die?'

'Be quiet, Adam. We're just going to have a nice walk.'

'I never thought my daddy would be so mean and cruel as to let a kitten die.'

At that moment his father turned around, returned to the spot at the side of the road. He bent down to pick up the kitten. The poor creature was just skin and bones, but when Adam's dad reached down to pick it up, with its last energy the kitten bared his teeth and claws. *Ssst! Sssst* went the cat. Adam's dad picked up the kitten and brought it back to the car and said to Adam, 'Don't touch, it's probably full of disease.'

When they got home, they gave the kitten several baths, about a pint of milk, and Adam begged, 'Can we let it stay in the house just tonight? Tomorrow we'll fix a place in the shed.'

His father said, 'Okay.'

Adam watched quietly in the corner as his father fixed a comfortable bed, fit for a prince.

He called their new pet Rex. He loved Rex, but his father didn't. Several weeks passed. Then one day his father walked into the house and felt something rub against his leg. He looked down and there was Rex. He reached down towards Rex, carefully checking to see that Adam wasn't watching. When Rex saw his hand, it did not bare its claws and hiss. Instead it began to lick Adam's father's fingers. From that day on, he became every bit as fond of Rex as Adam.

Every morning, Mr Golden put a grain of sugar on Adam's

tongue and another on the top of both his ears. He thought that if he did that, it would help Adam say nothing but nice, sweet words all day and hear nothing but good news and kind words all day.

At night he would put a grain of sugar on Adam's head so that he would have sweet dreams. Then he put a grain of sugar on his eyebrows so that the last thing he would see before he went to sleep and the first thing he would see when he woke up was something nice.

Adam found it very sad that his father refused to believe in Christmas. Mr Golden was a very successful businessman who treated all those who worked for him very well indeed. He was used to dealing with money and things he could buy and sell. He had no faith in all that nonsense which Christians celebrate at Christmas: the idea of God becoming human was too far-fetched to be seriously considered by any thinking person.

He kissed his wife on the cheek as she headed out to church for the midnight service. As she drove off in the car, snowflakes began to fall, timidly at first, then gathering momentum as the shyness appeared to wear off them.

At that moment, he heard a strange sound coming from the side of the house. Three little birds had been frightened by the sudden heavy snowfall and in their panic had sought to find shelter by flying through the sitting-room window. *It wouldn't be right to leave these poor little creatures out here in the freezing cold*, Mr Golden thought. He decided that he would put them into the bicycle shed at the bottom of the garden, where they would be dry and warm. He put on his coat and his big boots and marched through the deafening snow to the shed. He opened the door wide and turned on the light. But he could not persuade them to come into the shed.

Then he got a brainwave. Food will tempt them in, he thought.

He rushed back to the house, stumbling a few times on the way in the blanket of snow. In the kitchen he got a few slices of bread and chopped them up into tiny pieces, which he sprinkled on the snow to make a trail into the barn. However, the birds paid no attention to the crumbs and remained in the exact same spot. He tried to direct them into the shed by walking around and waving his arms and shouting at the top of his voice. They scattered in every direction except into the lighted shed. 'They must find me a weird and frightening creature; there is no way I can make them trust me,' he said to himself. 'If only I could become a bird myself for a few minutes, then I could lead them to safety.'

At that very moment, the church bells began ringing. He raised up his hands to heaven. 'Now I know why', he whispered. 'Now I realise why You had to do it.'

The following morning, Adam listened attentively as the preacher gave his Christmas sermon.

He said: 'The simple truth of Christmas is that God sent his only son to become human like us, so that we might be saved.'

Adam looked up at his father, who was sitting beside him. He winked back at him. Adam smiled to himself and thanked God for answering his Christmas prayer.

HOME THOUGHTS FROM ABROAD

Christmas came early for me last year. By that I don't mean when the first Christmas stores opened in July or when the advertisements for Christmas parties first started on the radio in August. Instead it came when I visited Kenya.

On a sweltering hot day, I found myself in Kibera, the second biggest slum in the world. In Kenya, rural to urban migration is responsible for the high unemployment and the increased development of informal housing on the outskirts of the city of Nairobi. The cost of education, housing and healthcare is rising. Many children have no alternative but to roam the streets, exposed to crime, violence, drugs and prostitution. Some sixty thousand children (one in six being HIV positive) live on the streets of Kenya's capital city.

In Kibera, there are over two million dwellers in the slum. There, the key words in the Christmas story 'there was no room in the inn', hit me with the force of a punch in the stomach. The hardest thing emotionally was to see the many neglected children with no hope of ever gaining a proper job. Theirs is a lost childhood and their only hope is for someone to give them the opportunity to go to school.

Yet I did not come away depressed. In his song 'Anthem' Leonard Cohen wrote about how the crack in anything is what will let the light in. In this place of abject, back-breaking, gut-wrenching neglect, the nuns I saw working there were cracks to let the light in. The code of their humanity was that not even great deprivation can shackle the human spirit.

The nuns in Kibera make it their life's mission to care for the plight of Kenya's forgotten children and to provide them with all those basic needs in life which we all take for granted; food and water, clothing, shelter, healthcare and education. My one regret is those media commentators who are so dismissive of the place of the Church in today's world did not get the opportunity to see the nuns' work at first hand.

From the outset, Jesus publicly aligned himself with the poor and the outcasts. Jesus formulated an alternative model of society. Our search for the face of Christ cannot be authentic until we honestly confront the social structures that, for example, cause parents to feel that there is no option for them but to reluctantly send their children into hostel accommodation. It is surely a damning indictment of us all that over three thousand Irish children this Christmas will be caught up in the ghastly nightmare of homelessness.

That is why the Christmas story is so important, because it takes us back to the birth in a stable of a baby for whom 'there was no room in the inn'. Rather than bemoan the two-tier society of the 'have yachts and the have nots' Christmas is a challenge to each of us to take practical action to live in solidarity with, in particular, the most vulnerable sectors of our society. St James in his letter (1:27) reminds us that 'authentic religion' is taking care of widows and orphans.

The Gospel tells us the story of the rich young man, a good young man, a young man who had kept all the commandments from his youth, whom, nevertheless, could not become a follower of Jesus, could not be admitted to the early Christian community, because his unwillingness to share what he had for the sake of those in need was a contradiction to everything that Jesus lived and preached.

The baby in the stable calls for decisive measures in word and deed. An ounce of action is worth a ton of theory. My visit to Kibera, Kenya, was a clarion call to me that the best way I can celebrate Christmas this year is by reaching out in concrete ways to those who are finding no room for them in the inn.

POETRY
FOR
CHRISTMAS

Christ's Bounty

I pray you, Christ, to change my heart
To make it whole;
Once you took on flesh like mine,
Now take my soul.

Ignominy and pain you knew,
The lash, the scourge,
You, the perfect molten metal
Of my darkened forge.

You make the bright sun bless my head,
Put ice beneath my feet.
Send salmon swarming in the tides,
Give crops of wheat.

When Eve's wild children come to you
With prayerful words,
You crowd the rivers with fine fish,
The sky with birds.

You make the small flowers thrive
In the wholesome air.
You spread sweetness through the world.
What miracle can compare?

BRENDAN KENNELLY'S TRANSLATION OF
AN EIGHTH-CENTURY POEM

A Thousand Welcomes

O Son of God, it would be sweet
a lovely journey
to cross the wave, the fount in flood
and visit Ireland:
The fields of Ireland I have loved
and that's no lie.
To stay with Comgall, to visit
Caindech
it would be sweet.

A POEM ATTRIBUTED TO COLUM CILLE, D. 597 AD

Christmas is a time for . . .

Christmas is a time for celebration,
to spread love, to offer friendship, for reconciliation.

Christmas is a time for reflection,
to illuminate hope, to alleviate suffering, for
communication.

Christmas is a time for happiness,
to wash away sorrow, to embrace a neighbour, for
tenderness.

Christmas is a time for giving,
to accept gifts, to give thanks, for living.

Christmas is a time to cast differences aside,
to pardon transgressions, to forget grievances, to abandon
foolish pride.

Christmas is a time to remember,
all the children of God who are suffering in December.

ANON

Nativity

In time it came round, the time
ripe for the birth of a boy.
Much as a bridegroom steps
fresh from the chamber of joy,

arm in arm he arrived
entwining the sweetheart he chose.
Both in a byre at hand
the pleasant mother reposed . . .

Such a dazzle of tears! – this gift
all that the bride could bring?
How the mother was struck at so
topsy-turvy a thing:

distress of the flesh, in God!
in man, the pitch of delight!
Pairs never coupled so;
different as day and night.

'OF THE NATIVITY' – ST JOHN OF THE CROSS

Silent Night

How silently, how silently,
the wondrous gift is given.

'O LITTLE TOWN OF BETHLEHEM'
— PHILLIPS BROOKS, 1835–1893

The Incarnation

Then He called
The archangel Gabriel
And sent him to
The Virgin Mary

At whose consent
The mystery was wrought
In whom the Trinity
Clothed the Word with flesh

And though three work this
It is wrought in the one;
And the Word lived incarnate
In the womb of Mary.

And He who had only a father
Now had a Mother too,
But she was not like others
Who conceive by man.

From her own flesh
He received His flesh
So he is called
Son of God and of man.

ST JOHN OF THE CROSS

No Strange Land

The angels keep their ancient places; –
Turn but a stone, and start a wing!
'Tis ye, 'tis your estrangéd faces,
That miss the many-splendoured thing.

FRANCIS THOMPSON, 1859–1907

Seek Yourself in Me

It was by love that you were made,
Lovely and beautiful to be.
So, though it's true that you have strayed,
Upon my heart you are portrayed –
Soul, seek yourself in me.

In you, dear Soul, I am confined.
You are my dwelling and my home,
And even if one day I find
Closed-fast the portals of your mind,
I'll beg for entrance when I come.

O search for me not far away
For, if you would attain to me,
You only need my name to say
And I am here without delay,
Soul, seek yourself in me.

ST TERESA OF AVILA

The Holy Bath

Blessed are those for whom grace is waiting.
When you rise up from the most holy bath
Of your new birth.

LINES WRITTEN BY TERTULLIAN BETWEEN 200 AND 206 AD

PRAYERS
FOR
CHRISTMAS

The Saviour's Day

Dúirt an t-aingeal leo 'Rugabh Slanaitheoir daoibh inniu I gcathair Dháiví, is é Críost an Tiarna é.

(The angel said: 'A saviour will be born in Bethlehem who will be Christ the Lord.')

Blessings

Beannachtaí na Nollag agus Síocháin san Athbhlian.

(Merry Christmas and a happy New Year.)

Prayer for Open Hearts

We turn to God in prayer at the start of this new day. We ask you Lord to take care of us all and of all those we love and care about.

Help us Lord to always be loving, caring people. In the scriptures we are told:

'O that today you would listen to his voice. Harden not your
    hearts.'
From a spiritual point of view, hardness of heart is one of
the worst things that can happen to anyone.
To adopt a hard-hearted attitude is to maim oneself.
A hard heart can't feel, can't respond, can't love.
A hard heart can't experience joy.
A hard heart is a closed heart.
A hard heart is a barren heart.
A soft heart, on the other hand, is a blessing.
A soft heart can receive and can respond.
It can be saddened, but it can also be deliriously happy.
Softened by the rain of God's grace,
And warmed by the sun of his love,
The human heart can be turned from a desert into a garden.

Morning Prayer

At the start of this brand-new day we pause to pray:
Before we begin our work, we turn to you, O Lord.
For it is your work that we do, the work of your gospel.
We know this but we often lose sight of it.
We begin to rely on our own efforts only.
Or we lose sight of the vision and get absorbed in the
details.
And so today, we bring to our work a lively sense that you,
    Lord,
Are the ground and the goal, the inspiration of all that we
do.
In this awareness may we do our work lovingly.
In this awareness may we do our work joyfully.
May we not be too quick with our judgements,

Our agenda, our interpretations.
May we pause patiently, to open up to your wisdom,
To see with your eyes.
And may we not be so absorbed in our tasks
That we forget our co-workers and those for whom we
struggle.
May the way in which we carry out our work
Make for healing and reassurance for all.

Prayer for New Year's Day: Let's Build a New Tomorrow

Let's build a new tomorrow
Let's forget about the past.
An end to hate and sorrow
Let's build a peace that lasts.

No more pain
No more sorrow
Let's build a new tomorrow

Let's build a world like heaven above
Let's build a world united in love.

No more children in tears
No more famine or fears.
Our world can resonate with new sounds
Instead of darkness, let love and beauty abound.

Let the force of peace
Silence the stormy seas
let love and laughter
Echo from the highest trees.

Prayer for Peace

We pray for peace . . . in our hearts, our homes, our country and our world.

We pray for each one in our community, especially those who are sick or troubled in any way.

Lord, we pray, help us throughout this day . . . to be a comfort to the sad . . . to be a friend to the lonely . . . to be an encouragement to those who are down . . . to be a help to those who are stressed.

Help us all through this day . . . to do nothing which would be a cause of temptation to someone else or which would make it easier for someone else to go wrong. Help us not to discourage anyone who is doing their best.

Help us not to dampen anyone's enthusiasm or to increase anyone's doubt.

HUMOUR
FOR
CHRISTMAS

Horse Sense

Sr. Aoife was exhausted.

Every Christmas Eve she organised a big party for the children in the local orphanage. It was always the highlight of the year for them. Every evening, since the first of December, she had been busy baking all kinds of the most delicious cakes and buns for the feast at the finish.

She also arranged for the local shops to donate toys and presents so that each child could get a special gift and then she wrapped them in her own dazzling display of Christmas decorating paper.

Every child's favourite part of the day at the party was when Sr. Aoife told a story.

After the party, Sr. Aoife was sitting by the window in the huge hall on the ground floor, with two chambers for sleeping above it, as she opened a letter from home and found a £20 note inside as her Christmas gift from her family in Kerry.

Sr. Aoife was a big believer in knowing the true meaning of Christmas. While reading the letter she noticed a poor beggar sitting in the rain outside. She jumped out of her seat and wrapped the £20 note in a piece of paper which carried a simple message: 'Have courage. Sister Aoife.' She threw it out the window and the beggar accepted it gleefully.

On St Stephen's Day, Mother Caoimhe, the cross-looking Mother Superior, approached Sr. Aoife in the study and, with a raised eyebrow and a strong sense of disapproval, told her that 'a shabby man' was at the door, who was insisting on seeing her. Her face was black with anger as she left the room, and her irate muttering remained audible even as she walked purposefully down the corridor. Dark clouds massed over the leafy darkness of the convent, promising an early dusk and rain before morning.

A puzzled Sr. Aoife found the beggar waiting. He handed her £200 without a word.

'What's this?' she asked.

'Have Courage came in at ten to one in the one-thirty at Leopardstown.'

Do You Know it's Christmas?

In the past, obedience was to the Mother Superior and her biases and prejudices ruled supreme. To take one example, after Christmas dinner in one of the convents, the Mother Superior graciously passed around a box of sweets and instructed: 'Take plenty. Take two.'

The Sound of Silence

A young idealistic man joins a monastery of a silent order.

He was allowed to speak just two words every ten years.

After the first ten years he said to the Abbot: 'Terrible cold.'

Ten years later he went to the Abbot again and said: 'Food awful.'

Ten more years passed and he went to the Abbot and said: 'I'm leaving.'

The Abbot smiled with joy: 'Thank God. You have done nothing but complain since you arrived here.'

Wisdom

The abbot's annual Christmas joke was: 'A baguette in a zoo is an example of bre(a)d in captivity.'

Nativity Story

Little Molly was disappointed because she was not cast as an angel in the nativity play in her kindergarten class. Instead she was cast as the Virgin. She turned to her friend Sandra for consolation. Sandra rose to the occasion: 'My mother told me it is much harder to be a virgin than an angel.'

A Christmas Treat

Sr. Margaret was loved by all because of her big heart and generous nature. She had a particular soft spot for her grand-nieces. Their favourite treat was Romantica ice cream. On Christmas Day they religiously came to the convent to give her a Christmas present. It was always a woollen scarf. Sr. Margaret always gave them some ice cream. On Christmas Eve, she went to the local shop to buy some ice cream. The shop was crammed with last-minute shoppers. Everyone smiled at Sr. Margaret as she made her way to the counter. Unfortunately, in the excitement, she had a temporary loss of memory and could not remember the name 'Romantica'. After a protracted pause, there was a collective intake of breath all around the shop as she said: 'Can I have a big packet of Erotica please?'

LETTERS
FOR
CHRISTMAS

Christmas is the season when we are aware of those for whom 'there is no room in the inn'. For this section I invited Ireland's best-known campaigner on Homelessness, Fr. Peter McVerry, to write a letter to his parents.

Letter to My Parents

Life is a lottery; none of chooses where we will be born. I could have been born in Syria with bombs falling all around me, wondering whether I was going to be still alive in the morning. Or in Sub-Saharan Africa, where I might be lucky to get one meal every two days. Or my parents could have had a drug or alcohol addiction, which might have sent me into a spiral of addiction, crime and jail.

But I was lucky to have you as my parents. You, my father, were a doctor in a small town. For many years you did not have a 'practice', with assistants or partners to help share the burden at nights or weekends. You were on duty twenty-four hours a day, seven days a week. Even when we went on holidays in those early years, we went to a seaside town six miles away so that you were still available for your patients. I remember the phone ringing during the night and you would get up and go out to see a patient, and I never heard you ever complain. Sometimes, that phone would ring twice in the same night and you would still get up and go out to your patients. You were always there for them. I learned a sense of service from you, that life is about helping others and making the world a happier, healthier place.

And you, my mother, you were a Welsh Protestant, who met my father while working in a hospital in England shortly after he had qualified. In those days, if my father, a Catholic, married a Protestant, the Catholic Church would condemn him to hell for all eternity! To spare my father that fate, you became a Catholic, and like many converts, you became more Catholic than the Catholics themselves. So we were brought to Mass every Sunday without fail. Attendance at the family Rosary every night was compulsory, no excuses accepted. I got a strong sense of faith from you.

I think it was a huge sacrifice for you to become a Catholic – I always suspected that you were ostracised by your own family, as I never heard you talk about them, or visit them or phone them or write to them. Your family was always a mystery to me, an unknown and unknowable part of my history. In those days, the most sinful thing you could do in that strong Welsh Protestant tradition was to become a Catholic.

You shaped my future life for me. When wondering what I would do in life, a sense of service, motivated by faith, seemed to me to be the obvious path I should take. I told you I wanted to join the Jesuits, and you questioned me to make sure that this was really what I wanted to do, and then you supported me all the way.

When I went to work with homeless people in the inner city of Dublin, I think you found that a bit confusing. When people asked you what I did, you wanted to be able to say I was a teacher, or a parish priest or something with a recognisable label. But all you could tell them was that you didn't know exactly what I did – I worked with robbers or something! I remember you, my father, coming up to my flat in the inner city one day, and there was a young lad sitting on the floor, drawing on a sheet of paper. Trying to make conversation, you asked him, 'And what does your father do, young fellow?'

'Me da was murdered,' he answered.

That was your first and last visit to the inner city! I never told you that, later, that young fellow was also murdered.

I am just so grateful to you both for the life you gave me and the learning I received from living with you.

Peter

PART SIX

SPRING AGAIN

W̲E END THIS COLLECTION OF CELTIC wisdom as we
began, with spring.

Spring is coming again.

We live in an era when everything is compartmentalised.
The Celts could not have understood that. As Celtic art strik-
ingly illustrates, they believed that everything is inextricably
intertwined: the living and the dead; past, present and future;
the beginning and the end; nature and supernature; the secular
and the sacred; old and young; darkness and light; despair and
hope. They believed in the circle of life so that the year never
really ended – it simply rolled into the next one. In that spirit we
return to spring to stress a crucial tenet of the Celtic tradition –
the central importance of interconnections.

Ar scáth a chéile a mhaireann na daoine.

This literally translates as: people live in each other's shadows.
We are shielded from the sun by each other, we rely on each
other for shelter. People need another.

This was one of the great insights of St Patrick.

THE VOICE OF THE VOICELESS

While the *Confession* is the main element of Patrick's literary
legacy, there is one other addition. In his *Letter*, which he wrote
to Coroticus, a king in southern Scotland who had taken some

of Patrick's newly confirmed Christians as captives, we see a different side to Ireland's patron saint.

Patrick was irate because Coroticus, who professed to be a Christian, treated these Christians whom he had enslaved extremely badly. Patrick knew he was obliged to speak out against the injustice. In his *Letter*, he pulls no punches in his criticism of Coroticus and quotes liberally from the scriptures to justify his position. Moreover, the *Letter* was an open one. Patrick was anxious that it would be read out in public. It was actually addressed to the soldiers, but Patrick wanted them to read in the presence of Coroticus, their commanding officer. He had to be shown that he was responsible for what had happened. Innocent people were wronged and Patrick appears to have made their pain his own.

'What am I to do, Lord? Lord, I am thoroughly despised. See, your sheep are torn to pieces around me and are carried off by the raiders, as ordered by the evil-hearted Coroticus.'

Patrick went even further. Not alone was Coroticus and his soldiers guilty, but anyone who colluded with them or supported them in any way shared in their guilt.

'You must not associate with them, or seek any favours from any of them. It is not right to eat or drink with them. No one ought to receive any gifts or alms from them. Such fraternising must not take place until they make amends to God and pay painful penalties, until they set free these servants of God and these baptised handmaids of Christ for whom he was crucified.'

Patrick was not afraid to be sharply critical of society. He had the courage of his convictions and never hesitated to speak out – secure in the knowledge that what he was doing was what his Father wanted. 'Let anyone laugh and revile me who wants to. I will not keep silence nor will I conceal the signs and wonders which have been shown me by the Lord.'

Patrick was unequivocally taking the side of the down-trodden, the oppressed and the marginalised, regardless of the personal cost or threat to his physical wellbeing. Can the same be said of his followers in Ireland today? Whose side are we on? What price are we willing to pay for championing unpopular causes or standing up for what we know to be right? While there is a remarkable generosity today towards organisations like the Peter McVerry Trust and Concern, are we, like Patrick, willing to really put our comfort on the line?

A central component of this new project would be to re-examine the place of symbols. The example of Mary Robinson as Irish president is instructive in this context. Her celebrated light in the window in Áras an Uachtaráin was an early indication of her approach. Little things really do mean a lot. A simple lighted candle encapsulated the reaching out of the president to all Irish people at home and abroad.

At her inaugural address as Irish president, Mary McAleese observed: 'We know our duty is to spread the benefits of our prosperity to those whose lives are still mired in poverty, unemployment, worry and despair. There can be no rest until the harsh gap between the comfortable and the struggling has been bridged.' One of the most positive contributions of Catholic theology in the last century has been its emphasis on social justice. This theological evolution was captured by Pope John Paul II with his emphasis on 'solidarity' and 'the indirect employer'.

Perhaps, though, the time has come to revisit this whole area. The notion of 'the option for the poor' has brought a welcome focus on the fact that the social dimension is not an optional extra, but a constituent part of the gospel in a fundamentally formative sense. However, does this phrase not suggest a form of spiritual imperialism? Are we sure the poor really want us?

Have we ever asked them? The problem with this phrase is that it suggests we should be the voice of the voiceless rather than helping the voiceless to find their own voice. Is it now time for us to take the option with the poor? Or, in the words of Peter McVerry, do we need a 'radical imperative for the poor'?

Patrick challenges us to rediscover our prophetic role as Christians, a quality of life which attempts to give renewed heart to the Christian life by a radical commitment to simplicity, sharing and intimacy. He dares us to be double agents – people who observe the world as it is while in tandem imagining other worlds which might yet be. With his sense of symbol, his rich spirituality, his humility and his bold moral courage, Patrick has many important messages for us today.

Please come back, St Patrick.

Spring in the Celtic year is a time of thresholds, doorways in our lives that offer the possibility of beginning anew.

WISDOM
FOR
SPRING

Outer and Inner

The outer man is the swinging door
The inner man is the still hinge.

MEISTER ECKHART

The Still Point

Nothing in all creation is so like God as stillness.

MEISTER ECKHART

Seekers

Search your heart and see the way to do is to be.

LAO TZU

The Big Five

Five enemies of peace inhabit with us – avarice, ambition, envy,
anger, and pride; if these were to be banished, we should infal-
libly enjoy perpetual peace.

PETRARCH, 1304–1374

Honours

It is better to deserve honours and not have them, than to have them and not deserve them.

MARK TWAIN

Falling Slowly

If you don't stand for something, you'll fall for anything.

GUSTAVE FLAUBERT, 1821–1880

Pause for Thought

The right word may be effective, but no word was ever as effective as a rightly timed pause.

MARK TWAIN

At Peace

There is one thing that stands the brunt of life throughout its course: a quiet conscience.

EURIPIDES, 480–406 BC

Pride

Generosity is giving more than you can, and pride is taking less than you need.

KAHLIL GIBRAN

Giant Haystack

Do not overlook negative actions merely because they are small; however small a spark may be, it can burn down a haystack as big as a mountain.

BUDDHA

Strength in Weakness

The weak can never forgive.
   Forgiveness is the attribute of the strong.

MAHATMA GANDHI

Be the Best

No longer forward nor behind
I look in hope or fear;
But, grateful, take the good I find,
The best of now and here.

JOHN GREENLEAF WHITTIER, 1807–1892

What Lies Beneath

What lies behind us and what lies before us are tiny matters
compared to what lies within us.

RALPH WALDO EMERSON, 1803–1882

Success

To leave the world a bit better,
Whether by a healthy child, a garden
Patch or a redeemed social condition;
To even know one life has breathed
Easier because you have lived:
This is to have succeeded.

RALPH WALDO EMERSON

Give Thanks

Be grateful for whatever comes
Because each has been sent
As a guide from beyond.

RUMI

In Between

Between God and soul there
Is no between.

JULIAN OF NORWICH, 1342–1416

The Music of the Soul

A man should hear a little music, read a little poetry, and see a fine picture every day of his life, in order that worldly cares may not obliterate the sense of the beautiful which God has implanted in the human soul.

JOHANN WOLFGANG VON GOETHE, 1749–1832

Have a Little Faith

The way you see people
Is the way you treat them
And the way you treat them
Is what they become.

JOHANN WOLFGANG VON GOETHE

Practice Makes Perfect

An ounce of practice is worth more than two tons of preaching.

MAHATMA GANDHI

The Truth Shall Set You Free

Truth never damages a cause that is just.

MAHATMA GANDHI

When Silence is Not Golden

The cruellest lies are told in silence.

ROBERT LOUIS STEVENSON

What is the Name of the Game?

Truth is the cry of all, but the game of few.

GEORGE BERKELEY, 1685–1753

A Different Perspective

We make a living by what we get, but we make a life by what we give.

WINSTON CHURCHILL, 1874–1965

Restraint

Virtue debases itself in justifying itself.

VOLTAIRE, 1694–1778

The Real Deal

True happiness comes from the joy of deeds well done, the zest of creating things new.

ANTOINE DE SAINT-EXUPÉRY

Radiate

Those who bring sunshine to the lives of others, cannot keep it from themselves.

J.M. BARRIE, 1860–1937

Acceptance

Let us act on what we have, since we have not what we wish for.

ST JOHN HENRY NEWMAN

Don't Look Back in Anger

Finish each day and be done with it. Tomorrow is a new day. You shall begin it serenely and with too high a spirit to be encumbered with your old nonsense.

RALPH WALDO EMERSON

The Last Words

Be good to yourself.

TALES
FOR
SPRING

SOLITAIRE

He was born in an obscure village, the child of a peasant. He grew up in another village, where he worked in a carpenter shop until he was thirty. Then, for three years, he was an itinerant preacher.

He never wrote a book. He never held an office. He never had a family or owned a home. He didn't go to college. He never lived in a big city. He never travelled two hundred miles from the place where he was born. He did none of the things that usually accompany greatness. He had no credentials but himself.

He was only thirty-three when the tide of public opinion turned against him. His friends ran away. One of them denied him. He was turned over to his enemies and went through the mockery of a trial. He was nailed to a cross between two thieves. While he was dying, his executioners gambled for his garments, the only property he had on earth. When he was dead, he was laid in a borrowed grave, through the pity of a friend.

Twenty centuries have come and gone, and today he is the central figure of the human race. I am well within the mark when I say that all the armies that ever marched, all the navies that ever sailed, all the parliaments that ever sat, all the kings

that ever reigned – put together – have not affected the life of
man on this earth as much as that one, solitary life.

ATTRIBUTED TO JAMES ALLEN FRANCIS

MERCY STREET

Carraig Rua was a great Celtic hero and warrior. There was
never a braver man in all the world.

One day, to relax after all his battles, he went walking in the
country. On his wrist sat his favourite hawk. As he turned for
home he felt very thirsty because it was a hot day. His pet hawk
had flown away, but his master wasn't worried because he knew
it could make its own way home.

He knew there was a spring somewhere nearby. He went in
search of it. At last he saw some water trickling down over the
edge of the rock. He knew there was a spring farther up. Carraig
Rua took a little silver cup from his pocket. He held it so as to
catch the slowly falling drops.

It took a long time to fill the cup; and the king was so thirsty
that he could hardly wait. At last it was nearly full. He put the
cup to his lips, and was about to drink.

Suddenly there was a whirring sound in the air, and the cup
was knocked from his hands. The water was all spilled upon the
ground.

The great hero looked up to see who had done this thing. It
was his pet hawk.

Carraig Rua picked up the cup, and again held it to catch the
trickling drops. When the cup was half full, he lifted it towards
his mouth. But before it had touched his lips, the hawk swooped
down again, and knocked it from his hands.

By now Carraig Rua was very, very angry. He filled his cup a
third time, but before he tried to drink, he drew his sword.

'Now, my former friend, beware. You wouldn't do this to me again and live.'

He had barely finished speaking before the hawk swooped down and knocked the cup from his hand. But Carraig Rua was ready and struck the bird as it passed. The hawk fell and lay dying on the ground.

The great hero went looking for his cup only to discover that it had fallen down behind the rocks where he couldn't reach it. He had no choice but to climb up to the spring. It was a tough climb, but at last he reached his destination. There indeed was a pool of water; but what was there in the pool, and almost filling it? It was a huge, dead snake full of poison.

Carraig Rua let out a great scream. 'That poor hawk saved my life. But how did I repay him? He was my best friend, and I have killed him.'

He climbed back down and took up the dying bird in his arms and whispered softly to him until the hawk was dead. Tears fell from the great hero's eyes like a great river.

He was still sobbing softly when he got home late that night. His wife asked, 'What's wrong?'

In a sad voice Carraig Rua replied, 'I have learned a great lesson today. Never, ever do anything in anger.'

WHAT IS LOVE?

February is a great month for those who sell chocolates and flowers because of the feast of St Valentine's day. It is indeed right and fitting that we have a special day to celebrate its importance in the Christian calendar, because love is at the very heart of our faith. Why? Love is God's definition. While St Valentine is the saint most associated with love there is one other, often-forgotten great champion of love.

Sometimes St Valentine's day falls in Lent. Flowers, chocolate, red hearts and romance. That's what Valentine's day is all about, right? Well, maybe not. The origin of this holiday for the expression of love really is not romantic at all. Valentine was a Roman priest at a time when there was an emperor called Claudius who persecuted the Church. He also had an edict that prohibited the marriage of young people. This was based on the theory that unmarried soldiers fought better than married soldiers, because married soldiers might be afraid of what might happen to them or their wives or families if they died. The idea of encouraging them to marry within the Christian Church was what Valentine was about. And, because of the edict, he secretly married them. Valentine was eventually caught, imprisoned, tortured and martyred for performing marriage ceremonies against the command of the emperor.

As countless pop songs have illustrated, contemporary society uses the word 'love' very easily. But what is love? One of the most significant writers about love was the thirteenth-century mystic, Mechthild of Magdeburg (ca. 1207–1282). She was born to an aristocratic family in Saxony. Apart from the paltry biographical information that she provides, we know very little about the details of her life, but her masterpiece, *The Flowing Light of the Godhead*, offers many penetrating insights into the spiritual life, which continue to merit our attention today. It comprises seven books in total and she began writing in 1250 and finished it in the prestigious convent of Helfta only a few years before her death.

Mechthild received her first vision when she was twelve years of age, and for the next thirty-one years this event occurred on a daily basis. This experience left her with powerful feelings of sorrow, love, and even the desire to be treated with contempt. At the age of twenty-three, she said goodbye to her family in order to serve God without distraction. For forty years she lived as a Beguine in the city of Magdeburg. The Beguines were reputedly founded by Lambert le Begue, a priest of Liege (although there is a school of thought which said they had no founder), who exhorted women to live together in a community and minister to the sick and poor. They were not cloistered and it was not necessary for them to bring a dowry. At that time there were thousands in Germany alone. In the light of their mendicant lifestyle, they were of special interest to the Dominicans, who lived similarly. One Dominican, Meister Eckhart, preached to the Beguines on a regular basis. Unlike many of his male contemporaries, Eckhart was happy to recognise the spiritual and intellectual capabilities of women.

Although the Beguines lived the lifestyle of nuns, they were not actually nuns. They were viewed as outsiders and did not take irreversible vows. They lived simply by the work of their hands, embracing poverty and chastity, and served the sick and destitute in their community. They did not come under the any jurisdiction from male religious establishments. However, this created suspicion from the secular clergy and religious orders and on the most flimsy of evidence they were accused of hypo-critical virtue and sexual immortality.

After her death, in around 1282, Mechthild's work was largely forgotten by the fifteenth century. That is, until the nineteenth century when Gall Morel, a Benedictine librarian at Einsiedeln, worked on a translation and produced the first edition. Her work has been increasingly studied, both for its academic interest and as a work of devotional literature.

God compelled her to write down what she saw. Her percep-tion of God, the object of her love, was manifold. God was the emperor of the universe and is vitally present in creation, being all things to all people. God is three persons in one nature, with

a rich interior life whose intimate conversations she was allowed
to overhear. Most frequently, though, God appears in her writings as the human lover and divine bridegroom, passionately
seeking spiritual union with the soul. Mechthild wrote:

> And he speaks:
> Dearest love, think of the hour
> When you may grasp the full treasure.
> Do not let the time seem too long.
> After all, I hold you constantly
> Embraced in my arms.'
> Then our Lord says to his chosen bride:
> 'Come, my beloved, come. You shall be crowned'.

She was always keen to show that longing is not just on one
side of the relationship, but an equal reciprocation of feelings
and desires on the other. There is a palpable longing between
the person and the God and the hope that they will be granted
what each of them is yearning for. Again she wrote:

> Lord, now I am a naked soul
> And you in yourself are a well-adorned God.
> Our shared lot is eternal life without death.
> Then a blessed stillness
> That both desire comes over them.
> He surrenders himself to her,
> And she surrenders herself to him.
> And that is fine with me.
> But this cannot last long.
> When two lovers meet secretly,
> They must often part from one another inseparably.

There were many times when she felt cast down into the deepest gulf, until she was lower even than the souls in purgatory, the damned and Satan himself. Yet in her accounts of her visions, she tried to describe, in what is said to be 'unusually original and wide-ranging imagery that shows her common sense', and far from abstracted knowledge of human behaviour, how this God with burning desire attracts a soul that is so very sick with love, until we are joined in a union that takes the soul through human history and lifts us above everything ever known.

Mechthild would have agreed with the late Michael Paul Gallagher SJ, who likens Christian faith to the first smile of an infant:

'For weeks you smile and express your love . . . then one day your baby smiles back. He or she has entered into a different relationship, has responded to all you have given. It is a moment of recognition, of love. Our life of faith is exactly like that in its core simplicity. God loves us in Christ and one day we must realise it . . . there is a danger of reducing faith to morality or to the externals of religious belonging. If that happens religion becomes a matter of "I thought" or "I ought not". Needless to say, the commandments come alive and make best sense if God's love is received and recognised – like that first smile.'

Mechthild believed that loving Christ means loving Him in His living Church in the here and now. It is in the face of this reality that we collectively formulate our response as Christians and as members of a religious community who share in the mission of Christ – to serve and to save. They are close to people, healing and nurturing, challenging oppressive systems and structures, reaching out to those who need help and hope, praying with people rather than for them.

She seemed to share the view of St Francis of Assisi: it is

in giving that we receive. She would have approved that, in February, we especially recall St Brigid. She would have thought it was a beautiful thing that her monastery in Kildare was known as the City of the Poor, because of its reputation for hospitality, compassion and generosity. God loves a true faith in those with a pure heart.

Christian love means that in the intermingling of faith and life we want to be attentive to where God is today. We are searching for a way to live that is authentic and which offers an alternative to an individualistic way of life, which is increasingly prevalent in the modern world. In responding to the needs of society we are striving to witness to Christ and to reveal His love to struggling people.

The force of love, of unexpected and invigorating vitality rather than some judgemental doctrine, is what ought to animate Christians and all good people. Only true love carries memorial weight, regenerates moments of tenderness, of unions of spirit. Such a love is never encountered in stony walls or architectural masterpieces rising to an impassive sky. Mechthild showed us that the primary obligation is not to build memorials to the dead, but to give food to the living. She will always be a reminder that the secret of life is that only in love for the living is the spirit praised forever.

DUTY OF CARE

Gandhi said: 'I like your Christ. I do not like your Christians. Your Christians are not like your Christ.'

I suppose for me, listening to and observing people, it seems we are great at talking it but not great at living it. I remain a great believer in the philosophy of Christianity. What we need are people to live it.

When Pope John XXIII was a cardinal, one night he was sitting down for his supper in Venice and his secretary came in with the file of a priest who was in trouble for a minor disciplinary issue. The assistant was very disdainful as he spoke about the priest, who was having a bad time. John pointed at his glass on the table and asked his secretary who it belonged to. 'You own it, your Eminence,' replied the puzzled secretary.

Then John picked up the glass and threw it on the ground where it smashed into smithereens. 'Who owns it now?'

'You still own it, your Eminence.'

'And I still own that priest too,' said John.

ALL IN THE GAME

Some years ago, at the Seattle Special Olympics, nine disabled contestants assembled at the starting line for the hundred-yard dash. At the gun, they all took off in haste. Things were going according to plan until one little boy stumbled on the asphalt, fell, and started to cry. The other eight heard the boy cry. They slowed down and looked back. They all turned around and went back, every one of them. One girl with Down Syndrome bent down and kissed him and said, 'This will make it better.'

Then all nine linked arms and walked together to the finish line. Everyone in the stadium stood and cheered.

IF IT BE YOUR WILL

O Lord, remember not only the men and women of good will, but also those of ill will. But do not remember all of the suffering they have inflicted upon us.

Instead remember the fruits we have borne because of this suffering – our fellowship, our loyalty to one another, our humility, our courage, our generosity, the greatness of heart that has grown from this trouble.

When our persecutors come to be judged by you, let all of these fruits that we have borne be their forgiveness.

FOUND IN THE CLOTHING OF A DEAD CHILD

AT RAVENSBRUCK CONCENTRATION CAMP.

THE CREATIVE ONE

It was the biggest news ever in our parish. We were not just to get a mere parish priest – we were to get – a canon. A priest, even a parish priest, was one thing, but a canon was the ultimate in ecclesiastical and social grandeur. People spoke about the canon's soutane, with the red buttons down the front and silky red satin peering demurely from under the flaps. Others remarked about the delightful swish of a resplendent red monsignorial cassock. The cynics said it was the ultimate clerical status symbol for those who knew deep down that they would never rise to the elevated status of a bishop.

Everyone seemed to be talking about the great honour for the parish to have a canon. In truth, no one knew exactly what the difference was between a canon and a parish priest. There were some more sceptical voices that read all kinds of Machiavellian schemes behind this honour. These plots ranged from a shrewd ploy on the part of the bishop to raise more money from the Sunday collection to a plot to bring back the Church to its former glories before the aberrations of the Second Vatican Council.

The canon was an enigma, a fascinating mixture of conservative and liberal, sinner and saint, intellectual and eccentric. With his grey hair, weather-beaten face, commanding presence, he was not a man to take lightly. He ruled the parish with a fist of iron though underneath he had a heart of gold.

The first time the canon spoke in public at our Mass the atmosphere was electric, like a revivalist meeting with a touch of fanaticism.

One of the people who was to benefit most from the canon's kindness was the late Muireann Moody. She was a music teacher in the convent school and the president of the local branch of the Irish Countrywomen's Association. She sat on the front seat at first Mass every Sunday. She was a small, ascetic woman with grey hair and a very big, booming voice.

A proud woman, the highlight of her life was when her son Conor entered the seminary in Maynooth. When he was ordained a priest seven years later, she was walking on air. From that day on, when she was talking to any of the neighbours, she always prefaced her important comments with: 'As my son the priest says . . .'

But then came disaster. Conor left the priesthood. Muireann was distraught. Her world had collapsed overnight. She stopped going out. Although she went to Mass every Sunday, she sneaked in late and sat on the back seat and she was too embarrassed to go up and receive Holy Communion. She thought everyone in the parish was laughing at her. Her grief went on unabated for weeks. At that point the canon decided it was time to take decisive action to restore Muireann's pride and morale. It would have to be handled very subtly as Muireann would spurn anything which smacked of charity.

Eventually he came up with a masterplan, even though it required him to tell a lie, or at the very least bend the truth substantially. He went to Muireann's house and confided in her that his lifelong ambition had been to learn to play the piano. This year instead of 'giving up something for Lent' he was going to 'take on something for Lent'. He asked her would she be willing to teach him. Every morning of Lent, he went up to her house for an hour lesson. On Holy Saturday, he declared that he had achieved his life's ambition and that he could now play the piano with ease. He bowed humbly before his host and then blessed her formally as he told her that she was the best teacher ever. Muireann felt twenty feet tall.

On Easter Sunday, she took her old place at the front of the church with her old gusto and the whole parish could see that her rehabilitation was complete when she received Holy Communion at Mass again. For the first time in almost a year she talked to her neighbours effusively. She began every second sentence with the words: 'As my best pupil the Canon says . . .'

SILENCE IS GOLDEN

Once a great preacher was coming to visit a remote village in the mountains for the Easter celebrations, bringing a sudden end to the fascinating spectacle of people hurling insults at each other in the street. So excited were the local villagers that they spent days preparing the questions they were going to put to the holy man. His calm, sober manner and his reluctance to become embroiled in a public squabble with the most trying people, had won the admiration of many. It was said that he had more goodness in his little finger than was to be found in the souls of a hundred monks.

He had qualities that were hard to define, but easy to recognise. A man of self-reliance, of candour, he was not a prisoner of the uncertainties, nor the enforced servility, of the previous decades.

His strong accent gave him an exotic quality. Despite the best efforts of Father Time, his 63-year-old face was still exquisitely handsome. His features were flawlessly chiselled; his grey hair was tinged with flecks of ginger, his skin was smooth and hinting of a tan.

He was tall, with long, bony extremities and a strangely disproportionate round belly. His dark green eyes were unreadable or shyly sensitive, depending on whether you took the trouble to get to know him or not.

His house was spartan-like in its frugality. The only exception was the parlour, a honeycomb of boxes filled with great books. Pride of place was reserved for the Bible.

When dawn came before he set off on his journey, it was with a blaze of colour. The sky lightened gradually, then distant clouds were painted grey, orange and pink, and finally gold. The preacher awoke early, although there were lines under his eyes that suggested he had slept badly, but he was still cheerful and patient with everyone. He was never sharp-tongued. Indeed, he had the patience of a saint when dealing with people many would have regarded as unworthy of such courtesy, even when they were remarkable only for their arrogance, self-interest and ambition, although in exceptional circumstances his eyes could turn dangerously cold.

The preacher walked to his destination with a heavy heart, barely acknowledging the greetings of people he knew. He met an old friend mostly recovered from his drunken revelry, but did not feel like lingering to chat.

It was a pretty day, with a crisp scent of late spring in the air. The trees were red and gold, and showers of leaves drifted across the road each time the wind blew. A pheasant croaked crossly from deep in the woods, and a cow lowed in a nearby meadow. A woman smiled thinly as she demanded the latest gossip. There was ice in her voice. A neighbour gave her a look of such disdain that she felt herself bristle. Her husband suspected that his hostility was fuelled by her animosity to her next-door neighbour, twice removed, Mary. If gossip had been electricity, she would have been a power station. Given the poison that emanated from her tongue, her husband referred to her in private as Attila the Hen.

The preacher tipped his head back and took a deep breath, savouring the smell of damp leaves and sweet soil. Instead of speaking he looked into the eyes of everybody in the group. He gave an empty grin, full of misshapen teeth, and waved. Then he began to softly hum a strange melody. Soon everyone began to hum with him.

After some time the preacher started to sway and dance in solemn, measured steps. His audience did likewise. Gradually the crowd became so immersed in the dance that they forgot all their problems and anxieties. Nobody dared to blurt an interruption and people's faces visibly softened towards their enemies, and they laid apologetic arms across each other's shoulders.

An hour later, the dance slowed to a dead halt. By that time the crowd were totally relaxed and at peace with themselves. They savoured together the sense of peace and community that the preacher had created. Then, with a careless shrug, the preacher spoke the only words that passed his lips all evening: 'I come to you this Easter because I had been asked to voice concern for you, my brethren. I hope that I have answered all your questions.'

SUSPICIOUS MINDS

A farmer lost his cow. He immediately thought the neighbouring farmer down the road had stolen it. When he saw the neighbour walking by, the farmer looked like a fellow who had stolen a cow; while he listened to the neighbour's words, they sounded like those of a man who had stolen a cow. All his actions and manners were those of a man who had stolen a cow. Later, when walking deep in the forest, the man found the lost cow.

The next day he again saw his neighbour's son, but in all the man's manners and actions, there was nothing like a man who had stolen a cow. The man had not changed, but the farmer himself had changed. And the only reason for his change lay in his suspicion.

PLEASE, PLEASE ME

There was once a little word named 'Please'. Pleases live in everybody's mouth, though a lot of people forget they are there. All Pleases like to be taken out of people's mouths from time to time, just to feel that they are alive.

One Please lived in the mouth of a girl called Saoirse; but seldom did it get the chance to get out because Saoirse was a very bold and rude girl. She almost never said 'Please'.

Whenever she needed something she just said: 'Give me sweets. Give me chocolate.'

Her parents didn't like this because they were very polite. Saoirse's poor Please was in awful state because it was sitting up in the roof of Saoirse's mouth without ever getting any use. It was growing weaker day by day.

Saoirse had a sister called Maebh. Maebh was a very nice, polite girl. Her Please was very happy because Maebh used her all the time.

One day at breakfast, Saoirse's Please felt that she must have some fresh air, and decided to run away. So she ran out of Saoirse's mouth and right into Maebh's.

At first Maebh's please was annoyed because it didn't think there was enough room for two Pleases in the one mouth. Saoirse's Please begged to be allowed to say and when Maebh's Please heard what it had to say it took pity and allowed it to stay for the day. Maebh's Please said: 'When Maebh uses me, will both go out together. She is kind, and I'm certain she would not mind saying "Please" twice.'

At lunchtime, Maebh wanted some water and she asked, 'Dad, will you pass me the water, please – please.'

Everyone, including Maebh herself, were puzzled by the second Please. Shortly afterwards Maebh wanted some more potatoes, so she said, 'Mum, pass the potatoes please – please.'

Her mother laughed and as she passed the potatoes she asked, 'Why do you say "please" twice?'

'I don't know,' answered Maebh. 'The words just seem to jump out for no reason. Saoirse, please – please, some more water.'

Her father said, 'Don't worry, pet. You can never be too polite.'

Saoirse was jealous that Maebh was getting all her parents' attention, so she decided she would see what happened if she said please – please. She asked, 'Mum, can I have more potatoes, p-p-p?'

She was trying very hard to say Please even once, but how could she when her own Please was in Maebh's mouth. So she tried again, and asked for some peas, 'Dad, will you give me more peas, p-p-p?'

That was all she could say. This went on all day with Maebh saying, 'Please. Please' all the time and Saoirse trying and failing to say Please. By night-time everyone in the house was getting tired of the whole thing.

As agreed, Saoirse's Please left Maebh's mouth at midnight. Saoirse's Please never felt so well because it was used so much during the day.

The next morning at breakfast it got a huge surprise when Saoirse said, 'Dad, will you get me some orange juice, please.' Saoirse was thrilled. The word had come out as easily as could be. It sounded every bit as good as when Maebh said it and Maebh was only saying one 'please' that morning. And from that day on, Saoirse was every bit as polite as her sister.

YOU CAN COUNT ON ME

Once a monk decided to test the honesty of his friends, so he called them together and asked a question.

'What would you do if you were walking along and found a purse full of money lying in the road?' he asked.

'I'd return it to its owner,' said one friend.

His answer comes so quickly, I must wonder if he really means it, the monk thought.

'I'd keep the money if nobody saw me find it,' said another.

He has a frank tongue, but a wicked heart, the monk told himself.

'Well, monk,' said a third friend, 'to be honest, I believe I'd be tempted to keep it. So I would pray to God that He give me the strength to resist such temptation and do the right thing.'

Aha, thought the monk. Here is the man I would trust.

A RELIGIOUS OCCASION

The announcement of the parish mission was greeted with some excitement. It became a distant second to the weather as the most important topic of conversation in our parish.

'We'll never feel it till the mission,' was the standard comment. Fr. Mick tried to drum up some enthusiasm and spiritual fervour by describing it as 'an occasion of grace'. Not that grace was ever much in evidence on those days. Public enemy number one was sin. The preparation beforehand was a fastidious enterprise.

The trappings and ceremonial elements of services were

more elaborate and formal than normal and all the component parts were done with enormous care for detail. Even the choir's attention to musical offerings of praise were better than usual, rising from the truly awful to the simply bad.

Nevertheless, for most people, my grandfather included, the mission was one of the parish's great social occasions, serving as a fashion show, a community centre, a place of entertainment and two opportunities per day to meet with the locals. Some of the women even wore shiny new hats.

The sermons went on and on. Now and again a crying or crawling child gave a bit of diversion to the rustling and waiting congregation. For all his piety, my grandfather was sceptical about the real value of the priests who specialised in giving parish missions.

'They only make the pious a bit more insufferable and the sinner more despairing. Those priests are only strolling players. There's nobody so right as the righteous. Trying to get people to change their life by ranting and raving is about as sensible as trying to cut turf with a razor blade. But sure they are the only entertainment we get in the chapel all year.'

I could not understand why my grandfather could be so blasé about the whole thing. I found all the haranguing of sin and vice by the hell-fire merchants very disconcerting. The talk was a blend of threat and fear. Those terrifying sermons lingered maddeningly with me. I found it all very confusing and very different from the pieces of the Gospel we read at school. The Jesus of the scriptures was a loving and merciful man, the milk of human kindness, especially to those on the margins, a saviour who came to call upon not the just but the sinners. Accusation and reprisal were the twin characteristics of the God of the preachers, not a compassionate healer but a grim reaper. Their God purified through terror. The locals had a competition about the quality of the preaching. Somebody who really excelled earned the distinction:

'He'd make the hair stand on your head.'

A truly remarkable sermon merited the ultimate accolade:

'He'd make the hair stand on your head even if you were bald.'

By contrast, someone who was more intellectual and spoke in abstractions was dismissed in savage terms: 'He was so wishy-washy he was worse than watery tea.'

My fondest memories are those when I was engaged on a sensual level. There always seemed to be a chorus of shrouded coughing coming from the pews from nervous parishioners, answering awkwardly to the priest's promptings. In silence and solemnity the priest climbed towards the tabernacle.

My abiding memory of the mission was when I accompanied my grandfather to the Stations of the Cross, at six o'clock on a Friday evening. Three altar boys journeyed with the priest as he walked solemnly to each of the stations, two carried candles, and one a big wooden cross. Then the priest forcefully boomed out the chant at each station:

'O Jesus, for love of me didst bear thy cross to Calvary

In thy sweet mercy grant me to suffer and to die with thee.'

It endures with me today, because it reminds me that the heart of my faith is that a man came who loved us so much that he was prepared to give up his life for us.

AN EASTER PEOPLE

When I was a young boy, my grandfather told me the story of a man who had lived in our village. During the Great Famine, he was one of seven local men who were hung for stealing on Good Friday. Six bags of potatoes were stolen from the pit of the local landlord. Six local men with large families and no food had crept into Lord MacNicholas's farmyard and stolen a bag each, but the other man did nothing. This poignant story of an innocent man unjustly hung for the failures of others enabled me to think of Good Friday in an emotionally significant and humanising way.

On Good Friday we are asked, 'Were you there when they crucified my Lord?' It is an uncomfortable question and one most of us would rather avoid. Jesus died and is buried and all is apparently over. We recall the Lord going forth to sacrifice so that we too may win the laughter of Easter Day. On Easter Sunday, we marvel at the miraculous. The crucified Jesus has unexpectedly become the risen Christ. The eternal has invaded the transient. The Jesus of Good Friday has shown once and for all that God's relationship with each of us transcends the limitations of this life.

Easter is the time we are given the breathing space to prepare for the real presence. It is a gentle call to slow down and reflect on the bigger picture. Who is the God of the Paschal Mystery for us today?

This is a time when, more than any other, we are aware of the life that makes us live, the expectation of a new beginning, new birth and hope, and the inexhaustible, now accessible divine potential that is all around us. It is a welcome opportunity to savour the energy, joy, and trust of the unique Easter laughter.

HANGING ON THE TELEPHONE

When I was quite young, my father had one of the first telephones in our neighbourhood. I remember well the polished old case fastened to the wall. The shiny receiver hung on the side of the box. I was too little to reach the telephone, but would listen with fascination when my mother used to talk to it.

Then I discovered that somewhere inside the wonderful device lived an amazing person – her name was 'Information Please' and there was nothing she did not know. 'Information Please' could supply anybody's number and the correct time. My first personal experience with this genie-in-a-bottle came one day while my mother was visiting a neighbour. Amusing myself at the tool bench in the basement, I whacked my finger with a hammer. The pain was terrible, but there didn't seem to be any reason in crying because there was no one home to give sympathy. I walked around the house sucking my throbbing finger, finally arriving at the stairway.

The telephone!

Quickly, I ran for the footstool in the parlour and dragged it to the landing. Climbing up, I unhooked the receiver and held it to my ear. 'Information Please,' I said into the mouthpiece just above my head.

A click or two and a small clear voice spoke into my ear. 'Information.'

'I hurt my finger. . .' I wailed into the phone. The tears came readily enough now that I had an audience.

'Isn't your mother home?' came the question.

'Nobody's home but me,' I blubbered.

'Are you bleeding?'

'No,' I replied. 'I hit my finger with the hammer and it hurts.'

'Can you open your icebox?' she asked. I said I could. 'Then chip off a little piece of ice and hold it to your finger,' said the voice.

After that, I called 'Information Please' for everything. I asked her for help with my geography and she told me where Philadelphia was. She helped me with my math. She told me my pet chipmunk that I had caught in the park just the day before would eat fruits and nuts. Then, there was the time Petey, our pet canary died. I called 'Information Please' and told her the sad story. She listened, then said the usual things grown-ups say to soothe a child. But I was unconsoled. I asked her:

'Why is it that birds should sing so beautifully and bring joy to all families, only to end up as a heap of feathers?'

She must have sensed my deep concern, for she said quietly, 'Paul, always remember that there are other worlds to sing in.' Somehow I felt better.

Another day I was on the telephone. 'Information Please.'

'Information,' said the now-familiar voice.

'How do you spell fix?' I asked.

All this took place in a small town in the Pacific Northwest. When I was nine years old, we moved across the country to Boston. I missed my friend very much. 'Information Please' belonged in that old wooden box back home, and I somehow never thought of trying the tall, shiny new phone that sat on the table in the hall. As I grew into my teens, the memories of those childhood conversations never really left me. Often, in moments of doubt and perplexity, I would recall the serene sense of security I had then. I appreciated now how patient, understanding and kind she was to have spent her time on a little boy.

A few years later, on my way west to college, my plane put down in Seattle. I had about half an hour or so between planes. I spent fifteen minutes or so on the phone with my sister, who lived there now. Then without thinking what I was doing, I dialled my hometown operator and said, 'Information, Please.' Miraculously, I heard the small, clear voice I knew so well, 'Information.'

I hadn't planned this but I heard myself saying, 'Could you please tell me how to spell fix?' There was a long pause.

Then came the soft-spoken answer, 'I guess your finger must have healed by now.'

I laughed. 'So it's really still you,' I said. 'I wonder if you have any idea how much you meant to me during that time.'

'I wonder,' she said, 'if you know how much your calls meant to me. I never had any children, and I used to look forward to your calls.'

I told her how often I had thought of her over the years and I asked if I could call her again when I came back to visit my sister. 'Please do,' she said. 'Just ask for Sally.'

Three months later, I was back in Seattle. A different voice answered, 'Information.' I asked for Sally. 'Are you a friend?' she said.

'Yes, a very old friend,' I answered.

'I'm sorry to have to tell you this,' she said. 'Sally had been working part-time the last few years because she was sick. She died five weeks ago.' Before I could hang up she said, 'Wait a minute. Did you say your name was Paul?'

'Yes.'

'Well, Sally left a message for you. She wrote it down in case you called. Let me read it to you. The note said, "Tell him I still say there are other worlds to sing in. He'll know what I mean."'

I thanked her and hung up. I knew what Sally meant.

Never underestimate the impression you may make on others.

AUTHOR UNKNOWN

LEST WE FORGET

This year, 2020, marks the seventy-fifth anniversary of the death of Anne Frank. In 1999, *Time* magazine named Anne Frank among the heroes and icons of the twentieth century on their list *The Most Important People of the Century*, stating: 'With a diary kept in a secret attic, she braved the Nazis and lent a searing voice to the fight for human dignity.'

Anne lost her life in the concentration camp of Bergen-Belsen when she was just fifteen. However, her diary gave her immortality. The writer, Roger Rosenblatt, described her legacy with the comment:

'The passions the book ignites suggest that everyone owns Anne Frank, that she has risen above the Holocaust, Judaism, girlhood and even goodness and become a totemic figure of the modern world – the moral individual mind beset by the machinery of destruction, insisting on the right to live and question and hope for the future of human beings.'

He notes that while her courage and pragmatism are admired, her ability to write was exceptional. He claims:

'The reason for her immortality was basically literary. She was an extraordinarily good writer, for any age, and the quality of her work seemed a direct result of a ruthlessly honest disposition.'

In her introduction to the diary's first American edition, Eleanor Roosevelt described it as, 'One of the wisest and most moving commentaries on war and its impact on human beings that I have ever read.' John F. Kennedy discussed Anne Frank in a 1961 speech, and said, 'Of all the multitudes who throughout history have spoken for human dignity in times of great suffering and loss, no voice is more compelling than that of Anne Frank.'

As Anne Frank's stature as both a writer and humanist has grown, she has been discussed specifically as a symbol of the Holocaust and more broadly as a representative of persecution. Hillary Clinton, in her acceptance speech for an Elie Wiesel Humanitarian Award in 1994, read from Anne Frank's diary and spoke of her 'awakening us to the folly of indifference and the terrible toll it takes on our young,' which Mrs Clinton related to contemporary events in Sarajevo, Somalia and Rwanda.

After receiving a humanitarian award from the Anne Frank Foundation in 1994, Nelson Mandela addressed a crowd in Johannesburg, saying he had read Anne Frank's diary while in prison and 'derived much encouragement from it'. He likened her struggle against Nazism to his struggle against Apartheid, drawing a parallel between the two philosophies: 'Because these beliefs are patently false, and because they were, and will always be, challenged by the likes of Anne Frank, they are bound to fail.'

Anne Frank is frequently identified as a single representative of the millions of people who suffered and died as she did because she moves us more than the countless others who suffered just as she did but whose faces have remained in the shadows.

Simon Wiesenthal expressed a similar sentiment when he said that the diary had raised more widespread awareness of the Holocaust than had been achieved during the Nuremberg Trials, because: 'People identified with this child. This was the impact of the Holocaust, this was a family like my family, like your family and so you could understand this.'

Anne Frank remains a compelling reminder that the way forward for our troubled world can only be built by mutual acceptance by all parties, not by domination. Her life and, in particular, the manner of her death is a clarion call to a mutuality of understanding, a sense of belonging, a union of spirits, a loving appreciation of others and a deep communion to the common good.

Faith is not knowing what the future holds but knowing who holds the future. It is not given to us to peer into the mysteries

of the future, but we can safely predict that in the coming years
Anne Frank's rich legacy will endure.

TRY A LITTLE TENDERNESS

There was once a poor slave whose name was Eoghan. His
master was a cruel man, and so unkind to him that at last
Eoghan ran away.

He hid himself in caves for days. One time he was sleeping
when he was woken by a great noise. A lion had come into the
cave, and was roaring loudly. Eoghan was very much afraid, for
he felt certain that the beast would kill him. Soon, however, he
saw that lion not as angry, but that he limped as though his foot
hurt him.

Then Eoghan grew so bold that he took hold of the lion's
lame paw to see what the matter was. The lion stood quite still,
and rubbed his head against the man's shoulder. He seemed to
say, 'I know that you will help me.'

Eoghan lifted the paw from the ground, and saw that it was
a long, sharp thorn which hurt the lion so much. He took the
end of the thorn in his fingers; then he gave a strong, quick pull,
and out it came. The lion was full of joy. He jumped about like
a dog, and licked the hands and feet of his new friend.

Eoghan was not at all afraid after this. And, when night came,
he and the lion lay down and slept side by side.

For a long time, the lion brought food to Eoghan every
day, and the two became such good friends that Eoghan had a
wonderful time. He knew things were too good to be true. And
then something terrible happened.

One day some soldiers were passing and spotted Eoghan.
They captured him and brought him back to Dublin. It was the
law at the time that every slave who ran away from his master

should be made to fight a hungry lion. So a fierce lion was shut for a while without food, and a time was set for the fight.

When the day came, thousands of people crowded to see the sport. The door opened and poor Eoghan was brought in. He was almost dead with fear, for the roars of the lion were ringing in his ears.

Then the hungry lion rushed in. With a single leap he reached the slave. Eoghan gave a great cry, not out of fear, but of gladness. It was his old friend, the lion of the cave.

The people, who had expected to see the man killed by the lion, were filled with wonder. They saw Eoghan put his arms around the lion's neck; they saw the lion kneel down at his feet and lick them lovingly; they saw the great beast rub his head against the slave's face as though he wanted to be petted. They could not understand what it all meant.

They asked Eoghan to tell them about it. So he stood up before them and, with his arm around the lion's neck, told how he and the beast had lived together in the cave.

When he had finished everyone was in tears. They clapped and shouted, 'Let this man go free. Let this man go free.'

Others cried, 'Let the lion free too. Let them both go free.'

And so Eoghan was set free and the lion was given to him as his own. And they both lived happily together.

THE GOOD NEWS

At the beginning of his public life in Galilee, Jesus proclaimed the Kingdom of God. This was his 'Good News' to the poor, a kingdom into which the excluded are brought in, the blind are given sight, the paralysed walk and sinners are forgiven. The evidence for this kingdom was to be seen in everything he said and did. His miracles were not simply demonstrations of his power, but symbols of God's will for the world. A world where the work of healing has priority, where the hungry are fed, where the poor are no longer pawns in the games of the rich and powerful. In short, a world where our demons are faced and defeated.

Isn't it striking then that there were no miracles in Holy Week? We are not treated to any signs of his divine power to convince the leaders about his claims. So Pilate remained unimpressed by his notion of the truth and Herod went home disappointed that the holy man had not performed for him.

All we have this week is Jesus being faithful, faithful to his mission. Faithful to the kingdom's ideals of justice and peace, but isn't God is to be found in this as surely as in any miracle Jesus ever performed?

It's sometimes easier for us to believe in the Jesus of the miracles because we know we are not expected to perform any. But we are expected to live like the Jesus of Holy Week, faithful to a kingdom that is always and only a work of compassion and love.

ENDURANCE

A little steam engine had a long train of cars to pull.

She went along great until she came to a steep hill. But then, no matter how much she tried, she just couldn't move the long train of cars. She pulled and pulled. She puffed and puffed. She backed up and tried again. Choo! Choo! Choo! Choo!

Alas to no avail. The cars just couldn't get up the hill.

At last she left the train and started up the track alone. She wasn't giving up. She was seeking help. Over the hill and up the track went the little steam engine.

Choo, choo! Choo, choo! Choo, choo!

Soon she saw a big steam engine standing on a side track. He looked huge and strong. The big steam engine laughed at her: 'Don't you see that I am through my day's work? I have to get ready for tomorrow. I've no time to be helping the likes of you.'

The little steam engine was disappointed, but on she went.

Choo, choo! Choo, choo! Choo, choo!

Soon she came to a second huge steam engine on a side track. He was huffing and puffing, as if he was exhausted.

He may help me, thought the little steam engine. She ran up to him and said, 'Will you help me bring my train of cars over the hill? It's too heavy for me.'

The second big steam engine snapped, 'You stupid, tiny train. Don't you see I'm exhausted. Can't you get some other engine to help you?'

Again the little steam engine was sorry, but she kept going.

Choo, choo! Choo, choo! Choo, choo!

Much later, she came to another little steam engine. She rang alongside and said, 'Will you help me over the hill with my train of cars? It's too heavy for me.'

'Yes, indeed! said the second little steam engine. 'I'll be glad if I can.'

So the little steam engines started back to where the train of cars had been standing all this time. One little steam engine went to the head of the train, and the other to the end of it.

Puff, puff! Chug, chug! Choo, choo!

Gradually the cars began to move. Gradually they climbed the steep hill. As they climbed, each little steam engine began to sing.

'I-think-I-can! I-think-I-can! I-think-I-can! I think-I-can! I-think-I-can . . .

And they did!

Soon, they were over the hill and going down the other side. Soon they were on the plain again, and the little steam engine could pull her train hertself. So she thanked the little engine who had come to help her, and said goodbye.

And as she went merrily on her way, she sang to herself:

> 'I-thought-I-could! I-thought-I-could! I-thought-I-could!
> I-thought-I-could! I-thought-I-could!'

THE SUFFERING SERVANT

Jesus surprised and maybe even shocked his followers when he got down on his knees to wash their feet, but they must have been horrified at what transpired in the Garden of Gethsemane. Here they see Jesus making an impassioned plea that things might be different: 'Father, everything is possible for you, so let this cup pass from me.' The God man is on his knees again, but this time torn apart by a decision he must make. Should he just give up now and escape into the wilderness or should he stay, trusting in the prayer that he taught his disciples: 'Father, your will be done'?

In teaching them to pray this way, he was not instructing them to be passively resigned to all the forces over which they have no control. On the contrary, he was teaching them to want what God wants. Sadly, too often in the Christian tradition the phrase 'God's will' has been used in ways never intended by Jesus. He never told anyone in pain it was God's will for them.

No, he taught his disciples to pray that God's will be done and to commit themselves to doing it, because he knew, even in Gethsemane, that God's will is always to save and not to destroy.

In Holy Week, Jesus, the Word made flesh, makes it clear that God's only desire for us is that we should have life and to have it to the full.

LOOKING DOWN ON EMPTY STREET

In the final scene of the medieval epic *La Chanson de Roland*, the great Christian hero Charlemagne sat exhausted in Aix, his battles with the Moors over. According to the poem, he was more than nine hundred years old. An angel wakened the old man from his sleep and told him to get up again and return to battle because the work would not be finished until the end of time. Charlemagne, sighing, says: *Dieu, si penuse est ma vie.* (O God, how hard is my life.) The work of the hero remains unfinished, but who will do it if not (s)he?

POETRY
FOR
SPRING

The Gift

It came slowly
Afraid of insufficient self-content,
Or some inherent weakness in itself,
Small and hesitant,
Like children at the top of the stairs,
It came through shops, rooms, temples,
Streets; places that were badly lit,
It was a gift that took me unawares,
And I accepted it.

BRENDAN KENNELLY

The Scribe

Over my head the woodland wall
Rises; the ousel sings to me.
Above my booklet lined for words
The woodland birds shake out their glee.

There's the blithe cuckoo chanting clear
In mantle green from bouth to bough!

God keep me still! for here I write
A scripture bright in great woods now.

CELTIC POEM FROM THE EIGHTH CENTURY

The White Lake

When holy Patrick full of grace
Suffered on Cruach, that blest place,
In grief and gloom enduring then
For Eire's women, Eire's men,

God for his comfort sent a flight
Of birds angelically bright
That sang above the darkling lake
A song of unceasing for his sake.

'Twas thus they chanted, all and some,
'Come hither, Patrick! hither come!
Shield of the Gael, thou light of story,
Appointed star of the golden glory!'

Thus singing all those fair birds smite
The waters with soft wings in flight
Till the dark lake its gloom surrenders
And rolls a tide of silvery splendours.

CELTIC POEM FROM THE EIGHTH CENTURY

The Lark

Learned in music sings the lark,
I leave my cell to listen;

His open beak spills music, hark!
Where Heaven's bright cloudlets glisten.

And so I'll sing my morning psalm
That God bright Heaven may give me
And keep me in eternal calm
And from all sin relieve me.

CELTIC POEM FROM THE EIGHTH CENTURY

Be Thou My Vision

Be thou my vision, O Lord of my heart,
Naught is all else to me, save that Thou art.
Thou my best thought by day and by night,
Waking or sleeping, Thy presence my light.
Be Thou my wisdom, Thou my true word;
I ever with Thee, Thou with me, Lord.
Thou my great father, I Thy dear son;
Thou in me dwelling, I with Thee one.
Be Thou my battle-shield, sword for the fight,
Be Thou my dignity, Thou my delight.
Thou my soul's shelter, Thou my high tower;
Raise Thou me heavenward, power of my power.
Riches I heed not, not man's empty praise,
Thou mine inheritance now and always.
Thou, and Thou only, first in my heart,
High King of heaven, my treasure Thou art.
King of the seven heavens, grant me for dole,
Thy love in my heart, Thy light in my soul.
Thy light from my soul, Thy love from my heart,
King of the seven heavens, may they never depart.
With the high king of heaven, after victory won,

May I reach heaven's joys, O bright heaven's sun!
Heart of my own heart, whatever befall,
Still be my vision, O Ruler of all.

NINTH CENTURY, AUTHOR UNKNOWN

From East to West

From east to west, from shore to shore,
Let every heart awake and sing
The holy Child whom Mary bore,
The Christ, the everlasting King.

Behold, the world's Creator wears
The form and fashion of a slave;
Our very flesh our Maker shares,
His fallen creature, man, to save.

For this how wondrously He wrought!
A maiden, in her lowly place,
Became, in ways beyond all thought,
The chosen vessel of His grace.

CAELIUS SEDULIUS

The Living Flame of Love

O lamps of fire bright-burning
With wondrous brilliance, turning
Deep caverns of my soul to pools of light!
Once shadowed, dim, unknowing,
Now their new-found glowing
Gives warmth and radiance for my Love's delight.
Ah! Gentle and so loving

You wake within me, proving
That you are in secret and alone;
Your fragrant breathing stills me,
Your grace, your glory fills me,
so tenderly your love becomes my own.

ST JOHN OF THE CROSS

Boundless, Bottomless Love

My soul melts away
In the madness of Love,
The abyss into which she hurls me
Is deeper than the sea:
For Love's new deep abyss
Renews my wound.

HADEWIJCH OF ANTWERP, B. 1200

Greatness

Everybody can be great because anybody can serve.
You don't have to have a college degree to serve.
You don't have to make your subject and verb agree to
serve.
You only need a heart full of grace.
A soul generated by love.

MARTIN LUTHER KING JR., 1929–1968

A Different View

So often in life we ought to slow down and not try to fix
everything at once! To travel in patience means these things:
  It's giving up hope that we can solve everything.

It's making an effort, but understanding that one person
cannot do everything.

And it's putting the myth of efficiency into perspective.

POPE FRANCIS, B. 1936

Easter Night

All night had shout of men and cry
Of woeful women filled His way;
Until that noon of sombre sky
On Friday, clamour and display
Smote Him; no solitude had He,
No silence, since Gethsemane.

Public was Death; but Power, but Might,
But Life again, but Victory,
Were hushed within the dead of night,
The shutter'd dark, the secrecy.
And all alone, alone, alone,
He rose again behind the stone.

ALICE MEYNELL, 1847–1922

Homeward Bound

Thee, God, I come from, to thee go . . .
What I acknowledge of thee I bless
As acknowledging thy stress
On my being and as seeing
Something of thy holiness.

GERARD MANLEY HOPKINS

Ocean Deep

Here is love vast as the ocean,
Loving kindness as the flood,
When the Prince of life, our ransom,
Shed for us his precious blood.
Who his love will not remember?
Who can sing his praise
He can never be forgotten
throughout heaven's eternal days

On the mount of crucifixion
Fountains opened deep and wide;
through the floodgates of God's mercy
flowed a vast and gracious tide.

Grace and love, like mighty rivers,
poured incessant from above,
and heaven's peace and perfect justice
kissed a guilty world in love.

WILLIAM REES, 1802–1883

The Dark Night of the Soul

In darkness, hid from sight
I went by secret ladder and sure
– Ah, grace of sheer delight! –
so softly veiled by night,
hushed now my house, in darkness and secure.

Hidden in that glad night,
regarding nothing as I stole away,
no one to see my flight,

no other guide or light
save one that in my heart burned bright as day.

Flame, white-hot and compelling,
yet tender past all telling,
reaching the secret centre of my soul!
Burn that is for healing!
Wound of delight past feeling!
Willing, you give me life for death's distress.

ST JOHN OF THE CROSS

Don't Quit

When things go wrong as they sometimes will,
When the road you're trudging seems all up hill,
When the funds are low and the debts are high
And you want to smile, but you have to sigh,
When care is pressing you down a bit,
Rest if you must, but don't you quit.
Life is strange with its twists and turns
As every one of us sometimes learns
And many a failure comes about
When he might have won had he stuck it out;
Don't give up though the pace seems slow –
You may succeed with another blow.
Success is failure turned inside out –
The silver tint of the clouds of doubt,
And you never can tell just how close you are,
It may be near when it seems so far;
So stick to the fight when you're hardest hit –
It's when things seem worst that you must not quit.

JOHN GREENLEAF WHITTIER, 1807–1892

Poet's Corner

There is a danger of an excessively misty-eyed approach to the 'golden age of Irish monasticism'. This era was not without its 'dark spots'. The monasteries were very often under the control of local chieftains and there are quite a few examples of monasteries going to war with each other.

The local nature of Irish monasteries brought the weaknesses of its strengths. One of the problems with the Irish Church at the time was that it was so identified with local lords that the original Christian impetus was lost. Sometimes the monasteries became little more than pawns in the local wars going on between the local chieftains.

A warm welcome was not always welcomed in Celtic Ireland. There is a story of a beautiful young woman who was pursuing St Kevin. According to legend not alone did he reject her advances, he threw her into a lake and she drowned.

The poetry of the monks shows their willingness to meditate on the qualities that make them deeply human and also relating to the superhuman. The problem of their sexual nature is a recurring theme in their poetry and the challenge they faced was to transform their sexual energy into religious energy. Of course, this is not to imply that the religious and sexual are mutually exclusive, but the monks treated their sexual longings in a way that those feelings were converted into a longing for God. This is not unusual. One of the greatest poets in the English language, John Donne, was a very accomplished metaphysical poet and went on to become a great religious poet, as well as a sensual one.

As we have seen, one of Ireland's national treasures, Brendan Kennelly, translated many of the poems written by the Irish monks. One was a short poem called 'The Bell', which furnishes us with a revealing insight into the preoccupations of the monks:

I'd sooner keep my tryst with that sweet little bell,
the night of a bad winter mist,
than risk a ravenous female.

It is a very strong poem, with very definite anti-woman feelings. Yet it equally shows that they gave their natures their full attention and were able to reflect on the difference between a woman and a bell – two different kinds of chiming attractions it might be said! Fifteen hundred years later in his poem 'Temptation in Harvest', Patrick Kavanagh would write of his struggle to abandon his vocation as a poet: 'I go to follow her who winked at me.'

Like Kavanagh, these monks inspire us to reflect on human relationships and whatever relationship we have with what is beyond the human.

PRAYERS
FOR
SPRING

Disturb Us, Lord

Disturb us, Lord, when
We are too pleased with ourselves,
When our dreams have come true
Because we dreamed too little,
When we arrived safely
Because we sailed too close to the shore.

Disturb us, Lord, when
with the abundance of things we possess
We have lost our thirst
For the waters of life;
Having fallen in love with life,
We have ceased to dream of eternity
And in our efforts to build a new earth,
We have allowed our vision
Of the new Heaven to dim.

Disturb us, Lord, to dare more boldly,
To venture on wilder seas

Where storms will show Your mastery;
Where losing sight of land, We shall find the stars.

We ask you to push back
The horizons of our hopes;
And to push back the future
In strength, courage, hope, and love.

This we ask in the name of our Captain,
Who is Jesus Christ.

SIR FRANCIS DRAKE, C. 1540–1596

The Flame

Be Thou a brilliant flame before me,
Be Thou a guiding star above me,
Be Thou a smooth path below me,
Be Thou a kindly shepherd behind me,
Today, tonight and for ever more.

PRAYER OF ST COLUMBA

A Prayer for Love

God, Father, Son and Spirit
Through your love dwelling within us
May we always be willing to share the hope that lifts our
    hearts
May we always be generous in our service of others,
    especially those who are most in need
May we always seek the wisdom that comes from above and
    resides within
May we always have the courage to stand up for what is right

May we always have the humility to ask for pardon
May we always trust that our efforts for good are never in
   vain
And may we always draw confidence from your joy in us.
   Amen.

Prayer for Healing

Gracious and merciful God, the problems facing our human
family are very grave and we are no longer isolated from
one another. We are confronted daily with our addiction to
violence, our hatred and our greed. We are heartbroken.
The media are relentless in their presentation and critique
and we all long for some good news. It is so easy to forget
that your Son, Jesus, is always the good news and that
He has given us the remedy for our brokenness. 'Father,
forgive them, they don't know what they are doing.' He
spoke so clearly. We ask your Holy Spirit to remind us of
this again and again. We ask you for the gift of hope in our
lives and know that we need to turn to one another for the
confidence and assurance that we will emerge from situa-
tions, that, in the short term seem hopeless. Banish fear and
anxiety from our hearts.

   Tonight we gather to affirm one another and to remove
the barriers that seem to sour our relationships and keep
us at a distance. Heal the short tempers and the grudges
we hold, against one another, against our political system,
against our Church, against our financial institutions. We
could go on and on. Prompt us to be beacons in the present
darkness, and especially beacons to one another. We are all
guilty of some selfishness, many of us have lived beyond our
means and we become angry and irrational and embrace

ideologies that protect our acquisitions. We need your help to stop contributing to the larger greed that tears at our world. We believe in the power of your grace to change our lives and we promise tonight to be once again open to that grace. Bless us with a peaceful spirit and a desire to be reconciled with one another.

Amen.

Be Not Afraid

The Lord is my light and my salvation;
Whom shall I fear?
The Lord is the stronghold of my life;
Of whom shall I be afraid?

The Confessions of St Patrick – an extract

So I am first of all a simple country person, a refugee, and unlearned. I do not know how to provide for the future. But this I know for certain, that before I was brought low, I was like a stone lying deep in the mud. Then He who is powerful came and in his mercy pulled me out, and lifted me up and placed me on the very top of the wall. That is why I must shout aloud in return to the Lord for such great good deeds of his, here and now and forever, which the human mind cannot measure.

St Patrick's Breastplate

I arise today
Through a mighty strength, the invocation of the Trinity,
Through belief in the Threeness,

Through confession of the Oneness
of the Creator of creation.
I arise today
Through the strength of Christ's birth with His baptism,
Through the strength of His crucifixion with His burial,
Through the strength of His resurrection with His
ascension,
Through the strength of His descent for the judgment of
doom.
I arise today, through
The strength of heaven,
The light of the sun,
The radiance of the moon,
The splendour of fire,
The speed of lightning,
The swiftness of wind,
The depth of the sea,
The stability of the earth,
The firmness of rock.
I arise today, through
God's strength to pilot me,
God's might to uphold me,
God's wisdom to guide me,
God's eye to look before me,
God's ear to hear me,
God's word to speak for me,
God's hand to guard me,
God's shield to protect me,
God's host to save me
From snares of devils,
From temptation of vices,
From everyone who shall wish me ill,

afar and near.
Christ with me,
Christ before me,
Christ behind me,
Christ in me,
Christ beneath me,
Christ above me,
Christ on my right,
Christ on my left,
Christ when I lie down,
Christ when I sit down,
Christ when I arise,
Christ in the heart of every man who thinks of me,
Christ in the mouth of everyone who speaks of me,
Christ in every eye that sees me,
Christ in every ear that hears me.

Prayer for Ireland

Heavenly Father, as we prepare to celebrate the feast of St Patrick, we ask a blessing on our country at this time.

May all our people come to know their unique worth and dignity in your sight and may this knowledge inspire them to become compassionate adults, happy and willing to use their gifts in the service of others.

Like St Patrick may we learn to live with gratitude in our hearts for all the ways in which we have been blessed.

We make our prayer through Christ our Lord.
Amen.

Prayer for those in Religious Life

We pray for those who are consecrated to God by the vows of chastity, poverty and obedience.

May they always reveal the love of Christ to those they encounter and continue to enrich our world by their dedicated lives of prayer and service.

We pray that the life and mission of the women and men in consecrated life be a means of sanctification for them and building up the kingdom of God.

We pray that all those living consecrated lives may get the strength to answer God's call every day of their lives.

Amen.

HUMOUR
FOR
SPRING

Heaven Sent

While walking down the street one day, a head of state is tragically hit by a car and dies. Her soul arrives in heaven and is met by St Peter at the entrance.

'Welcome to heaven,' says St Peter. 'Before you settle in, it seems there is a problem. We seldom see a high official around these parts, you see, so we're not sure what to do with you.'

'No problem, just let me in,' says the lady.

'Well, I'd like to but I have orders from higher up. What'll we do is have you spend one day in hell and one in heaven. Then you can choose where to spend eternity.'

'Really, I've made up in my mind. I want to be in heaven', says the head of state.

'I'm sorry, but we have our rules.' And, with that, St Peter escorts her to the elevator and she goes down, down, down to hell.

The doors open and she finds herself in the middle of a golf course. In the distance is a clubhouse and standing in front of it are all her friends and the politicians who had worked with her. Everyone is very happy and in evening dress. They greet her, hug her, and reminisce about the good times they had while getting rich at the expense of the people. They play a friendly game of golf and then dine on lobster. Also present is the Devil, who really is a very friendly guy, who has a good time dancing and telling jokes. They are having such a good time that, before she realises it, it is time to go. Everyone gives her a big hug and waves while the elevator rises. The elevator goes up, up, up and reopens on heaven, where St Peter is waiting for her.

'Now it's time to visit heaven.'

So twenty-four hours pass with the head of state joining a large number of contented souls moving from cloud to cloud, playing the harp and singing. Before she realises it, the twenty-four hours have gone by and St Peter returns. 'Well then, you've spent a day in hell and another in heaven. Now choose your eternal destination.'

She reflects for a minute, then the head of state answers, 'Well, I would never have expected it. I mean, heaven has been delightful, but I think I would be better off in hell.'

So St Peter escorts her to the elevator and she goes down, down, down to hell. The doors of the elevator open and she is in the middle of a barren land covered with garbage. She sees all her friends, dressed in rags, picking up the trash and putting it in bags. The Devil comes over to her and lays his arm on her neck.

'I don't understand,' stammers the head of state. 'Yesterday I was here and everyone was on the golf course and clubhouse and we ate lobster and caviar and danced and had a great time. Now it is a wasteland full of garbage and my friends look miserable.'

The Devil looks at her, smiles and says, 'Yesterday we were campaigning. Today you voted for us!'

The Odd Couple

An American tourist and his wife were visiting a cemetery. They were a bit surprised at one inscription they read on an old tombstone which said, 'Here lies a politician and an honest man.'

The wife said, 'Fancy burying those two in the same grave.'

Prayer for Good Humour

Grant me, O Lord, good digestion, and also something to digest.
Grant me a healthy body, and the necessary good humour to maintain it.
Grant me a simple soul that knows to treasure all that is good and that doesn't frighten easily at the sight of evil,
but rather finds the means to put things back in their place.
Give me a soul that knows not boredom, grumblings, sighs and laments, nor excess of stress, because of that obstructing thing called 'I'.
Grant me, O Lord, a sense of good humour.
Allow me the grace to be able to take a joke to discover in life a bit of joy, and to be able to share it with others.

ST THOMAS MORE, 1478–1535

Driven

The story was that Pope Francis was so excited about his visit to Ireland for the World Meeting of Families that he decided to visit the Irish College in Rome to learn a few words in Irish. Not a man to bother with formalities, Francis told his driver that he would drive himself and he instructed his driver to take his place in the back seat.

Pope Francis was getting so absorbed thinking about his speech that he completely forgot about the speed limit. That all changed when an angry-looking policeman pulled up beside him on his motorcycle and waved him down. Pope Francis was a little surprised that instead of approaching his car the policeman spoke into his phone. The cop explained to his boss that he had pulled over a dignitary for speeding, but he did not think it would be wise to charge him.

The chief of police asked, 'Who have you got there, a Member of Parliament?'

The traffic cop replied, 'Bigger.'

Chief: 'Not the President?'

The traffic cop replied, 'Bigger.'

'Well,' said the chief. 'Tell me who is it then, for God's sake?'

Traffic cop: 'Well, that's just it. I think it is God.'

Chief: 'Why do you say that?'

Traffic cop: 'Well, he's got Pope Francis as his chauffeur!'

Sleeping Beauties

There are two types of people: givers and takers. Takers have more, but givers sleep better.

LETTERS
FOR
SPRING

For this final section I decided to write a letter to my own father.

Letter to My Father

Dear Daddy,

My earliest memory is of you.

When I was three, you brought my mother and me to the Ballinasloe Horse Fair. I had never heard of Disneyland at that point, but this was my equivalent. I was looking around me with all the wonder of a child after Santa visits on Christmas morning. In fact, so absorbed I was by all the distractions that I walked smack bang into a big pole. As I was sobbing hysterically, you quickly melted away my tears like snow in a sudden thaw when you bought me the absolute treat – a whole Flake bar for myself. This was sheer bliss. I could not have been happier.

It is literally a sweet memory and all these years later I still smile when I hear the words in the advertisement: 'Only the crumbliest flakiest chocolate, tastes like chocolate never tasted before.'

The second happiest day of my young life came when I was five and my mother brought me on the train from Athlone to see you in St Vincent's Hospital in Dublin. I still remember the big smile on your face and the wink you gave me when we were leaving. I was happy because I knew you were going to be home with us soon. The doctors told us that the operation would make you better.

But it didn't.

Instead something unexpected happened and you took your last breath on the operation table.

You were just thirty-five.

Hearing the news was an act of cognitive violence. Who knew my deepest certainties were so fragile? All was changed, changed utterly. My rocklike convictions were brutally assassinated.

You gave my hurting heart a love for Gaelic football and your last gift to me was to mark my card about a young player who had burst on to the scene. You said he would become Roscommon's greatest footballer. You were so right. His name was Dermot Earley.

I would like to have inherited your wry sense of humour. Like your description of one of our neighbours: 'He's just built a henhouse – for his ducks.'

Long before we heard of health and safety you once let me jump from a high wall into your arms. It never crossed my mind that you would not catch me. I believed in you absolutely.

The heart that loves is always young. You are forever young.

Life is a battle between two thieves: regret over the past and fear of the future. I mourn for the unfinished business between us. So many things I would have liked to say to you but never got the chance. I am too numb for feelings of grief but not too numb for guilt. The living of grief would come quickly and linger forever.

Let me be brutally honest, I still feel cheated that you were taken from me when I was so young. You were my shining star and my man mountain. I looked up to you in a way that I have looked up at nobody since.

Your funeral will live with me forever – looking down on a

gathering for an occasion almost unbearably sad; a centre of my life gone as I quietly uncoiled on the edge of the living world. I was near to tears and in my heart there was something stirring, a sense of outrage, a feeling of total despair. It was one of those moments that can derange the emotional life.

I could not bring myself to think of you in the past tense but I had seen the evidence of the previous night as you lay in your coffin. You seemed so calm as you smiled and held your rosary beads in your hand.

I hope fervently your soul has been set free and that you have found peace in a higher, more perfect world.

In the softness of the western mist as I walk these fields in our family farm in Roscommon from which my heart can never be departed (yours neither I am guessing), I see your face. This land opens questions, often violent questions, about my history and identity and goes even further to some secret compass point which directs me to somewhere I do not know – crossing boundaries where sadness and pain meet so dramatically. As I walk in this field I try to listen to its secrets of lives gained and lives lost, strange riches and sadness. It has a music of its own. The melody which enters my consciousness is a melody of loneliness, poignant cries of quiet despair. In these fields, people long dead live again, somehow speaking to years that belong to people not yet born. Your ghost will always linger in these fields.

In my greatest triumphs and on the bleakest days I have felt your breath softly whispering in my ear.

Somewhere between the land of the living and the risen, there is a garden. In another existence I will meet you there again.

Until then watch over me, please. Help me to make you proud of me.

Your son.

Letter from Mother Teresa

In the 1990s, I had the great good fortune to correspond with Mother Teresa. One section of the letter is relevant for this collection.

Dear John

People are often unreasonable, irrational, and self-centred. Forgive them anyway.

If you are kind, people may accuse you of selfish, ulterior motives. Be kind anyway.

If you are successful, you will win some unfaithful friends and some genuine enemies. Succeed anyway.

If you are honest and sincere people may deceive you. Be honest and sincere anyway.

What you spend years creating, others could destroy overnight. Create anyway.

If you find serenity and happiness, some may be jealous. Be happy anyway.

The good you do today, will often be forgotten. Do good anyway.

Give the best you have, and it will never be enough. Give your best anyway.

In the final analysis, it is between you and God. It was never between you and them anyway.

Mother Teresa

A LEGACY
FOR ALL
SEASONS

This book recalls our Celtic tradition not only for our past or even for our present but equally importantly for our future.

Recently I visited Clonmacnoise, the great city of early Irish monasticism, which is today a world heritage site. To visit this extraordinary place is to breathe in a special spirit. These ruins open many questions about our identity today.

The Celts were not content to be chaplains to the tribe. They wanted to be prophets to the society. For too much of recent Irish history our politics have demeaned our religion. The Celts believed that our religion should enhance our politics. I grew up in Ireland where there was an orthodoxy of religion. Perhaps, though, today we need an orthodoxy of humanity. The Celtic Church points to how an orthodoxy of religion could illuminate an orthodoxy of humanity.

Apart from their relevance to the wider society, the Celtic Christians have much to offer us to reflect on in our spiritual and personal lives. Their spirituality was very scriptural and it is interesting to read the prayers they composed and observe in them their great love of the scriptures. They were also very imaginative, as is evident in their rich artistic legacy including the Book of Kells, the Derrynaflan Chalice, remnants of wall paintings in certain churches and the very high crosses. Could the church today benefit from an infusion of such creativity and imagination?

I had the privilege of exchanging occasional correspondence with Seamus Heaney. On the first of September 2013, before the All-Ireland semi-final between the two titans Kerry and Dublin in Croke Park, the GAA displayed a photo of Seamus two days after his death and asked for a minute's silence. You could have heard a pin drop and at the end eighty thousand people clapped for over a minute. In what other country would a football crowd clap for a poet?

The inscription on Seamus's tombstone is: 'Walk on air against your better judgement.' One of the phrases he used in his 'Republic of Conscience', was 'the Celtic Marvels'. In poems such as 'Postscript', he alludes to the richness of the Celtic imaginative tradition. He saw his role not to be a propagandist but to be someone who 'weighed up' rather than 'weighed in'. However, he acknowledged that the Celtic tradition had the capacity to 'catch the heart off guard'. In his poem 'Man and Boy', he uses the phrase 'Blessed be' a number of times, which has striking echoes of his Celtic roots.

Indeed, in his final note to me, he observed that 'the biggest shift in my lifetime has been the evaporation of the transcendent from all our discourse and our sense of human destiny'. While he had moved away from the faith he was born into, he had never shut the door on it. Seamus's final words to me were:

'And yet I cannot disavow the inner expansiveness of consciousness, a sense of grace and God-filled space and a universe drenched in radiance nor can I disavow words like "Thanksgiving" or "host" or "communion bread". They have an undying tremor and draw, like well water far down.'

Indeed, it is telling that Heaney's very last words were in a text message to his wife: *Noli timere* – be not afraid. These are words Jesus repeats many times in the gospels.

MORE THAN WORDS

Beatha teanga i a labhairt.
The life of a language is in its speaking.

In the Celtic tradition, God was understood as appreciative of and protective of every single human life. The Celtic description of a disabled person as God's own person (*duine le Dia*) is a good illustration of that point. In the Celtic tradition, old life, injured life, disabled life: every life is God's own life, God's special gift and task.

One of the big buzz phrases today in social and political life is the democratic deficit – the frustration 'ordinary people' have because they are denied any real power in the society they live in, with little or no say in the decision-making processes. For the disabled person, the possibility of making decisions for themselves is often little more than a pipe dream. Decisions about their welfare are often taken by people who have no direct experience of what it is like to be disabled.

Much lip-service is paid to people with disabilities, which fails to yield any practical benefits. The problem is resources, or more precisely lack of resources. Many medical and technical advances have presented new and exciting treatment options – the use of art and music therapy to help people cope with mental illness is just one such innovative example. However, across the globe there is a major shortage of funding, which leaves many disabled people seriously disadvantaged. It is too easy, though, to talk about action for disabled people in terms of aspirations. What is needed are specific targets and specific action programmes.

For all our talk of equal rights, a significant minority of people living throughout the four corners of the world have not achieved legal, economic or cultural parity. The economic, political and cultural disadvantages suffered by these 'outcasts' are serious violations of justice.

A number of questions present themselves about the place of disabled people in our world today. In our society, are all people equal, or are some, like those with disabilities, seen as less equal than others? How many disabled people are institutionalised? How many have a home of their own? How many have access to the specific, particular education that they may require? How many have a job? The Celts knew how to cherish those who we might view as disabled. By our actions, and often inactions, we often do not.

DYING AND BEHOLD WE LIVE

The Celtic understanding of the cycle of life and death is crucial to the inner growth of the soul. In the Celtic tradition, each new day is seen as a new beginning, a gift from God. Today this insight needs to be retrieved. Ours is an age which is obsessed with youth. The growth of the cosmetic surgery 'industry' reveals that so many people seem petrified of ageing, let alone dying. We need a new culture of dealing with the reality of death. The Celtic tradition has many insights to offer to this debate. Columbanus wrote in one of his sermons, 'I am always moving from the day of birth until the day of death.' St Brendan echoed a similar sentiment. Death is not the end of the story, but another phase in the soul's journey, an entrance into the wider life, endlessly stretching out. As Christians we ought to be forefront of the development of this new understanding of death as we profess to believe that the eternal life in which we pray to be resurrected has long begun. It is striking that the Celtic phrase for dying was *dul ar shlí na fírinee* (literally, to go on the path of truth).

AMONGST WOMEN

In the sixth-century, St Brigid's foundation was unique in that it was a double monastery for women and men. Each group followed the same rule and used a common church, with the government of the whole community held jointly by the abbess and the bishop-abbot. The Celtic Church of this time was one of those rare periods in Irish history when women were given a meaningful role and could claim to have equality.

Pope John Paul II's *Mulieris Dignitatem* (The Dignity of Women, 1988), noted that one of the recommendations of the 1987 Synod of Bishops was for a 'further study of the anthropological and theological bases that are needed in order to solve the problems connected with the meaning and dignity of being a woman or a man.' Unfortunately, that challenge has not been adequately taken up. There is a need for a new approach which takes account of the need to build new relationships of mutuality and reciprocity between women and men in the Church. Today, people's faith is threatened by many factors including poverty and family break-up. Many women, though, feel that their faith life is endangered by a patriarchal church.

Despite a massive amount of essential equality legislation, many women echo the type of sentiments expressed by Mary Robinson in her inauguration speech as Irish president in 1990: 'As a woman I want women who have felt themselves outside of history to be written back into history, in the words of Eavan Boland, finding a voice where they found a vision.'

THE CELTIC WEB OF LIFE

The Celtic understanding of the divine was never merely of a transcendent presence, but also an immanent reality in the world of people's everyday lives. While they did retain the traditional Christian doctrine of a transcendent God – that is, the God who watches us from a distance – the Celtic Christians laid particular emphasis on the immanence of God: the closeness of God to us and an involvement with nature and with the world, a vital presence in the world, animating all of creaturely life.

Of course, this stress on the immanence of God's ongoing creative project in everyday life did lead to distortions in the same way as theologies which placed heavy emphasis on the transcendence of God neglected the immanence of God.

A WINDOW INTO GOD

The Celts saw creation as offering a window into God. Columbanus stated, 'If you want to know the Creator, understand created things.' This heavily experiential understanding of God was beautifully summed up by An tAthair Donnchadh O Floinn as a 'breathing in and breathing out of God'. Seamus Heaney has written about the legendary story of St Kevin, one which tells of him praying with outstretched hands for so long that a blackbird came to make a nest and lay an egg in one of them. According to Heaney, at that moment Kevin was 'linked into the network of eternal life'. Another legend is about the monk who had a fly who kept the page of his manuscript open as he designed it.

In Celtic times, for example, it was believed that all wells had their source in one great well deep inside the centre of the earth. These were sacred places, protected by protective feminine spirits. In this tradition, a rainbow was understood as a love letter from God. John Macquarrie claimed that the Celts were 'intoxicated with the love of God'. Patrick Kavanagh had a similar insight in his poem 'Auditors in'.

CARING FOR THE EARTH

Bíonn siúlach scéalach.
Travellers have tales to tell.

Many of the early Irish monks were filled with missionary zeal. Among them were people like St Kilian who went to Germany. It would be fascinating to investigate the extent to which these early Irish monks may have sown some of the seeds of the modern green movement. For example, one of the people who would have inherited the spiritual tradition of these early monks was Hildegard of Bingen, who was born in Bermersheim, Germany, in 1098, to a noble family, the tenth of ten children. From an early age, mystical experiences formed an integral part of her life, and it may have been on account of these visions that her family sent her at the tender age of eight to the care of a Benedictine monastery. In due course, she became a Benedictine sister herself and in 1141 she received the divine command to record her visions.

What is most startling to the contemporary eye is the relevance of her message, despite its antiquity, to the concerns of today. Particularly fascinating is her insight into what in today's parlance is termed creation spirituality – best summed up in her use of the concept of *viriditas* or greenness, which is representative of the creative power present in nature, humankind and having its ultimate source of expression in God. Humankind, despite its special place in creation, has a special responsibility to nature, and abuse of our position would upset this dynamic of interdependence. Accordingly, she showed that humankind is entrusted with a caretaker role. Hilda claimed: 'Although the creatures have been made in order to serve our needs, we too are answerable to them.' These sentiments represent to a considerable extent the spiritual inheritance of Celtic Christianity and still have an important message for our lives today.

ALL CREATURES MEEK AND TALL

The literature of the early Irish Christians is full of celebration of the fact that God and nature are closely intertwined. *The Voyage of Brendan*, for example, is the story of Brendan's quest to find the Promised Land of the Saints. The work itself is an indication of how Christianity appropriated the indigenous culture as it borrows heavily from the *Immram*, a pagan tale of the seafaring Celts who had boldly explored the mysteries of the mighty and threatening Atlantic Ocean.

The Book of Kells have many pictures which remind us of Columba's love of birds, horses, dogs, cats and many species of fish. The scribes liked to include all sorts of small pictures as they wrote. Birds fly down and land on certain words. Sometimes these drawings have a definite use. Other times they are inserted as a joke. Two handsome peacocks, with many-coloured feathers, surround Christ's head. Peacocks often stood for immortality or life-everlasting in the art of this period. Indeed, the intricate, interwoven designs and natural motifs that so adorn the Book of Kells themselves make a bold theological statement: that a web of life connects God's creative activity and the natural world.

In the Celtic tradition, the robin redbreast is a sacred bird, as he sought to relieve the sufferings of Christ by using his beak to pull out the thorns piercing our Lord's head. These tales have clearly been romanticised, but they convey an important message more fully and more entertainingly than a dry factual account. They pay homage to the sanctity of the earth and all of creation, as it is imbued with the divine presence that can inspire us to live in greater harmony with the natural world.

THEIR TIME
The future keeps arriving.

The leading theologian Hans Küng has argued that if the Church is really in sympathy with the world, a sympathetic attitude and sympathetic words will not be sufficient; a passive, more or less peaceful co-existence will not be sufficient. There will have to be pro-existence rather than co-existence, involvement rather than disengagement.

Küng suggests that the Church's understanding of the world will be unfruitful and its links with its useless unless they lead to an active assumption of responsibility for the world. If it truly follows its Lord, the Church is called to the active service of its brethren, who are all created by the one Father. Such a Church, which only lived and worked for itself, would not be the Church of Christ. In this perspective, the Church has the gift and the responsibility of sharing in responsibility, not merely in words but in deeds also, for the world, its present and its future. Accordingly, the Church has a future; it has *the* future. This is the eighth day, which passes description and cannot be foreseen, the day on which God will complete his work. Küng's vision for the Church of tomorrow has striking similarities with the Celtic community of yesterday.

Could it be that the Celtic Church had some significant emphases which we could profitably retrieve to the enrichment of our society and Church today? Their reverence for their environment; their recognition of the equality of women; their respect for people with disabilities; their emphasis on the creative and imaginative and their belief in the centrality of hospitality are as applicable for our time as theirs. For those landing in ageing's long dusk or approaching the shores of middle age, the Celtic tradition is particularly reassuring. To those of us who are slaves to time it points us in another direction. It offers a light to our imagination and a signpost to our path.

Notwithstanding the enormous social, economic, cultural and political differences between the early years of the third millennium and the period of the fifth and ninth centuries could it be that, in some respects at least, our future is in our past?

TRIBUTE TO
JOHN O'DONOHUE

One of the most formative influences on my understanding of the Celtic tradition was the late, great John O'Donohue. He was a man with a word-store as large as Shakespeare's. As a tribute to John's memory, I am publishing for the first time one of my most prized possessions: a letter I received from John almost twenty years ago.

Dear John,

Thanks for your lovely letter. My apologies I had meant to write to you and thank you for the wonderful and incisive review you wrote on *Anam Cara*. You really got it and you got me! Not everyone does!

I am not going to respond to your questions in a systematic way but I hope you will get what you need from these random thoughts. Let us start at the beginning. Beginnings are new horizons that want to be seen.

We need to remember. Memory rescues experience from total disappearance . . . the grooves in the mind hold traces and vestiges of everything that has ever happened to us. Nothing is ever lost or forgotten . . . a ruin is never simply empty. It remains a vivid temple of absence.

The way you look at things is the most powerful force in shaping your life. I was born in a limestone valley in the West of Ireland. The Irish landscape is an ancient landscape; it is full of ruins and traces of ancient civilisation. There is a curvature in the landscape, a colour and a shape that constantly resists that which is too clear or over linear. Every few miles the landscape changes; it always surprises, and offers ever new vistas where light and colour conspire. This landscape seems always to veer away from that which is too direct or flat, and in a sense, this is the nature of the Celtic consciousness.

I used the Celtic vision of life to examine the landscape of the soul. I overturned the contemporary perception of spirituality and argued that instead of seeking to satisfy our spiritual hunger on an everlasting journey of exploration, we should seek an understanding that the soul is the house of our belonging. It is ever-present and is ever-ready to dispense peace and wisdom to enhance our life experience. This presence is nurtured in silence.

The mystery never leaves you alone. Behind your image, below your words, above your thoughts, the silence of another world waits. A world lives within you. No one else can bring you news of this inner world. Through our voices, we bring out sounds from the mountain beneath the soul.

Anam Cara, meaning Soul-Friend from the Gaelic word 'anam' for soul and 'cara' for friend, is the name given in the Celtic tradition to the friend of your soul, your soul mate. The one with whom you share a deep bond of friendship unbroken by space or time. When people love they open their life to an Other and, as the body is in the soul, when they let someone near, they let them become part of their very selves. In the sacred kinship of real love, two souls are twinned. God is always our divine *anam cara*, but our soul longs to share this gift of love and friendship with another person and in them our own *anam cara*.

The body is the home of the soul on earth and through our

senses we feel the presence of the divine. Our bodies are made of the clay of the earth and so our souls are inextricably bound to the landscape. We are part of nature, but the inner landscape of the soul is a secret world, a territory only to be explored alone.

To be wholesome, we must remain truthful to our vulnerable complexity. In order to keep our balance, we need to hold the interior and exterior, visible and invisible, known and unknown, temporal and eternal, ancient and new, together. No one else can undertake this task for you. You are the one and only threshold of an inner world. This wholesome is holiness. To be holy is to be natural; to befriend the worlds that come to balance in you.

We live in an era where we pay homage to image. In the Celtic tradition each new day is seen as a new beginning, a gift from God. However, in modern life, we are often trapped on a treadmill, exhausted from work which numbs creativity and feeling, investing all our energies in a destructive environment where our souls are never engaged. We must be aware of the spiritual danger of investing our energy and sense of belonging in that which is not worthy of our dignity. If you sell your soul, you ultimately buy a life of misery. The world of possibility is silent, yet dense with the dreams of what could be.

We should have no fear of death, as it has been with us since birth and is only the completion of our life's cycle. By releasing ourselves from the earth of death, which is the root of all our fears, we free ourselves to live our lives more fully. New possibility, instead of constantly engaging with fixed givenness in order to reveal and release new potency, is now itself offered as the fruit of an assurgent and passionate givenness. The veil of experience is lifted. Everything can become pure source!

This belief is not, of course, confined to the Celts. The Chinese Buddhist poet Wu-Men (1183–1260) wrote:

> Ten thousand flowers in the spring.
> the moon in autumn,
> A cool breeze in summer.
> snow in winter.
> If your mind isn't clouded by unnecessary things
> This is the best season of your life.

In Connemara, the phrase used to describe popularity and admiration is *tá aghaigh an phobail ort* – 'the face of the people is towards you'. This is particularly relevant in Irish society given the evils of sectarianism and the need for an ecumenical approach to the search for truth. The phrase ought to be a presence for reconciliation in a country which has been disfigured by violence and it serves as a constant reminder that we must all intensify and improve still further our efforts for lasting peace. There is a rich ethical fragrance to this phrase, reminding us of our responsibilities to other people. In a sense, it is prophetic – challenging us to create a society where, in the words of the Irish poet John Hewitt, 'each may grasp his neighbour's hand as friend'.

At the heart of this theological enterprise will be finding a worthy role for the environment. William Butler Yeats had a keen appreciation of this insight: 'Everything we look upon is blest.'

Many will see such a root and branch reform of the Church and theology as a threat because of all the problems, real and imagined, that might surface. I often speak of the tale of the man condemned to share a cell for one night with a deadly snake coiled taut in the corner. The man daren't sleep, move or even breathe deeply for fear of attracting the snake's attention. As dawn lit the horizon, the man relaxed. In the full light of day, he saw that the snake was but a length of old rope. There are hundreds of lengths of ropes thrown in different corners of our minds. Then our fears begin to work on them. They grow into monsters. Fortune favours the bold.

It is not what you asked for, but I hope this helps. Always remember that a horizon is something towards which we continually move but then discover that it moves with us.

Nearly there! Those lines you mentioned that I finished my talk with from that night in All Hallows you allude to were:

> This is where your life has arrived,
> After all the years of effort and toil;
> Look back with graciousness and thanks on all your great
> and quiet achievements.
> You stand on the shore of new invitation
> To open your life to what is left undone;
> Let your heart enjoy a different rhythm
> When drawn to the wonder of other horizons.
> Have the courage for a new approach to time;
> Allow it to slow until you find freedom.
> To draw alongside the mystery you hold.
> And befriend your own beauty of soul.
> Now is the time to enjoy your heart's desire,
> To live the dreams you've waited for,
> To awaken the depths beyond your work
> And enter into your infinite source.

Thanks again for your wonderful review.
Keep up your good work.

As the wind loves to call things to dance
May your gravity be lightened by grace . . .

May your prayer of listening deepen enough
To hear, in the depths, the laughter of God.

And so many a slow wind work these words of love around you,
An invisible cloak to mind your life.

John

P.S. I was very taken reading your piece about the Troubles. It
is filled with a quiet intensity which makes it even more powerful.
I hope you like my prayer which says some of the same things
perhaps – albeit in a different way.

We pray for those who suffered violence today
May an unexpected serenity surprise them.
For those who risk their lives each day for peace
May their hearts glimpse providence at the heart of history.
That those who make riches from violence and war
Might hear in their dreams the cries of the lost.
That we might see through our fear of each other
A new vision to heal our fatal attraction to aggression.
That those who enjoy the privilege of peace
Might not forget their tormented brothers and sisters.

BENEDICTUS

A Response to John's Letter:

Goodbye to you, my trusted friend.

If Jimmy Magee was still around to describe her he would have summed her up as: 'Different class.' She has to be the woman of the year.

A close contender has to her daughter, Linda Golden, who said goodbye to a career in teaching this year after a lifetime of dedicated service. Generations of grateful students are in her deep debt.

Easter 2020 was the most unique Easter since the very first one. The message of new life though was confirmed with the birth of Noel Graham Spence Rice and Nevin Jackie Abel Rice to their proud parents Emma and Peter. I hope they will know many great days.

There was great sadness in July for the family of Mary O'Brien. As she leans over the bannisters of heaven her memory will continue to live on in the hearts of the many people who loved her.